Beyond Paradise

Beyond Paradise

Encounters in Hawai'i
Where the Tour Bus Never Runs

Peter S. Adler

FROM THE LIBRARY OF:

SALLY LUNA

Ox Bow Press
Woodbridge, Connecticut

Published by
OX BOW PRESS
P.O. Box 4045
Woodbridge, Connecticut 06525
(203) 387-5900   Fax (203) 387-0035

Cover art by Carli Oliver

Library of Congress Cataloging-in-Publication Data

Adler, Peter S., 1944–
    Beyond paradise : encounters in Hawaii where
the tour bus never runs / Peter S. Adler.
        p.   cm.
    ISBN 1-881987-01-9 (acid free paper)
    1. Hawaii.   I. Title.
    DU623.25.A32   1993   93-13728
    919.6904′4—dc20   CIP

The paper in this book meets the guidelines for permanence
and durability of the Committee on Production Guidelines for
Book Longevity of the Council on Library Resources.

Printed in the United States of America

For Carolyn, Corey, Dana, and Kelly Adler,
who endured the dark moods and strange
ecstasies that attended the birth of this book

Acknowledgments

When you conclude something important in Polynesia, says Steven Goldsberry, it is very important to thank everybody for everything. Honoring that tradition to the fullest, my list begins with Carolyn, Corey, Dana, and Kelly Adler, whose support was constant and love unconditional. Without them, none of this would have happened.

Other thank yous are in order to people who read, listened to, or were otherwise subjected to early versions of these chapters: my brothers Bob and Tom Adler; Randy Roth and Joanne Punu from the Richardson School of Law; Ha'aheo Mansfield and Greg Owen, colleagues from Hawaii Bound days; Kem Lowry from the Department of Urban and Regional Planning; and Jim Paul, Karen Takahashi, Bill Wood, Joanne Yukimura, Ted Riley, Steven Montgomery, Warren Haight, Holly Bakke, Tom Fee, Dan Hatch, Jackie Young, Maile Meyer, Neal Milner, Guy Fujimura, Sonja Franzel, Puananai Burgess, Walter Bradbury, and Dee Dee Letts, all of whom plowed through various portions of the manuscript and offered sage advice.

Three other people are in a category by themselves. The first is the late Fletcher Knebel, candid commentator on the human condition, free spirit, and a true man of letters. His unceasing encouragement and support inspired me to complete the manuscript at the very moment I started to lose heart.

The second is Holly Henderson, a woman with soul and intelligence who is also a courageous community activist and superb editor. Mercifully, Holly undertook the task of damage control and helped me de-bungle some ideas that, with hindsight, were headed for true disaster. Last, there is Lucille Stein, editor and owner of Ox Bow Press, who said she would do it, and she did.

Mahalo nui ia kākou.

Contents

No alien land in all the world has any deep, strong charm for me but that one, no other land could so longingly and so beseechingly haunt me, sleeping and waking, through half a lifetime, as that one has done. Other things leave me, but it abides....

Mark Twain on Hawai'i, 1889

Introduction

The urge to travel to faraway places can seize you at any time. Hawai'i stirs that need within us. The Hawaiian Islands are a lei of earthly flowers floating on the broad waters of the world's greatest ocean, a necklace of Pacific landfalls, the legendary children of the first Polynesian gods. They are the remotest islands on Earth.

Steep, dark forms of volcanic islands rise from the depths. Blue-green waves curl down a stretch of sand. The sky is crystalline. The sun sparkles. Gracious people dwell there. The dream summons.

So people from all over the world awake and come to Hawai'i, millions of them, surging in from Asia, America, and Europe to luxuriate in the sun. They seek the serenity of being by the sea and the beauty that seems to spring from the land. They are searching for paradise ... and perhaps something beyond paradise.

But questions arise. Are those who travel to Hawai'i truly enriched by their visit? Are they amazed by the archipelago's flora, surprised by its fauna, intrigued by its people? Are passions aroused by their encounters? And what about those of us who live here? Are we open to discoveries about the soul of the place in which we live?

Consider the way encounters in Hawai'i are supposed to be, the way all of us wish they would be.

Imagine you are a stranger, cut off from family and friends. You go to the beach, visit the museums, browse through the stores, and watch a few sunsets. Still, something is missing. There is more to Hawai'i, you suspect, than exotic dining and the pulsating Polynesia of a nightclub. Whatever it is, it eludes you. So you wander.

In your meanderings, you walk down a neighborhood side street. It is a warm summer evening. Soon you come to a house with forty pairs of foot gear jumbled up in a pile on the doorstep. Most are rubber slippers, but there are also running shoes, heels, loafers, construction boots, and the reddest, smallest plastic boots imaginable. There are lights on inside. The sound of ukeleles and guitars accompanied by a chorus of extraordinarily sweet voices comes drifting into the night. Normally you are not a nosy person so you try to resist, but it's impossible. You wander closer, catch a glimpse, and stare incredulously.

An amazing group has gathered together. Their faces — engaged in various combinations of talking, singing, and drinking — range from brown to yellow to black to white and all possible shades in between (including a few older guys with red noses and silly grins surrounded by empty beer bottles). People are also eating. Some have brought main dishes: barbecued beef sticks, deep-fried won ton, ginger chicken, *kālua* pig, Korean-style shortribs, pork tofu with slices of gobo, logs of sushi wrapped in dried seaweed, bowls of white rice, pots full of dumplings and noodles, baskets with buns and sweet potatoes, and trays with smoked, broiled, fried, pickled, and raw fish. There are also home-grown mangos, papayas, guavas, mountain apples, lychees, and bananas. Still others have brought desserts: malasadas, ensemadas, haupia, guava chiffon and coconut cream pies, ice cream, chocolate sheet cake with Kona coffee icing, almond float in paper cups, and a couple of dozen DeLite Bakery glazed doughnuts.

Off in a corner three men with a guitar, a ukulele, and a bass are singing. Some of their songs are in Hawaiian; others are in English; some are in both. One song is about the blossoms of the *'ōhi'a* tree. Another is about a waterfall and the mists surrounding it. Massive, splendid, older women in *mu'umu'u* are dancing with the cadences; so, too, are beautiful younger women and girls in shorts, T-shirts, and braids. Everyone embraces or shakes hands or touches one another gently when they say *mahalo* and *aloha*.

As you stand there craning your neck, transfixed by these offerings of hearth and home, a beefy looking half-Hawaiian, half-Asian man with squinty eyes, a bald head, and big muscles steps out on the *lānai* for a smoke and sees you spying. You look at him and he looks at you and in that instantaneous fraction of a nanosecond, you know he thinks you are lusting after one of his willowy, long-legged, dark-haired daughters who just danced to the song about the waterfall (and whom, to tell the truth, you've kind of noticed and admired in an aesthetic sort of way for a few minutes).

Realization comes quickly. You've bought the farm. You say your good-byes in the language of your childhood religion. Then, suddenly, your death preparations are interrupted. The man's face — the size of a large hubcap — erupts into a smile. "Hey brah, try come inside," he says. "We get plenty music and food. No need fo stay out heah." Nervously at first, you accept his invitation to the party and over the next few hours learn — for the first time, perhaps — the true meaning of hospitality.

What you have just encountered is a special aspect of Hawai'i, a type of cordiality and graciousness not found in many parts of our rapidly shrinking world. Offering a hearty welcome to outsiders does not necessarily have to center on food, although eating and drinking together is, and always has been, a benchmark of common courtesy even in the poorest and most barren of cultures. Hawaiians, however, have elevated this open friendliness to an everyday art form. Local people — a term that, for my purposes, includes non-Hawaiians who are Hawaiian in spirit — are always ready to drop what they are doing and use the most minor of comings and goings as a reason for celebration. We like parties because they affirm the bonds of family and friendship, both of which are critical to long-term survival when you live on an island.

Real sharing, however, can only evolve in a climate of reciprocity. "Before receiving," opined Lao-tzu, "there must be giving." What he seems to have meant was this: for both the giver and the receiver there must be an open moment and what takes place must come from the heart. Giving must be guileless and offered without pretension or expectation.

Comes a moment, then, when you contribute something of your own. A song or story, perhaps. Help with some task. Flowers or food or a present that has special significance. Or perhaps you will return the hospitality to other sojourners who come your way. Regardless, you will now begin to understand how much is really embraced in the concept and practice of *aloha*.

Unfortunately, these kinds of exchanges are increasingly rare. More often tourism intrudes on everyone, visitors and visited alike, in ways that are better forgotten. Crowds of people roam formerly remote beaches. Roads are choked with buses. Housing tracts creep up the mountainsides and more and more of the city's streets look like concrete canyons. Massive parking problems occur regularly. Locals shun tourists and tourists avoid locals. And too frequently when the two happen to mingle, there is congestion, irritation, and a host of upraised middle-finger resentments.

Which is not the way it is supposed to be, or has to be, and that brings us, in a roundabout way, to this book.

In the simplest sense, the essays that follow are the record of certain expeditions and encounters in Hawai'i. A few years ago I started to jot down some impressions about what I had seen, heard, and learned on a trip to Kaho'olawe, the Hawaiian island that was used by the U.S. Navy for bombing practice. I was, for all practical purposes, a tourist, though the tour group I had traveled with was unique. It was made up of young and assiduously independent Hawaiians who were, and still are, fighting for the return of native lands. Through their kindness and guidance, I was able to share, for a brief moment, the fierce and bittersweet pride that is so integral to their history, their culture, and their future.

Like the journey itself, the writing seemed important and proved enjoyable, and soon I began working on other essays, about a rare Hawaiian goose being rescued from the brink of extinction, an extraordinarily bountiful avocado tree, some peculiar local insects, hiking on Mauna Loa, whale watching, the selection of a State fish, and more. The doing and the writing took a long time but also satisfied a deep-rooted passion for ranging around on foot, some intense curiosities about Hawai'i, and a desire to get certain matters off my chest.

The results lie before you. Think of these serendipitous accounts of life in the Islands as reports from places where the tour bus never runs. Admittedly, you won't learn the secret of how to make big bucks speculating in local real estate or which hotel mixes the best mai-tai. What you will find are ten true stories about Hawai'i, some worries about the hurricane-like forces of change that are bearing down on the Islands, and many gentler thoughts that call to the voyager and traveler in all of us. If the book deepens your appreciation of the Islands, pleases your mind's eye, and occasionally nettles your conscience, then all of the writing will have been worth the effort.

1

Cairns

The body roams the mountains.
And the spirit is set free.

Hsu Hsia-k'o

"**C**OMES OVER ONE AN ABSOLUTE NECESSITY TO MOVE. And what is more," said D. H. Lawrence, "to move in some particular direction." My particular direction is south, along Route 11 past Kurtistown, Mountain View, and Glenwood, headed toward a smoking, lonely landscape filled with rare birds, fragile flowers, and cooling mists: Volcanoes National Park. A refuge on the "Big" Island, not just for small creatures and plants, but for the human animal as well — for me.

This need to push off into the wilderness, to lose myself and get away from the noise and frenzy of the city, both the physical city and the city inside my head, is periodic. "Where do you go on vacation if you live in Hawai'i?" a mainland friend once asked. It's not hotels and nightclubs I crave, or even spectacular beaches — it's isolation and solitude, time away from the human world and a chance to measure life on a different kind of yardstick. So I go back to the Big Island, which somehow is home; to a place of origins and births, to one of two living volcanoes spewing up new lands for Hawai'i and rattling the sensibilities of anyone who thinks stability should be — or actually is — the natural order of things.

The way up starts at 6,662 feet at the end of a ten-mile strip road in an alpine zone, a confluence of small *kīpuka*, dry niches, cool ledges, birds, flowers, and mists. Inevitably, there is an incipient drizzle here. The forest is soft and humid, a tangle of cold-

and warm-weather plants. Old friends, these plants, creatures I haven't seen for a long time: *kūkaenēnē* and *pūkiawe*; sagebrush; wild strawberries. Before my climb I pick a few sprigs of *'a'ali'i*, the strong waxy leaves that are a symbol of the ancient royalty of Hawai'i. I put them away in a side pocket in my pack where they are least likely to get mashed. I'll carry them to the top of the mountain for luck, for company, and for an offering. Who knows? It seems right, so I do it.

A few beer cans and empty shotgun shells are lying around, the leavings of locals and tourists alike. There are two fiberglass outhouses, a small parking lot with a few rental cars and pickup trucks, a shelter with dioramas and explanations of Mauna Loa's geology and ecology, and an overlook from which the casual visitor can gaze down on most of the Puna district. Twenty feet beyond the trailhead, there is the mountain.

The preparation is a familiar constellation of sensations, something special by itself. Slip into old, worn boots. Cinch them up. Check water, map, and compass. Tie everything down. Then shoulder the pack and push off up the mountain. The stony trail heading up Mauna Loa skirts an old lava flow. There are occasional boot prints in the dirt.

The thick, green vegetation of the alpine zone is a refreshing change from the shimmering heat below. Perceptions flood in and mix with memories. The green and earth-ocher colors of *hinahina* and bracken fern come back to me, and the red berries and red flowers of *'ōhelo* and *'ōhi'a*. And certain sounds. I hear the soft honkings of a *nēnē* hidden in the underbrush, the buzz of flies, and the sound of my breathing adjusting to unfamiliar altitudes. I can hear and feel my boots crunching up the trail on thousands of pebbles of lava. And behind and beyond all of these sensations there is a great and mysterious stillness that commands and baffles the senses.

A mile up the trail the forest gives way to open slope, to a vast expanse of rock rising up gently and steadily, an upgrading of land that appears horizonless. The path cuts across large flows of *pāhoehoe* lava, their billowy, ropy folds convoluted into the edges of other flows and layered down like rumpled sheets. The trail leads in a generally northern direction. Vegetation thins. At 8,300 feet I pass the last 'ōhi'a tree, a tough and gnarled old-timer whose roots cling to life in a crack of soil on the side of a small cinder cone.

The tension of the past months begins to dissipate. There is a physical letting go. Shoulders relax as my back flexes with the weight. Frowns flatten out, city thoughts drift away, and senses open up. The simple brute effort of walking begins to overtake and eradicate what's in the part of my mind that normally stays preoccupied with work.

Other sensations come into play. Brain and body seem to disengage, and legs, arms, and torso go on automatic pilot. The mountain's great emptiness starts to penetrate. Take away the stimuli we are used to and, for a time, the mind manufactures its own. The silence is filled with new descriptions and then, eventually, with no descriptions at all. I fade off into what I imagine is some version of aboriginal "dream-time," a trancelike lowering of the normal defenses erected by overly compulsive and rational minds. And slowly in the upward drift toward Red Hill I begin to notice something new — a feeling that I am not really alone up here even though there is nobody else on the trail; a feeling that I'm the observed instead of the observer.

Then, after a few miles, I notice them. I've seen them a hundred times before, here and on the other Islands where suburbs and pastures end and forests begin. Always they have been on the edge of consciousness, something seen but not really acknowledged. Now, for the first time, they enter my thoughts. They are no longer objects but beings in their own right, standing like sentinels, posting progress, watching my passage, and marking this strange, brief interlude. In Hawaiian, they are called *ahu*, heaps of stones built to direct the traffic of an earlier age when travelers in these parts crossed by foot instead of tour bus. In English, they are cairns. Simple, plain, everyday, run-of-the-mill trail markers. And yet … they seem to be more.

Islands in general — and the Hawaiian Islands in particular — teach us that things are rarely what they appear to be. The perspective is different, more rounded and interior, with everything cascading back onto itself. Perhaps this is true in any locale where large stands of free-ranging wilderness still exist. In Hawai'i, it seems especially so. Trails are not simply backcountry footpaths, and cairns are not just piles of rocks casually heaped together to mark them. Minimally, there are histories to consider. Mounds, in ancient times, might be dressed with a freshly killed pig laid down as tribute to a particular area's ruling chief. And even the word *ahu* itself relates to *ahupua'a*, recalling the old and fundamental mountain-to-sea land division system that the Hawaiians used for a thousand years.

Some cairns honor gods. Others mark the site of a special event: a birth, a death, a battle. And still others seem to have been set in place by the gods themselves.

The *ahu* on the flanks of Mauna Loa are part of a network pegging off more than two hundred miles of ancient and modern trails maintained by the National Park Service. Following the contours of the land, they lead through four environments, all within the park. At the tundra-summit of Mauna Loa there are cairns rising above the winter snow pack level, six, seven, even ten feet high, and the same across the base. In the rain forests and uplands of Kīlauea the cousins of these markers are smaller and squatter and choked by creepers and vines. Along the seashore and in the Ka'ū Desert, rattled by tremors and earthquakes, they are farther apart and quietly shrouded in broomsedge and *pili* grass.

I hike steadily, observing and pondering this complex network of living paths marked off as abstract, unexciting dots on the U.S. Geodetic Survey map. In the foot-after-foot rhythm of the journey, inner and outer geographies begin to merge. The solitudes of the forest and the fine desolations of lava are revealed slowly, a function of time, place, and distance from the city. It provides a form of decompression, this park, a renewal of noise-and-routine-deadened nerve endings. As pleasure and understanding of the wilderness deepen, as the preciousness of this particular island comes back to me, the *ahu* transform. First they are sculptures, human creations, textures and shapes that have been intentionally carved out from the land to mirror our innermost imaginings. And then later, much later, they assume lives of their own, becoming sentient beings, living creatures with individual identities and maybe some sort of collective soul.

Is it possible? Romantic drivel, says the left side of my brain, a figment of altitude and blisters. A probable case of imputing meaning where none exists. But then I see the rocks, carefully and intricately nestled against each other in the harsh and shimmering sunlight. And I imagine them at night, huddled together in the plunging cold that wraps the mountain in blankets of ice and fog. In pre-metal Hawai'i there was this belief: that stones are alive. Their latent power was understood and accepted on just these terms. Leave a male and female rock together and they will beget baby pebbles. Offer water to a stone in right proportion and it will grow to be a god. Feed and love the god, tend it from generation to generation, and it will always protect you.

So I watch and wonder about the cairns, another one every fifty or hundred yards. In the lava itself, in the folded wrinkles of this ancient material, feldspar sparkles and olivine glistens. Drops of trapped water shimmer like jewels. I stop to put a few stones back on top of a cairn. The rough slabs of basalt cut and chafe my hands. In the high, thin air it is slow work, this shifting and stacking of stones. And on a mountain of rock spewed up from a hot spot 15,000 feet below the surface of the sea in the middle of the Pacific, it is a minor and temporary act that will soon be eradicated by the weather, earth tremors, and the steady pressure of time.

But the idea remains. The stones and rocks really are alive. They are sentient and aware and as valid a life form as myself.

How far might this idea extend? Are the rocks alive when they come up from this roiling, shuddering volcano, when they are orange and liquid? When they have been weathered down to ten thousand tiny pebbles and crushed into dust by centuries of rain and wind? And if the volcano itself is a giant boulder, is it a life unto itself as well? If it is alive, is it a single organism made up of complex pieces or is it many creatures coming together to make something greater than the sum of all the individuals?

Questions and more questions. The cairns seem to evoke them. Maybe it's that there's nothing else to do when you walk along hour after hour by yourself. Or maybe it's just some gland in the neocortex reacting to the rarefied air. Whatever the reason, the cairns seem to mark the intermediate zone between wilderness and civilization, that boundary beyond which nature must be met on its own terms. The problem is that the rules for engaging this boundary aren't clear.

Living in the city seems to make many people, myself included, a little crazy. Conversely, traipsing up mountains periodically makes us feel more integral to nature's great web, as if we were a piece of the tapestry and not just a loose thread hanging off the edge. But what about nature on a day-to-day basis? What about when we are pushing papers, dodging traffic, buying or selling real estate, or quarreling with contrary, cunning, and obstreperous bureaucrats? Are we doing something that is somehow less than "natural" when we write on a computer and talk through a telephone?

If this were a larger-than-life national park on the mainland, a Yosemite or Yellowstone, answers to all these weighty questions might be more forthcoming. Continents display themselves on a grand and majestic scale. As a consequence, they often offer continental insights. There is a tradition for this, a line of writers like Henry Thoreau, John Muir, and Walt Whitman, all of whom thought hard about the nature of nature and came away from the process with important understandings. That tradition continues today in the essays and poems of people like Gary Snyder, Annie Dillard, Peter Matthiessen, Barry Lopez, and Wendell Berry.

All of these people make their homes on the large, sprawling continent of North America. I live on a little island, which in some ways seems to make things harder. Islands conceal and obscure. Secrets are kept in out-of-the-way places, tucked off in odd spots where they can't get stepped on and are free to take their own evolutionary course. Hence insights don't come in the same way. The view is smaller, filled with tiny habitats and microclimates hiding nuggets and kernels of life in the shadows or off in little crevices and cracks. People from continents, influenced by the grandness of big cities, tall mountains, vast prairies, and great basins have a hard time of it when they try to apply their native intelligences to Hawai'i. Often they look for "the big picture," only to find that they brought along the wrong tools: a pair of bin-oculars instead of a magnifying glass; a shovel instead of tweezers.

Perhaps a giant, snow-covered mountain rising up from a warm, blue-green sea just north of the equator offers a more appropriate vantage point for these kinds of matters. Mauna Loa matches the questions at hand. It is high enough to rise above all the day-to-day pettiness, central enough to offer a sight of the whole, and close at hand. It is also compelling. For thousands of years people have gone up mountains looking for vision or under-standing. At the very least, for a short chat with their gods. They plod up, bask in the clean, crisp air, and come back with a know-ing and far-away look in their eyes, as if they've been to the back of the beyond, gazed out over the boundary, and solved some essential mystery.

In my heart of hearts, I keep hoping that will happen to me one day when I'm off walking in my own physical and mental backcountries.

*   *   *

Hawai'i has true wild places, and Mauna Loa is one of them. At 13,680 feet above sea level and with 10,000 cubic miles of solidi-fied lava, it has a bulk larger than the entire Sierra Nevada range put together. From its roots on the bottom of the Pacific, it is the most massive mountain in the world and dominates, along with its sister volcano Mauna Kea, the entire Island of Hawai'i. Rising up to catch the prevailing trade winds, it generates its own weather, including fickle drafts that often reverse directions in midafternoon and a snow pack that can be six feet thick at the top in winter. There are frosty, brittle nights studded with bright white stars and scorching days under a relentless sun that can fry the brains of anyone who forgets to bring a hat. The sky is pure and wide and filled with clean, breathable air. So clean and pristine is Mauna Loa that the U.S. Meteorological Service observatory on the north-east side of the mountain at the 10,000-foot level can record dust particles thrown up into the air from a hiker's movements several miles away.

This particular journey up is a continuing study in contrasts. It is dominated by lava, by shapes and colors that can appear as distorted or as magnificent as anything conceived under the influence of opium, hashish, or LSD. Mauna Loa is a tidal wave of lava thrown up from the inner madness of the mountain and propelled down the slopes in textures that would make Miró, Picasso, and Giacometti delirious. Lava spatters over the edge of some long-dead cone and turns into green cinders. It arches out of a fissure and freezes into a puddle of glass. It seeps out of a crack and becomes a mile-long torrent. Lava flows, rolls, drifts, creeps, slides, and glides out of the mountain, always downhill and always coming to rest in some new and phantasmagoric form.

The hues and textures are a landscape pulled from the primordial dreams of our species. In great sheets and blocks lava becomes a placid lunar lake, a bubble of stone that has cracked in near-perfect geometric form. The colors are metallic: silvers, mauves, and blues that sparkle and dance in the sunlight, radiating the day's heat back into the atmosphere. It is thin as new ice and equally treacherous to walk on. And in other forms, fifty feet away, it is completely different; strong as steel and dappled a dull gray with rust and mottled brown striations. And next to that is still another slant of rock, deep purple like a ripe eggplant. In one place the lava has built itself into boobytrap trenches of jagged, razor-sharp edges. Next to this spot, perhaps from the same vent or crack, the stone is a polished mirror.

But it is on the open slope that the structural geology of the mountain becomes readily apparent. Mauna Loa is one of the most active volcanoes on the planet, a great hot hump that fires up every few years. Summit eruptions take place in Moku'āweoweo, the caldera at the top, and flank eruptions usually occur along one of the mountain's two main rift zones. The trail follows the northeast rift, the most active. It is dormant now, calm and quiet and overdue for an eruption that, on some uncertain day in the near future, could send a viscous river of molten lava pouring through the streets of downtown Hilo.

The rift up higher is a long line of cracks, cones, fissures, vents, faults, and fumaroles. Many are hot. Others are dead or dormant.

Steam rises from a slab of rock; I dump my pack and walk over to inspect. The entrance to a belching hole surrounded by yellow, oxidized sediments is stained with brown, pink, beige, and mustard deposits. Dull gray smoke pours out of a small nondescript cave. A closer look shows yellow-brown gas issuing up from a seemingly bottomless tube a few feet off at the side of the trail.

The lava itself is a geochemist's dream come true. It is made up of silicon, aluminum, ferrous iron, magnesium, titanium, manganese, phosphorus, potassium, sodium, and calcium. All of these are combined into rock forms that seem even more exotic: olivine basalt, labradorite, andesite, and plagioclase feldspar. The mountain is a furnace. Heat, pressure, and weather continue to mold its outer face; its inner chambers are a mystery. The trail, a momentary line stamped out just fifty years ago, juts across broken domes and jagged, mile-long blisters of basalt. Everywhere the land is pitted, scarred, and pockmarked. One sees all of this and assumes permanence. In truth, the remains of former lava activity have only temporarily solidified into these shapes.

The landscape I am seeing is a snapshot of a moment in time, a brief slice of some monstrously large life cycle that goes back several million years into the early part of the Pleistocene at the latest. Visualize the forces that are at play. Under the earth's surface there are enormous crustal plates holding up the oceans and continents, which have moved a few inches each year as far back as can be measured. These foundations are being shoved around by convection currents generated from the planet's molten interior. In our own age the plates go a long way toward explaining Pacific basin geology, including the "ring of fire," earthquakes, tsunamis, continental drift, and why San Francisco may not be with us one day.

Now transport yourself back to these geologic beginnings. Underwater, the Hawaiian ridge is a low, broad upwelling off the sea floor, 500 miles long, half a mile high. Beneath this ridge the Pacific plate is moving north by northwest over a "hot spot," an upwelling plume of molten material originating beneath the Earth's mantle. As the plate moves over the plume this rock-melting magma burns upward, forming vents leading to the surface. Back in what John McPhee calls "deep time," these vents are the volcanoes that are starting to make up the Hawaiian Islands.

As the archipelago moves over the hot spot, various islands form, rise up to maturity, and then weather away until they are reclaimed by the elements. Imagine the entire chain as puffs of smoke left behind by a locomotive. Those closest to the engine are fresh and full. Those farther back are more dissipated. So it is with the islands left in the wake as the plate moves over the hot spot.

Mauna Loa begins to grow. The upsurging magma spurts out from its hidden chambers and meets the cool, blue seawater of the mid-Pacific. For millions of years molten rock gushes up. Century after century in fits and starts it progresses, not violently, but steadily. Eventually, it reaches the surface and in long slow interludes is washed away. Again it builds, only to be flattened by wind, wave, and rain. However, inch by inch, foot by foot, mile by cubic mile, the land begins to rise. The mountain creeps up, steaming, cooling, erupting, cooling, and — again and again as if guided by some independent energy — pushing its way to the sky.

In the infancy of the island, hundreds of centuries slide by. Eons. Yugas. The land twists, heaves, and accumulates. It steams, bakes, boils, cools, cracks, and heats up again. And over time, this large fiery mountain starts to assume its current proportions. Through the long night of these uninhabited millennia, the sky is crimson and orange, a beacon that lights the way for spores, seeds, birds, insects, and canoes full of ancient Polynesian mariners.

All of this time other volcanoes are being born on top of the same underwater rift. The things we call "islands" rise up in youthful vigor and pronounce their presence to the world. Some are stunted. Others ripen and mature. Eventually, they all disappear. Through the seasons of these island lives, though, the archipelago survives. Always the fire is close at hand, waiting just below the surface.

Can this be what it was really like? Viewing the landscape as a calendar, trying to decipher the contours of time itself, the mind staggers and retreats, lost in the vortex, unable to follow this stream of thought very far. There are no detailed trails to follow, no cairns to mark the way. Instead there is the kaleidoscopic montage of the rift above Red Hill. In this montage, the colors are metallic and burnt: ocher, umber, reddish brown, dark blue, chrome, deep rust. The sky surrounding it is bright blue. Light glares. Crystals, cinders, and pumice lie scattered in random patterns. Everywhere the land is cracked and crooked, scarped, angled, and sharp. In these hours the solitary hiker stops more and more often, inspecting what lies underneath a ledge, dropping down on all fours to watch a small spider roaming across a few feet of rock, drinking cold water from the canteen, and gazing out, down, and up in the hope of finding some new diversion to break the growing monotony.

The land is eerie, the hiking slow and time-consuming. My feet are sore. My body hurts where the straps of my backpack have dug small trenches into my shoulders. The trail from Red Hill to the summit is 11.6 miles. Because I live at sea level, I can feel the increasing altitude. It causes a slow, throbbing tiredness that comes and goes. One moment I am mesmerized by images of lava. The next moment I am totally captured by the pain of a small blister on one toe. There is a balance here, a kind of rough justice. One comes to terms with the hurts or one doesn't. It is a small price to pay. I stop to patch the little wound. My foot is white and wrinkled from sweat, prunelike, foreign-looking. An alien's foot.

Very close to a grained, weathered board that marks the 12,000-foot level, there is a cave, a large lava tube with a pool at the bottom. Fresh, sweet, jaw-numbing, tooth-ringing ice water has precipitated out of the rocks, collected into a small pond, and is now, at the end of the day, frozen. On this particular trip, this is the place at which I have decided to spend the night. The cave itself is far too cold but just outside there is a large, half-collapsed rock bubble big enough to crawl under if it rains or snows and flat enough to offer relative comfort. The small ledge is my backup. I prefer to sleep outside.

In the late afternoon I set up my campsite and while away an hour reading an old, bizarre, and not-very-good science fiction book. Intermittently I set it down and daydream. Still later, the stove hisses as I melt ice for water. Dinner is simple: macaroni and cheese, a large, Bugs Bunny–style carrot, tea. Then I walk over to a small mound of stones I've propped up for a chair, wrap my sleeping bag around my legs like a comforter, and watch the sunset.

The temperature is below freezing. My breath vaporizes. The thermos of tea steams. In the west, the sun has dropped below the horizon and the sky is filled with a red afterglow. To the east, the first stars are rising. Tomorrow I'll be up early and on the summit by noon. For the moment, however, there is just the exquisite clarity of the mountain. I sit and watch and think. In the gathering embrace of night, in the quiet rhythm of sunset, there is no penetrating understanding or culminating flash of insight. Yet in the absence of answers to larger questions, my curiosities are satiated by the magic of rock and sky and the much simpler pleasures of solitude and hot tea.

*   *   *

The giant mouth of the crater called Moku'āweoweo is revealed at a point some 400 feet below the true summit of the mountain. I follow the cairns and move from marker to marker across the foot-deep snow. There is spice in the air, a renewed anticipation now that I'm so close to the top. It is a cold, clear morning. A dozen times I've crashed my boots down onto what looks like solid footing only to find myself sinking through crusts of snow and lava and into several feet of emptiness. The result is scratched legs and bruised shins.

I pass through a portal of two large and handsome cairns, twin architectures resembling miniature Japanese temples. Suddenly I can look across and down instead of up. The crater is three miles long and a mile and a half wide. Three hundred and fifty feet below me is a mix of old and new lava flows, of cinder cones, pits, craters, and cliffs. Steam is pouring out of dozens of fissures. The center of the caldera is visible in the distance and the source of the mountain's magnificent power is now fully displayed. And again, the cairns seem to be telling me something, beckoning and guiding me toward some other end.

But there are two more miles of hiking; I push on. From this first view of the caldera at Jaggar's Ledge to the cabin at Pendulum

Peak, the trail follows the rim skirting North Bay, the lava flows of 1935, 1940, and 1942, East Pit, and Lua Poholo (literally, "to sink, slip into, vanish, plunge out of sight, or miscarry"). Always there are cairns, and were they not here, there is a good possibility that several of these pits and sinkholes would be filled up with dead backpackers. The trail skirts sheer drops of several hundred feet. The footing is dangerous. The winds are treacherous. I walk with extreme caution, carefully planting my feet so that each footfall is straight and true.

Finally, I reach the cabin, a squalid little affair the best part of which is a genuine, old-time outhouse perched on the edge of the crater, a one-holer with no door. One sits, minding the body's business and gazing out on a prehistoric landscape whose larger business also seems to have something to do with bodies. It is, bar none, the greatest and most scenic toilet in existence anywhere, a room with a view. The only improvement I might make would be a few dinosaurs garumphing around for some high-altitude entertainment.

No one else is at the cabin. And now, in the early afternoon after lunch and a nap, I start down into the caldera. A mile south of the cabin there is an old avalanche that has peeled off from the crater's wall. I gingerly pick my way down a mass of tumbled rocks, taking the six-hundred-foot descent the slow, sure way. Then I hit bottom. There are no trails now, no cairns, altitude markers, or cabins. Step by step I test each foothold. The rock is 'a'ā, jagged clinkers that draw blood at the slightest touch. Finally, I am on the crater floor. I look around. The Coast and Geodetic Survey map I've brought along is only a general representation of what is here. The features have changed since government cartographers charted them a few years ago.

I have come to this place with only the vaguest of purposes. I want to walk across the floor of the caldera, ascend the rim on the opposite side of Pendulum Peak, and then circle back to the cabin. My pack is in the cabin but I'm carrying water, a flashlight, first-aid kit, a bag of M&Ms (Vitamin M), and the sprigs of 'a'ali'i I picked at the trailhead. Now that I'm here, the larger goal gets broken down into a more specific objective: a trip to that part of the crater that gives rise to the Curtain of Fire. I can see it in the distance, a mile-long fissure of steam and gas in the middle of the crater's floor. At the beginning of most summit eruptions, the inner magma chamber of the volcano inflates. This swelling may take days or even weeks. When the fissure finally opens it spews up a sheet of hot and very liquid lava. The curtain of fire is a long crack of fountains. At the moment it is dormant but signs of life are unmistakable. Steady streams of gas burp out from spidery cracks along this central seam. The vapors are pastel: light blue, gray-white, corn-yellow.

Pushing out across the caldera I again realize that there are no trail markers. Moku'āweoweo is no-man's-land, a kind of demilitarized zone in which the human intruder takes his or her chances. I approach with a certain blend of respect and cowardice that has always served me well. I am conscious of the imperative not to disturb things needlessly. If rocks really are alive, then they ought to be treated with courtesy. Even if they are not, respect is still in order. True wilderness has no tolerance for ignorance, however well-intentioned and rationalized. And nature here is in one of its rawest, most dangerous forms. It hasn't been roped off, posted, and made properly safe and pretty. There are no rangers and interpreters to translate the landscape into cute nature stories. It is a fierce, harsh place that is alive with possibilities.

This is the home of Pele, the legendary, mercurial lady who uses fire and magma to show her periodic displeasure with human affairs. Pele is a properly contentious and wholly appropriate symbol for a place like this. In the stories and myths that surround her, she is a relatively recent immigrant, a latecomer not loath to take what she wants or what she believes is rightfully due her. It is told that she migrated to the Big Island by way of Ni'ihau, Kaua'i, O'ahu, Moloka'i, and Maui. On the way she lured, loved, killed, and restored to life a handsome young chief from Kaua'i; fought and vanquished a number of demons; banished her allegedly duplicitous sisters without explanation; and struggled with other gods and humans who fell in love with her. After much journeying Pele at last came to the Big Island, where she now resides. Her two domiciles are Halema'uma'u, the crater at Kīlauea volcano, and Moku'āweoweo, the crater of Mauna Loa. Moving between these homes or roaming the larger domain of the entire Big Island, she assumes different forms. Sometimes she is a mysterious light spotted high up at night on the slopes of Kīlauea and Mauna Loa. At other times she is a moving fireball seen from Hilo. And on the saddle road between Mauna Loa and Mauna Kea she is sometimes an alluring siren veiled in steams and mists and at other times a decrepit old hag hitching a ride. Woe comes to those who refuse her request.

Unquestionably, Pele is a force that cannot be tamed and must be reckoned with despite her transformation into a tourist attraction. Crossing O'ahu's Ko'olau Mountains via the four-lane Pali Highway, for example, takes a matter of minutes now, but there are still some Hawaiians who refuse to carry pork in their cars when they do so. Not, at least, without stopping and leaving her some. And once in a while, someone will also leave Pele a rock wrapped in ti leaves or a shot of gin poured on a stone. Cars have been known to break down when these rituals are neglected. The offerings and ceremonies may differ in form from those of past centuries, but the memories and sentiment are deeply embedded in the culture.

Yet fierceness, it seems, is no longer a quality most people want or respect in the natural and supernatural worlds that encompass us. Perhaps it is we who have changed and not our gods and goddesses. Maybe it's our own connections that have been gnawed through, eroded, and confused by the tendrils of mass culture that are covering the planet in this century. We refuse to believe in and honor our gods yet we refuse to dismiss them entirely. So we try to bend them to our will. Twentieth-century mythology is a thin remnant of a much richer system of nature-thinking that sustained humankind for a period of 10,000 years and across a horizontal axis of some 1,500 cultures and language groups. Today, all of this seems to be dying out. In contemporary times fearsome deities with complex powers and strong passions have been reduced to decorations. We are enchanted by our own capacity to alter the natural scheme of things, and the gods of the deserts, mountains, forests, and oceans no longer seem to inspire or infuse us by their presence. Instead we treat them as benign artifacts that adorn the shallowest pieces of our lives.

In Hawai'i, however, the spirits are closer at hand. Somehow, they are more tangible and detailed, more real. Why else would Pele, along with a few others, compel us so? Pele bridges old and new. Pele is a survivor: a reminder of old Hawai'i, a harbinger of things to come, and a constant and abiding reflection of the protean permutations nature takes on volcanic islands. Pele animates the fire, rock, and earth of Hawai'i and allows us to see, in these fundamental elements, the diversity that is our natural inheritance.

To speak of Pele as a single creation, however, is a mistake. To the ancient Hawaiians she was actually many different but related beings. The idea of multiple, overlapping, and mutually dependent forms of nature was an integral concept in Hawaiian culture, an intrinsic and local honoring of the mysterious interconnectedness of life. *Kino lau* ("the body's leaves") was a Hawaiian system of thinking that established both the natural resemblances and affinities between things and the rules for protecting them. Mary Kawena Pukui, the dean of Hawaiian translators, tells us that edible tree ferns are part of the body of Haumea — who is, in different form, a part of Pāpa, the Earth Mother. Lizards are related to an ancient and formidable chiefess from Maui. Sharks are the brothers of Pele. Caterpillars are cousins of sea cucumbers and baby eels. All of this was part of an ecology of mind, nature, and spirit glorified and still remembered through the *Kumulipo*, the ancient creation chant. The logic-by-analogy thinking that permeated Hawaiian taxonomies extended from land to sea, from air to ground, and into the human web as well. The *'aumakua* or totem of each family was, in essence, a leaf on the body of a greater spirit. Hence that god or goddess was worshipped and the vast, supporting network of animals, plants, mountains, beaches, and forests held in sacred and inviolable trust.

Many *heiau* were erected to honor the deities in general and, on the Big Island, Pele in particular. Here, the bodies of the dead were offered to her in the belief that their spirits would join Pele in her burning home. Recently, before her own death, Pukui wrote that this tradition continues. Only those families connected with

Pele, however, have a right to such burials, which take place secretly by the edges of lava streams and craters.

Today, the essential Pele story is a continuous reminder of Hawai'i's volcanic roots. Not so long ago, in the midst of a bitter legal fight over geothermal energy development on the Big Island, Kīlauea began a multiphased eruption that sent tons of fresh lava rolling over several sites proposed for geothermal energy wells. A few older Hawaiians had warned developers not to puncture Pele's body to "steal away her breath." Testifiers on all three sides — private business interests, the State, and local community and environmental groups — were all, if only for a short while, hushed by the unspoken implications. And at least one lawyer, a grizzled veteran of several landmark environmental battles, referred to Pele as the trial's "final witness."

So now I am in Pele's home, on the crater floor. I walk parallel to the Curtain of Fire fissure looking for a proper place to complete what I now realize is a private, slightly scrambled pilgrimage filled with complicated metaphors I only dimly understand. And then I find it: a long, flat expanse of unbroken lava near a steaming fumarole. Peering down into the crack my face is engulfed in warm, moist steam full of hydrogen sulfide. It can be poisonous stuff in heavy, industrial-strength concentrations, but is not bad up here. "The smell of sulphur is strong, but not unpleasant to a sinner," said Mark Twain when he visited Kīlauea. The edges of this fissure are spattered yellow and brown; it is as fitting and proper a place as any. I take off my jacket and set to work. Nearby, there is a large bubble of lava that has shattered from internal stresses beneath the floor of the caldera. I find a big piece and drag it over to the spot I have chosen. Then I bring another, and another, and still more.

The mound rises. After an hour of work it is four feet high, not very big in the scheme of things, but solid enough to hold together through a few of the minor tremors that ripple the surface of the crater. In the high, rarefied air of Mauna Loa where one might expect to feel lethargic and sluggish, I feel energized. It is no great architectural accomplishment, my stack of stones, but I like it. And when I am finished, I take out the sprigs of 'a'ali'i, primp them up a little from the rigors of riding in a backpack, and then lay them in a crack of the cairn I have built. No prayers, ceremonies, incantations, or rituals. Just this meager offering of greenery, a small and temporary leaving that will desiccate quickly in the dry air and will soon be tumbled or melted back down into whatever shapes Pele chooses.

Before I leave I sit and rest by the *ahu* I have made, leaning against it as if to be part of the stones. The wind strums through the crater and is just as suddenly punctured by moments of stillness. A few clouds build and puff across the sky. In the late afternoon the sky darkens and the temperature drops. Tonight I'll cook rice and vegetables and boil tea and watch the sunset and perhaps read through the record book that the Park Service has left in the cabin for people like me to write in.

Rising up to leave I take a last look at my cairn and the small branches I have placed there. A fly buzzes down onto what must be, from the fly's perspective, a freshly tossed salad. On the horizon a cold, white mist is beginning to descend into the crater. The wind comes and goes. But even in its absence, in the silence of interludes, there is still a deep and delicate hum coming from someplace that still eludes me.

*　*　*

The way up is the way down. There are other routes but time is short. There are things to do in the city, a plane to catch, and a bit of business in Hilo before returning to Honolulu. Clomping down the mountain below Red Hill on the way back to the trailhead there is a quick, fierce, and thunderless rainstorm and then sunshine. The air is whipped and washed, the lava cleansed. My clothes are steaming. The cairns shimmer and gleam in the wetness, mist rising off slick surfaces from puddles trapped in basaltic pores. As I trundle down the mountain carrying less than I came up with I can feel the difference both inside and out. The passing notion of three days ago on the way up is haunting me. It is still difficult to wrap my mind around the idea that stones are alive. The idea, however, won't go away.

I am also aware of time passing and the transient nature of things. Perhaps it's the cairns that nudge me to think of it. Constantly shaken by earth movements and slowly ground down by the elements, they are a reminder that life is tenuous and impermanent. Faced with the additional uncertainties of our time, many of us inevitably turn to protection and stewardship of the environment as a bulwark against the incendiary technological changes that are sweeping the planet. Einstein once characterized this age as an "agreement on means and a confusion of ends." For myself, one of those ends is to ensure the preservation of some areas that are wild and untamed. We need empty, open spaces in which natural diversity can take its own course unplanned and uninterrupted by humankind. There must always be a few places that are left free, clean, and honored for their own sake.

The fact is, though, that "wilderness" is a strictly civilized concept, something that doesn't even occur to people until they are cut off from direct contact with the land. In this peculiar, topsy-turvy time it is the interstitial zone we need to come to grips with, the meeting place between our own wild natures and our impetus to control everything. In this one little park tucked off in the far corner of a far-flung island chain, perhaps that confluence could happen. Perhaps it's starting to emerge. The trail down Mauna Loa, after all, wends through the volcanic corridors of a large shrine — not a religious artifact sanctified and locked away like some saint's bleached-out bones, but a monument celebrating the pulse of life itself; not a tomb in which to pray to abstractions but a place of birthing, a place for human and nonhuman intelligences to meet and commune.

In the end, it isn't more predigested tour group interpretations we need but periodic opportunities to live close to and lightly on the earth. Wilderness isn't a place. It is a state of awareness. We require it, perhaps just as much as we need food, shelter, and human companionship.

Elsewhere in the park this same trail rolls over crumbling lava flows and into the rich grasslands of a high desert. I could follow an unbroken line of cairns from the summit of Mauna Loa down to the wheat-colored *pili* grass of Ka'ū and, finally, down to a cobalt sea where still more cairns mark off the remains of old Hawaiian temples at the shore. Always, there are places the cairns don't go, off the trail, away from the interstitial zone, and into the heart of the backcountry. In the wandering and pondering, the rocks are a line of questions and metaphors leading off to other places that could be explored.

But what if the questions aren't just allegorical? What if, just suppose, this entire trail system is a single tendril in an integrated complex of nerves extending out from the center of some larger but unknown presence, a real being and not just an imagined one? What if the contours of the land are wrinkles and folds on that being's living body, a skin that is sloughed off as pebbles and boulders instead of cells? What if lava is life-giving blood and sulphur its exhalings? And what if the body, the Big Island, is really the head of some much larger intelligence, the archipelago, whose existence we sense but can't really fathom even though it is pumping and breathing across unimaginable life spans?

Scientists and philosophers who know about these things tell us that there is some kind of cosmic architecture at play in stars and atoms even though the structure is obscured from view. They seek their truths in measurements and inferences beyond which lie educated leaps of faith. Meanwhile, we ordinary people, little motes of planetary dust that we are, simply dream of islands and search them out to take refuge. There is a sense of completeness in the isolation of an island, a roundness and boundedness that somehow makes things more manageable. We are constrained, held in check, and caught in a universe of horizons. It's a smaller, more precise kind of universe with built-in limitations. And I wonder sometimes if the quest to understand galaxies, cells, and molecules isn't just another compulsion for islands also.

Wallace Stegner says a person standing on an island can see both the edge and the source of his or her world simultaneously. When that happens, understanding has a rare chance to grow. So we follow the cairns to see where they lead and inevitably they lead us toward the boundary beyond which there are no markers.

On the trail, the weather changes by the minute. An azure sky is concealed by clouds. The fog rolls in. Vapor rises up from fumaroles. Plants drip in the rain. One by one the cairns drift by in the mist, steering me over a steaming landscape. I take great comfort from their presence. And something more than comfort as well.

With unremitting accuracy and grace, these stones, standing so starkly in the wet and heavy air, are guiding me down the side of one of the greatest mountains in the world and through a fog that is obliterating any other view of the landscape. I know for a fact that they offer other paths and destinations. It all comes down to the choosing.

2

The Feast

I saw that the sacred hoop of my people was one of many hoops that made one circle, wide as daylight and as starlight, and in the center grew one mighty flowering tree to shelter all the children of one mother and father. And I knew that it was holy.

Black Elk

T HE HOUSE I LIVE IN, THE HOUSE MY CHILDREN ARE GROWING UP IN, the house that shelters and sustains us, is located on a little plot of land in lower Mānoa, one of the lushest and most beautiful valleys in Hawai'i. Mānoa is a place of mists, clouds, and rainbows, a valley full of green and growing things and one that might fit everyone's fantasy of what a Hawaiian valley should look like.

The valley is also interesting. Not so long ago much of the land in Mānoa was an intensively cultivated agricultural area where taro was grown and then rice; later still, there were dairy farms and pastures full of cattle and sheep. Some fine old photos depicting Hawaiian-Chinese farmers can be found, believe it or not, at our local McDonald's. Drowning nostalgia in burgers and fries, sitting there with Chicken McNugget sauce smeared on the table, you can gaze into the face of a man tilling and hoeing his field with a water buffalo less than a hundred years ago. Before that, Kamehameha the Great sent a small flanking force of foot soldiers up what is now Mānoa Road just past my house to rout Chief Kalanikupule and conquer O'ahu at the top of Nu'uanu Pali. This event, however, is not commemorated by McDonald's.

Today, Mānoa is a fertile, shaded place filled with fine old college homes, the University of Hawai'i and several notable private schools, an arboretum, a large Chinese cemetery, and, way in the back of the valley, a few remaining flower and vegetable farms.

Sheltered on each side by high ridges, washed and fed by Mānoa Falls and its attending stream, Mānoa Valley has an aura and majesty and mystery few other places can offer. It also harbors a most stupendous avocado tree, which by the sheerest of coincidences happens to be in my backyard.

When the ultimate story of the valley comes to be written, Mānoa's physical and intellectual charms may pale into obscurity when mention is made of my tree. I refer to a tree that deserves the horticultural equivalent of the Nobel and Pulitzer prizes for guacamole and avocado-salad-boat production, a tree that is worthy of worship by avocado lovers worldwide, and a tree whose picture could most certainly find its way into the local McDonald's.

Like everything in life, however, there is a dark side. The simple fact is that the tree, leviathan producer that it is, makes leviathan demands on my time, energy, patience, and humility. World-class avos don't come cheap. I pay my dues (plus some) for every mouth-melting, stomach-pleasing spoonful of guacamole that slides down my gullet. People need to understand, for example, that the fruits we pluck and eat are as much a source of constipation as they are of inspiration and that the shade the tree provides in the steamiest part of the summer's heat is traded for in full in the fall by endless afternoons of raking leaves. And that even the fine details of a midsummer night's moon rising through the tree's branches are a debt to be billed later in perspiration and blisters when the tree needs pruning.

Not to say that the price is too high. I wouldn't trade the tree for anything. From my point of view, it is a central and perfect reason for living in Mānoa Valley and, for that matter, in Hawai'i. It's a constant and steady reminder of the vitality that rises up from the roots of the Island itself, a tough and stately plant life that permeates my animal life and the lives of Carolyn and our sprawling, squalling, broody horde of children. The tree is kinship and stability in a culture that seems to be insatiably hooked on speed and change.

Carolyn and daughters Corey, Dana, and Kelly each rejoice in the tree's presence, each in her own way, each for her own unspoken reasons. For myself, though, the seasons of my life no less than the seasons of the year are marked off by the changes I see outside my window in cycles, circles, and seeds. The flowers of spring are wistful dreams, half of them dashed to the ground in the first high wind. The small green buds of early summer are my ambitions, each an unfulfilled longing that I have known and still remember. And the fruits that do survive, those that ripen and finally become themselves, are lives of their own, close and fitting semblances to those few things in my world that are precisely, perfectly correct.

So the seasons come and go and I have spent more than forty of them with the tree. Five hundred and twenty weeks; three thousand, six hundred, and forty days; one hundred and twenty full moons. A useful measure of my own life, this avocado tree, a way of searching and finding and marking the deeper passages in which I am just a momentary swirl of energy in life's strange winds. The tree is my time manager, a set of reminders that forces self-consciousness and perhaps even a modicum of self-disclosure. It's a giant, two-ton, green-and-brown appointment book useful for remembering things that bear remembering. Not everything, mind you, just the few, rare things that perennially stay important.

* * *

The seasons. The Russians say spring is a virgin, summer is a mother, fall a widow, and winter a stepmother. Frankly, I think they have it wrong. In Hawai'i, at my house at least, the first season of the year comes roaring in like a fumigator. Carolyn's annual effort at sprucing the place up is a job something akin to laundering the federal deficit; a holy jihad in which all-out war is declared on cockroaches and dustballs. It's an ethnic matter actually, an Asian tradition in which the new year must be started out just right or else the entire house, lot, and environs will be swallowed up by an 8.5 earthquake.

What this means in practical terms is a two-week frenzy of mopping, dusting, sweeping, polishing, washing, repairing, and general house straightening in which it is expected that I take full part, with enthusiasm and cheer, I might add. From my point of view, however, all of this is a nervous and wasteful exertion that strains everyone involved. For myself it means two long weeks of groans, whines, snivels, sulks, and snits. (Plus the kind of aching whimpers old dogs make when they are about to die.) Carolyn, however, sees through me as though I were saran wrap. She simply sets me to tasks that keep me out of her line of sight: trimming hedges, painting, cleaning out the garage, tidying up the yard, and washing out garbage cans.

And this year, it's as if spring has moved in to stay. "Peter, guess who called today?" she asks as I walk in the door on a Saturday afternoon. At last, I think, my Presidential appointment is here. He's calling to see if I'll accept his latest job offer: Director of U.S. Scenic Spots; official spokesman on all matters pertaining to clouds, sunsets, and mountaintops; head of a newly created Department of Remote Points of Interest with a gargantuan travel budget and a staff of one: me. But before I can suggest all this, Carolyn answers her own question. No time for foolishness and flippery here. "Mrs. Hashinaga," she says with that I-told-you-so look in her eyes. "Mrs. Hashinaga," I repeat, the name sticking in my mouth. Fear wells up and I feel the blood draining from my face. "Mrs. Hashinaga," I say again in a croaking whisper. And now I know I'm in trouble.

Mrs. Hashinaga lives in the house in back of us and has a reputation for being direct and forthright with her neighbors when she's in a bad mood. Being Japanese, she's undoubtedly going through the same fanatic spring convulsions as Carolyn. Maybe worse because she's older and because her nature is basically confrontational. Generally we don't see or hear much from Mrs. Hashinaga throughout the year, let alone her husband. He appears, in contrast to his wife, to be an emaciated but well-trained house drone who is constantly down on his hands and knees pulling out strands of crab grass and snipping the edge of his lawn with a little scissors, getting rid of those little wisps of wildness that creep in and take over if you let them. Over the normal course of a year, the Hashinagas stay to themselves and mind their own business. But in the fall, regular as rain, Mrs. H. will call to say that large green bombs are dropping on her roof and that we'll soon be hearing from her lawyer.

In past years, when a stray fruit did actually fall her way, I've managed to stave off her complaints with what I view as truly creative diversions. Things like: "Mrs. Hashinaga, why don't you just keep that five-pound avo that came through your roof last night. Put a little in Mr. H's salad tonight. Looks like he could use some carbohydrates anyway." But this year it's all to no avail. I've been double-crossed. One very late ripening avo has dropped and Mrs. H. has called Carolyn. Now both of them are annoyed and it's two against one. So out I go to survey the situation and life in general. Hmmmmm. Our avo crop for last year is finished and, yes, the tree is overhanging a bit. It looks nice that way, but it *is* getting too tall. For efficiency's sake I'll either have to trim things down an eensy bit or buy a $350,000 avocado-picking machine from the John Deere Company. Trimming seems the better course.

So my next step is to make two phone calls. The first is to Jerry Vasconcellos, a good friend and prize-winning wood carver, to alert him that a large chunk of avocado log looms in his future and ask him does he want it? Answer: yes. Next, I call Bill Steinhoff, a more casual acquaintance, but a man I know to be a tree surgeon extraordinaire. Steinhoff is a house-husband whose wife is a professor of sociology at the University of Hawai'i. She travels and lectures across the world on Japanese terrorism, something she could easily study first-hand right here in my house if she were really interested in the subject. Bill stays home, takes care of the kids, does manly sorts of odd jobs around the neighborhood for a fee, and is writing an epic soldier novel about Vietnam.

I've heard that Steinhoff has been wanting to borrow my pick-up truck for a few weeks to haul rubbish off a work site. I call him. We talk. There's a bit of dickering about gasoline and some additional palaver about the value of avocado firewood, but a deal is struck and the date is set.

The next Saturday he rolls up in an enormous and ancient Ford station wagon, unloads several hundred pounds of tools (which it is my job to carry), and sets to work. Steinhoff asks me questions as he rigs up his ropes and saws. Which way does the prevailing

wind blow? Do you want the tree to spread out or be more direc-
tional? Do you want more shade over here or over there?

We discuss all this and then Bill says, "I'm going to start with
some big limbs first, move them out of the way, section down
about ten feet of trunk from the top, and then clean up some of the
smaller branches that are growing kind of crazy." Crazy like me, I
mumble to myself. Getting nuttier by the day as my life gets more
and more domesticated. Pretty soon I'll be down on the ground
with Mr. Hashinaga picking at the crabgrass with tweezers. "What
did you say?" asks Steinhoff as he cranks up his chainsaw. "Just
thinking it's a good time to prune the tree." "Yep," he agrees,
"that's what spring is for."

Thus over the next three hours the world's greatest avocado tree
gets a haircut, trim, and pedicure. For the record, Steinhoff is not
simply some rookie tree hacker practicing up for better-paying
jobs. On the contrary; he grew up in the trade in the formerly great
timber state of Michigan and knows his stuff. I watch as he takes
the problem carefully in hand and, through a series of intricately
choreographed steps, moves basic tree butchery into the realm of
fine art. For all of his 200-pound bulk, he is agile and graceful.
Moreover, he is extremely intelligent. He is constantly surveying
the tree, looking at the health of the leaves and bark, examining its
features, and noting the tree's basic desire to grow over and into
Mrs. Hashinaga's back window. (Which would be fine with me if a
plague of legal retribution weren't being threatened.)

For me the entire ritual is tinged with sadness and fear. I see half
a ton or more of wood descending from where Bill is working his
way through the tree's main limbs. Some of it rains down in chips,
flakes, and sawdust. More often, monster sections of trunk come
crashing down with a ground-quivering thump. I worry about my
tree like any parent frets about a sick child. Steinhoff assures me
that it is all in God's hands. "It will recover," he chirps, "or it
won't." Simple as that. His saw whines and slobbers its way
through more wood. Leaves, twigs, and other assorted knee-deep
rubble litter the ground. I have visions of my backyard looking like
a Weyerhauser forest that has been clear-cut with drag chains and
bulldozers and then burned for good measure. And me, looking

like Smokey the Bear on the day after, standing next to a charred stump with my shovel and wide-brimmed hat and a big photogenic tear glistening on my cheek.

At the end of the morning Steinhoff announces from the top of a now considerably shorter tree that the job is done. "That's that!" he says, as he climbs down. For some reason I expect more ceremony — maybe a prayer for the dead or a moment of silence with heads bowed. Instead, Bill unrigs his ropes, puts his tools back, partakes of one of my special-occasion Heinekens, loads up his Ford, and drives off.

I start cutting and stacking large limbs and loading rubbish for the dump. The tree looks naked and plucked, a sad remnant of its former green glory. In the late afternoon Jerry comes over. We recline on the deck to survey the carnage. "Here's the deal," I explain. "You see that big chunk down there? That one's for you. The littler one [a mere hundred pounder], that's mine." He nods, eyes dancing over and around the log destined for his workshop. Jerry and I have an understanding forged in beer and blood more than a year ago. He gets a piece of world-class avocado wood for a sculpture he intends to make. Over the next few months, in exchange, he must teach me something about wood carving and sculpting, a subject that interests me.

The agreement is reconfirmed. Peter Adler, I think to myself, you are the true and only Avocado King of Mānoa Valley and one hell of a wheeler-dealer and big-time avocado negotiator! We agree to meet next week at his house for lesson number one; exchange oaths of eternal and undying friendship; and then push, roll, and manhandle his share of our fortune into the gaping maw of his car's trunk.

As the sun goes down, I sweep the last remaining woodchips into a little pile, put away my saws and tidy up the deck. A soft trade wind blows down the valley. Birds skitter through the sunset. The tree really did need a trim, I admit. I walk into the house and wash up for dinner. That night, though, I dream of endless chainsaws biting into the soft, suffering, cream-colored flesh of the tree. And all night long I keep thinking I hear muffled screams and a long, slow moaning coming from the backyard.

* * *

Early on a Sunday morning two months later I take a drive up
to Jerry's for another lesson on carving and the next installment of
my continuing look at Jerry's avocado sculpture. Jerry's house sits
on a large tract of land at the upper end of another of O'ahu's
more beautiful valleys, ten minutes away from downtown. It lies
half hidden in a forest of ferns, rubber trees, lantana, bougainvil-
laea, hibiscus, guava, ironwood, kukui, and Java plum. Shafts of
sunlight slant down through openings in the vegetation overhead.
The ground is cast in deep shadows. It is a landscape made up of
a spectrum of different greens: emeralds, viridians, aquamarines,
and olives. In this sanctuary of towering foliage, Honolulu — just
two miles down the street — seems like a different time zone.
The air is thick and warm, rich with the spongy, earthy greenhouse smell of composting biomass.

As I drive up, a miscellaneous ball of fur, paws, and tails
comes flying down the hill to greet me. Five dogs, all of dubious
ancestry and all mightily pleased with themselves, descend on
me as I get out of my car to a chorus of frantic barking and hand
licking. From the rear of a stand of bananas, a voice calls them
off. Georgia, an eighty-pound German shepherd, reluctantly
removes her frame from mine. Great, muddy paws slowly slide
down my shirt and pants, leaving a wake of brown skid marks.
Jerry appears, shoos off the tangle of dogs, and escorts me up a
short trail.

Jerry's house looks like it has been transported by boat from the
rain forests of Africa but fell overboard a few times before getting
to Hawai'i. The combination house and workshop (better thought
of as a lair, actually) is a rambling, termite-eaten affair with no
clear and fully distinguishable boundary separating inside from
out. It includes a small slum of storage rooms holding on by sheer
instinct to a kitchen; a bathroom and brace of bedrooms; a sag-
ging lānai littered with tools, books, papers, and small carvings; a
leaky blue tarp attached to the house; and a quarter-acre of land
that is distinctly outside and covered with large wood and stone
sculptures in various stages of development or decay depending

on how you look at them. The house, savaged by years of humidity, is slowly returning to the elements. Rotten beams do their best to hold up a rotten shingled roof, out of which sprout several species of endangered ferns and mushrooms. Stumps and stones litter the ground, some partially carved, some simply weathering away under layers of lichens and moss. Spikes of green, red, and purple ti plants grow everywhere. Jerry collects them and has assembled maybe thirty different kinds.

Jerry is not entirely alone here. There are the dogs and there are also birds, lizards, frogs, toads, a three-legged cat, and great, black swarms of mosquitoes. Seeing fresh meat approach, the latter point their nasty noses my way and attack. One swat on the arm kills ten of them. Serves the little buggers right for being so casual and cocky.

Remarkably neat and organized amid all this biological chaos is Jerry himself, a former body-surfing champion and Hawaii Bound wilderness instructor, and now a genuine, full-time, unemployed, struggling-but-not-totally-ignored artist. "I have this perennial cash-flow problem," Jerry explains. "All my money is tied up in food and rent." In his portfolio, nonetheless, are several pieces that have sold for tidy five-digit sums, including one that sits in the Governor's office and others that grace the homes of Honolulu's most prominent people.

Jerry stands a shade under six feet and smokes Marlboros. He has a thin frame — now slightly paunchy as he approaches 45 — and brown hair, green eyes, and little crow's feet crinkling out from the corners of his eyes. A mature-sounding fellow, you might think, but the twinkling eyes and wry smile attest to an imagination that has yet to fully navigate the mysteries of adolescence. When he speaks he nearly always laughs. And when he laughs, it is the kind of laughter one associates with finger paints and PlayDoh — a hearty, full-bodied, infectious, spontaneous and open laugh tinged with a slight hint of adulthood. Nonetheless, Jerry is a master wood-carver, and the proof is just outside his back door.

The 300 pound chunk of avocado log that came crashing down under Bill Steinhoff's deft hand is now being transfigured into something new, something rife with artistic potential. Lying on the ground in upper Kalihi Valley, its weight has been reduced to approximately 125 pounds. Size: roughly five feet by three feet. Shape: not fully defined yet but something vaguely elliptical. For the past two months Jerry has been whittling away at it, chopping, slicing, and shaving off strips of wood as he searches for the log's essence. My role has been that of apprentice. Jerry won't let me touch his piece. Instead, I practice using various carving tools on old scraps he has lying around.

In the shade of a giant eucalyptus tree I lean into a remnant piece of *kamani* and try my hand with a Swiss shaping adze, a sort of giant, left-handed, Paul Bunyan meat cleaver used for shagging off bark. Jerry works away at the avocado log. The morning heats up. My effort is directionless, a simple fooling around with the tools. Like learning to play scales on the clarinet when I was ten years old — useful knowledge but not very pretty. Jerry's work is in earnest. He is sculpting although even he does not fully understand what it will become. "My carving," he says, "is never fully by aim. In fact, it is kind of illusory. What I want to do is get inside the wood. You can't force it though. Carving should be a nice, long, easy-going conversation. If you converse long enough and well enough the result is a finished piece."

Unlike many other sculptors, Jerry loves to work wood that is partially rotted. "What remains after a log has been lying around and decaying or after bugs and disease have attacked a tree is extremely tough and resilient. Rot is nature's way of beginning the carving process. The fibers that are left are clinging to life. I like to follow the direction set by nature herself, carve off the junk stuff, and then give new life to the wood that remains. In effect, I'm an agent. My job is to preserve the secret life of the tree that most people don't know about." And so we carve away, Jerry on the avocado log and me on the *kamani* piece, talking occasionally but more often just chopping and cutting in silence.

Late in the morning we take a break and adjourn to his kitchen by way of the tool room. Laid out on tables and shelves are the basic implements of a wood-carver's trade. Jerry tells me these are essential. The tools exist on a continuum. At one end are the "heavys" used for logging, chopping, and all-purpose large-scale wood whacking. At the other end are the precision instruments used for close-up detail work. In general, the overriding need is for tools that produce concave results. His workshop of essentials includes a medium-sized double-headed ax, a 12-inch McCullough chainsaw, the Swiss shaping adze, a large, New England-style hewing adze, four smaller homemade adzes, a variety of curved and straight gouges and chisels, four kinds of sureform rasps, flat and rat-tail files, a Rockwell speedblock sander, a Craftsman circular hand grinder, a Makita belt sander, miscellaneous scrapers, coping saws, clamps, brushes, rulers, pocketknives, wooden mallets, sandpapers, steel wool, oils, stains, waxes, and a Walkman player with headphones.

Eventually, we make it to the kitchen. Jerry sets some water to boil and then slouches into a straight-back chair as if someone had poured him off the ceiling. Two of the dogs come wandering in the back door and lie down in the corner to listen. The kitchen table is cluttered with small, roughed-out sculptures, notes, drawings, and dirty dishes. We drink coffee and talk story. The mood is lazy, the air humid, the mosquitoes buzzing and crazy with bloodlust. Jerry starts telling me about one of his teachers, Pius "Mau" Piailug, a master boat builder from Satawal Atoll in Micronesia and principal navigator for the first Hōkūle'a canoe expedition to Tahiti. Piailug taught Jerry how to use the Polynesian-style adze. Now Jerry is teaching me.

As he talks, weaving various stories together, my eyes are drawn to his hands. They are stubborn and chunky looking with undersized fingers and unartistically large and battered nails. Partly healed blisters the size of half-dollars are peeling away from his palms. The pads of his fingers are rimmed with callus. I watch his hands carefully as they move across the table in effusive gestures, shaping the air and punctuating the story he is telling me. "…so Piailug and I went up the valley a ways to look for an adze handle and he pointed to a guava tree that looked just about right…." I see Jerry's hands cleave the air around him, his fingers curling and unfolding, extending, and then curling again, disembodied, almost as if they were engaged in a separate conversation that had nothing to do with his mouth and brains. As if they belonged elsewhere, up in the mountains perhaps, grappling with fallen *koa*, or outside working on logs of *kamani* or *milo* or guava. Or avocado. Not, however, sitting at the kitchen table waiting for the jawing to stop. Working hands to be sure, alive with their own memories of saw handles, waxes, chisels, and oils.

The coffee gone, we go back out for another hour of work. Soon I discard my *kamani* piece and simply watch Jerry carve the avocado log. With a mallet he taps a large gouge through whorls and rings of wood, across lines of spalt, down into the various layers of sapwood and cambium. He moves with the grain of the wood, parting strips and chips from the mother log with sure and deft movements. There is rarely a wasted motion, rarely a missed stroke, rarely a sense of urgency. The shape of the sculpture becomes more pronounced. Jerry puts down the gouge and starts to carve a hole through the thinnest part of the log with a small adze. The very one, in fact, that Pius Piailug made for him out of a guava branch.

Jerry kneels down, raises the adze above the log, then guides it on its downward course. A small, neat chip of wood spins into the air. He repeats the move again. And then again, rocking on his knees. Each stroke is sure and true. As he works in the morning heat, in the lush splendor of the forest clearing, I notice his face. What is it about that smile? Where have I seen it before? A twenty-year-old memory of a serendipitous encounter suddenly comes back to me: I remember a white-haired holy man I met in India, a wandering *sannyasi* who invited me to go wading into a dirty river one morning for ablutions. The same rocking and bowing, the same enigmatic smile. Above all else, the same effortless concentration.

When Jerry stops to rest he shows me how the sculpture is starting to evolve in his mind. He might just mount the whole thing on a lovely lava stone with braided rope lashings, he says. Then he traces a pattern down the length of the wood to show me its future shape, an oblong wing form with a taper at one end. "Peter, I think this is what your tree wants to become," he says. He sets his adze down and gets a drink of water from a hose. "How can you tell?" I ask him. He gives me that quizzical finger paint and Play-Doh look, laughs, then picks up the adze and goes back to work.

* * *

Late in spring, the first flowers start to appear on the tree. Eagle-eyed Dana notices them one day when we're out in the backyard watering (resuscitating, actually) a half-dead papaya plant. Despite, or because of, the radical pruning, the tree is covered with flowers — a good omen; a sign of continuing health and vitality. Merrily buzzing away are hundreds of honey bees that have come from miles around to suck up some avocado goodness and do a bit of pollinating for us. Dana is intrigued by the number of falling flowers; each little puff of wind brings down more. Under one unpruned corner of the tree, the blossoms are thick on the ground. Dana and Corey scoop up handfuls and throw them in the air and at each other, the same way people on the mainland go out and enjoy the first snowfall before they have to attend to it with shovels and rock salt.

A month later only a few bees, drunk and swollen with pollen lust, are still buzzing around looking for flowers. Most of the petals have fallen. But everywhere on the tree are baby avocados, little green fruits that seem intent on defying marauding birds and gusty trade winds. In early summer, the heat is upon us. Each evening at sunset the kids and I go into the backyard to water some of the more parched plants: pots of Boston ferns and baby's tears, tropical violets growing under the small papaya tree, orchids hanging on a rack under the deck, white and yellow gingers, an oregano plant, some Maui roses, and, in the corner of the yard, a few Chinese banana trees.

It would be quite natural to think of all this vegetation sprawling out on some vast and genteel manor replete with gardeners, butlers, drivers, and maids. The truth of the matter is that our "estate" is 50 yards long by 20 yards wide, an undersized and — as Mānoa backyards go — rather puny example of Hawaiian living. The avocado tree dominates the scene. Everything else that is planted here must ultimately accommodate itself to the tree because it is so central. Our deck, a recent addition built on weekends, extends fifteen feet into the middle branches of the tree, eight feet off the ground. Looking out from our living room, sitting on the deck drinking beer, wandering around the yard, or even gazing over in our direction from the Hashinaga house, all you see is avocado tree.

When we first moved into our house a decade ago, I set off to find out whatever I could about avocado trees in general and our tree in particular. What emerged from my study was an interesting array of avocado trivia, much of which I later dismissed — temporarily — as unnecessary and irrelevant to real avocado philosophizing. Who cares that the first recorded introduction of the avocado took place well before 1850? Or that avocados currently rank fourth among fruits commercially produced in Hawai'i? Or that there was once a Hawaiian Avocado Company near Waimea, O'ahu? Or that between 1904 and 1907, Hawaiian avocados were gobbled down by people in Vancouver, Chicago, New York, and Washington? Or that in 1911 the Hawaiian Agricultural Experiment Station had more than sixty varieties under observation? Well, I do.

Then I found out that avocados have been classified into three races — Mexican, Guatemalan, and West Indian — and that the prevailing races in Hawai'i are the Guatemalan and West Indian. These races, in turn, are divided into subgroups called, to name but a few, the Nutmeg, Holt, Lehua, Ilialu, Wilder, Case, and McDonald. (Still another reason why my tree's picture should grace the wall of our local McEatery.) Given my dual interests in dark clouds and silver linings, however, I learned that the life of an avocado tree in Hawai'i can be just as difficult as in a third-world country like Mexico or Guatemala. Avo trees are vulnerable to a variety of nasty and sometimes fatal diseases, the names of which alone are enough to cause avocado tree heart failure: root rot, scab, algal spot, and black spot. Moreover, avo trees can be loved to death by any of a number of bugs including beetles, scales, thrips, mites, and fruit flies.

As to the tree in my backyard, I discovered that it is known locally as a "Beardslee" or "Ables," a variety of avocado grown from a parent seed by a certain L. C. Ables who once lived at 1627 Kewalo Street in Honolulu. Ables, whoever he or she was, planted the seed of a McDonald (there it is again!) avocado in December,

1911, and the new variety that came up was then named in honor of one Admiral Beardslee. How the son or daughter of the original Ables avocado came to my house is uncertain, but what is known is that my tree is a veteran. It's more than fifty years old. The fruits it produces are called "winter pears" because they ripen in October. A Beardslee avo typically weighs in at 1-1/2 to 2-1/2 pounds. The fruits on my tree, however, average 3 pounds and better. The yellow-and-green flesh has an oil content of about 12% and a pleasing nutty sort of taste.

So much for facts and figures. Avocados also have a more intimate life that is worth recounting. Yes, the great act itself, sex and fertilization. Unlike most other plants, avocados have flowers that open and close twice. On its first opening every flower behaves as if it were female, meaning that it can be pollinated but cannot shed pollen. Twelve to twenty-four hours after closing, the flowers open up again, but this time as males. Now they shed pollen but no longer receive it. To make its own life even more complicated, all of the flowers on a given tree — and all the trees of a given species — open and close at the same time. This makes natural diversity or interplanting essential.

All of this unrestrained sexual activity in the backyard doesn't seem to interest Corey, Dana, and Kelly. One afternoon while we are noodling around looking at the last of the flowers and the first of the fruits, I try to do a little explaining about the birds and the bees. A good opportunity, I think to myself. When I was Corey's age I would have paid hard-cash allowance money for a little accurate information on how all this works. So I start to give them Adler's Modified Lecture Number 4 called "Some Words Elucidating Sperm, Eggs, and Rock and Roll." I tell them about pistils, stamens, and pollen and how some of the flowers are boys and other ones are girls. And how the boys and girls get together when they are old enough and how each of them makes a half of their baby. This discussion leads into more complicated talk about seeds and eggs and how children grow inside of their parents. After ten minutes of this the two older kids look at me in utter disbelief, decide that I'm seriously jiving them, and walk off in search of bigger thrills. Kelly would too if she could walk yet.

By late July the weather has turned hot and dry — 90 degrees and more most days. Searching for a good place to recline one Sunday afternoon I grab Kelly under one arm, extract a beer out of the fridge with the other, and head down to the backyard. Kelly and I settle ourselves on the grass in the shade. I pop open the beer and lean back on the tree. Kelly reaches for the beer bottle. I notice her diaper is already wet. "Kelly," I tell her, "the first thing you need to know about beer is that you don't really drink it; you just sort of rent it for awhile." I check to see that Carolyn isn't around and then give her a swig. She wrinkles her little face and dribbles it all out on me. So much for sharing.

Then Kelly climbs down and starts grazing through the grass searching for something more substantial to shove in her mouth. She starts with grass, sticks, and old leaves and then, in a quick abandonment of vegetarianism, starts tasting bugs and worms. All of which, if I remember my African and South American anthropology correctly, are good for her. I settle back. The tree encompasses us in its shade, a great arch of branches hanging down in a semicircle around us, cooling the ground beneath and us at the same time. The new branches, a result of the Steinhoffian pruning process, are fruitless but have thick, leathery, and bright green leaves. The old branches, untouched by Bill's blades, are full of maturing avocados. The leaves that are left on these are purplish since most of the tree's nourishment is going into mainline avocado production.

Kelly navigates her way back to me on all fours with a big smear of dirt on her face, crawls into my lap, and promptly falls asleep. I gaze around. How fine and content to be here like this, I think. Sitting under the sweep of a fertile fruit tree and lazing in the heat and shade of this beautiful place in the middle of the blue Pacific is as close as one can get to heaven without actually going through the departure-from-earth process. Kelly obviously agrees. After a while Corey and Dana wander outside, and then Carolyn shows up with an old beach blanket. She scolds me for letting Kelly eat dirt, but it's a token scolding at best. Not much authority in her voice because of the drooping heat. Pretty soon Dana falls asleep. Then Carolyn's eyes start to close. Corey and I are still awake but fading fast, somewhere between slow motion and no motion. Corey is smiling drowsily on the blankets. I lie down on my stomach and look out sideways on their four assorted female bodies. The tribe. Our own new race of people. Dana scratches herself in her sleep. The preciousness of so much family washes over me and for a moment I feel like crying. And then sleep comes and the five of us have the easiest, laziest nap in the history of our clan.

*   *   *

August and September come and go. In October, the first truly mature avos come whistling down though the branches like the unguided missiles they actually are — dangerously close to, but not precisely on, Mrs. Hashinaga's side of the fence. We are now presented with our annual problem of what to do with too many avocados. To be exact, how to dispose of a ton of them without creating an instant avocado welfare economy. Over the next several weeks I start picking them and giving them by twos and threes to good friends. Later on, I start collecting them by the bucket and then, later still, by the bushel basketful. The idea is to snag them off the tree using a twelve-foot bamboo stick with a cloth and wire bag attached to the end. Moreover, it is imperative to do this before they fall themselves but after they have grown and ripened to their maximum. A delicate matter of timing and judgment. Do it too soon and you end up with a less than world-class avo; do it too late and they jump, hit the ground, and turn to avocado slime.

Those avocados that I miss, however, do not necessarily go to waste. They find their way down to the good earth of the yard and, slime or no slime, keep the rat, mouse, and mynah bird population in my neighborhood in first-class fighting trim. When an avo falls on the ground overnight, I typically find it half chewed in the morning. You can see where one of the critters gnawed, pecked, and/or clawed its way into the avo's innards and guzzled down half of the green meat inside. We don't begrudge the critters; they have to eat too. And this keeps us all in touch with nature even if it's in a strictly urban setting.

Nonetheless, even with the loss of, say, two hundred semi-trashed avos each fall we still have the problem of what to do with about a thousand other good ones. The answer lies in free enterprise. Over the last few years, I've developed a small but sophisticated market for a portion of my crop. My middle man is a guy named Andy Rodrigues, the proprietor of our own local Mānoa Health Food Store. Each year Andy and I go through the same basic buyer-seller ritual. I pick a couple of plump ones and drive down to the store. "Andy," says I, "have I got some avos for you this year!" Andy looks at them as if they were old tires and boards I'd just picked up at the dump. "Kind of puny," he says as he hefts a four-pounder with both hands and lofts it onto his scale. We talk for a while. And then, the pregnant moment comes. "Howmuchyawantferem?" I always pause for dramatic effect at this point. "Look," I tell him, "I don't want to haggle around with you because we've been doing business for a long time and these are, unquestionably, the best avos you will ever have. So for you, a special one-time price of 60 cents per pound." Then Andy pauses; "40," he replies. "You're a hard man," I answer. "How's about 55?" To which Andy always says 45. And so on and so on. Each year, no matter what the larger world and regional avocado markets are doing, no matter that Safeway is selling wrinkled little six-ounce avocados from California for $1.69 each, Andy and I always end up at 50 cents a pound.

But even selling off sixty or seventy pounds a week to the health food store barely makes a dent on the supply side of the equation. To take up the excess, we are constantly hunting for new things to do with avocados. What we've discovered includes delectables like avocado with hot chili poured over it, avocado mixed with grapefruit, golden avocado bread, and chilled avocado wine. Then there's avocado sponge cake with light green icing, avocado curry, avocado waffles, avocado milkshakes, avocado mocha mint coolers, avocado cream pies, and avocado tofu whip. Even our die-hard beer-and-meat friends go for avocado-papaya ice cream.

By mid-November, however, the end of the avocado season is in sight. Most of our fruits are gone, consumed by us, our friends and the walk-in traffic at Andy's Mānoa Health Food Store.

There's maybe one big picking left and then the tree will be clean. One weekday afternoon Jerry calls up and asks if he can stop by my office the next morning and pick up an avo or two. We set a time and that day after work I go out to pick a few for him. I snag several big ones off the side of the tree I have been saving, set them aside, and then pick a few extras that I leave on Mrs. Hashinaga's door step.

The next day Jerry shows up at the office with a large lumpy object covered in a sheet. The staff in my office gathers around and I introduce Jerry as a famous local sculptor. Jerry asks everyone to stand back and then pulls the shroud away from the lump. Underneath is the avocado-wood sculpture that he has worked on all summer; the same one that started out as a piece of trunk excised by Bill Steinhoff some months back. The log has been transformed into a gleaming, sweeping, robustly polished arch with a large, graceful twist in the middle. A free-form expression in wood that suggests the lazy flap of a wing on a large seabird. The style is pure Jerry — reminiscent of Hans Arp, Henry Moore, and Pablo Picasso — but an original Vasconcellos nonetheless. The carving seems flawless. It has been sanded smooth and oiled and rubbed until the darker grains stand out from the blond wood in deep and lustrous relief. The carving is attached to a large lava stone and held by handmade rope lashings. "Traditional lashings," says Jerry, "the same knots and wraps that the old Hawaiians used on their canoes."

He props his sculpture up on a table in the waiting area of the office and says he intends to leave it here for a while, maybe a month or two, maybe longer. We drink coffee and talk about other pieces he has in progress, including a *koa* altar for a church and a large free-form he is making ("just following the grain") from a fine piece of swamp mahogany he rescued from the City and County tree cutters near Waikīkī. I give him the avos I picked for him. Just before he leaves, I ask him if he's given his sculpture a name. "Yep," he says. It's called "I Flew Over Peter's Tree." And then Jerry departs with that ever-so-slightly maniacal grin tattooed on his face. I gaze at his statue and let its name and shape sink into my mind, and then I go back to work.

* * *

A few days before Thanksgiving I shove a ladder up against the tree, climb into the branches with a large sack, and strip off all the remaining avocados, about 100 pounds worth. I box them up and drive downtown to see Father Claude DuTeil. For many years DuTeil and his successors have run an organization called the Institute for Human Services, a food and shelter program for street people. Most of his two-hundred-per-day clients (he calls them guests) are people who are sadly down on their luck or whose mental processes have, for one reason or another, snagged up on some half-submerged cranial coral reef. Some are retarded. Others are alcoholics or slightly crazy but not so crazy that they need to be locked away. Few of Claude's people hold permanent jobs and not a one has a permanent address except for the Institute. DuTeil is a rare and remarkable man. He has devoted his life to the single-minded mission of taking care of those people that no one else wants to have around. He helps me unload the boxes and invites me in for a cup of tea, after which I wish him a happy holiday and take my leave.

Thanksgiving comes and goes. December rolls in and with it a change in the weather. Just north of the Hawaiian chain an old cold front — what weathermen call a shearline — is sending 30- to 45-mile-an-hour trade winds and lots of rain blustering across the Island. It's jacket and blanket time, cool, wet, and invigorating. One Sunday when Carolyn and the kids are out of the house for the afternoon, I step out into the backyard to complete a task un-attended to but not totally forgotten for many months now. In fact, some inner clock has been waiting for an auspicious time and that moment has now arrived with the change in weather. I walk around under the tree and inspect its leaves. I poke at the bark, tug a few dead branches out of the lower limbs, and rake away the leaves and twigs the storm has brought down. Then I pace around looking for a special spot on the ground in the tree's shade and when I find it I get a trowel and dig a small, narrow hole.

I push down about ten inches, down through the rich, humid, life-giving soil of Mānoa Valley and then take a small Tupperware box out of my back pocket that contains a dried scab of skin. The little black piece of flesh is a remnant of baby Kelly's *piko*, the umbilical cord saved from her birthing. I pluck it out of the box, drop it in the hole, and cover it with dirt. Kelly is now more than a year old and completion of that first year is important in Hawai'i. This same ritual is one I carried out for my other two daughters and one I need to complete now. It is a special, private ceremony that is, in Hawaiian culture, a father's responsibility. It pays homage to the earth and the great richness and continuity that permeates life.

Digging the hole, I think back to how it was with the other two. How when Corey was born I saved the tiny bit of umbilicus that dropped off her belly button after a week and a half of life and months later hiked back into the hills behind Kāne'ohe and left her *piko* in a shaded cleft of rock next to a wild taro plant. And then several years later, after Dana was born, I performed the same ceremony again, walking the hills and ridges behind Round Top until I found a special place as if I had been guided to it. And there I buried her precious *piko* in the soil under a beautiful, flowering 'ōhi'a tree.

And now, with my last child I complete the process. I cover the hole with a few handfuls of dirt, smooth it over, and transplant some strands of grass on top. Then I stand up, stretch, and gaze around. A sudden gust of wind comes whipping down the valley as if the spirits and gods of Mānoa were somehow pleased. The air is crisp and sweet, bringing a foretaste of rain that will sweep down across the land shortly. Kelly and Carolyn will never know exactly where I have buried this small portion of themselves and I will never reveal precisely where it is to anyone. Suffice it to say that it rests in the presence of the great avocado tree that centers and quietly grounds our day-to-day lives.

I head back toward the house, the wind rising, the first drops of rain brushing my face. The tree sways back and forth as if it were acknowledging this moment with a graceful hula of limbs and branches. As I pass under it I pause and clear my mind of everything except the ritual task I have just completed. I close my eyes, squeeze them shut as tightly as I can, and then relax in the inner darkness. For a moment there is silence, an absence of sight and sound. Then an image comes into place. I see Kelly grown up. There is a man standing by her and there are other children — Kelly's children — playing under our avocado tree. Then Corey and Dana and their husbands and children gather around as well. I watch my daughters and their families join hands in a playful circle on the very spot on which I am standing. I open my eyes and the image disappears. The rain comes down harder. I turn and walk toward the house and leave the sheltering branches of the tree.

Thus it is once more: on a cool, wet Sunday afternoon my family and I are bound over to the land that nourishes us — and, through this tree, we are again renewed.

3

Bugs

We hope that, when the insects take over the world, they will remember with gratitude how we took them along on all our picnics.

Bill Vaughan

IT'S SATURDAY AND I REALLY SHOULD BE DOING SOMETHING ELSE right now, something more manly and American, like mowing the clumps of crabgrass that constitute the farther dominions of our lawn or fixing the clogged gutters that spout cold water onto anyone who approaches the front door in a rain. I should be changing the oil in my ten-year-old Mazda and repairing the fence that I crushed while trimming avocado branches. Instead I'm down in the basement dealing with bugs, one of which is lying dead in front of me.

This particular critter is a cockroach. "He" — which a certain feminist friend tells me is the only proper pronoun for referring to cockroaches, dead or alive — belongs to a tribe of three-inch monstrosities that has taken up permanent residence with me, Carolyn, and the kids. His name is *Periplaneta americana*, known more commonly as the American Roach. Being progressive citizens of the emerging global village, we have German and Surinam roaches here as well. In fact, an entire international community of roaches (some of which are by necessity "shes") has moved in and now lives under, around, over, and inside our house in Honolulu.

All of this I accept. Roaches go with the territory and if you want to live in Hawai'i, you have to get used to bugs. They are as much a part of Paradise as we are and they outnumber us by millions to one anyway. Therefore, to my mind, the best policy has always been to strive for a state of peaceful coexistence. Carolyn, however, has a different disposition on this matter. Loathing any-thing that smacks of domestic disorganization, she brooks no non-sense from insects that walk, crawl, stump, wiggle, swim, fly, or otherwise stumble into our environs. It's nothing personal. She just thinks all insects are vile, dirty, and disgusting creatures that war-rant instantaneous destruction. Inescapably, I see this attitude being passed along to our daughters.

I tend to be more let-live, even with the roaches, whom I don't especially admire. In fact, cockroaches and I — cowards that we both are — usually get along just fine. They skitter around the darker corners and edges of our house on various types of roach missions until they see me or some other human coming. Then the little chickenhearts bolt for cover. While Carolyn's instincts are to hunt them down, I avoid thinking about them.

The one in front of me, however, was different. He made the mistake of running up my arm while I was eating a peanut butter sandwich. Perhaps it was a frontal assault on the peanut butter itself. Or maybe he was just too stupid or tired to know up from down. In any case, for a brief second, I got enraged at his unadul-terated audacity, brushed him off, slapped him into a tan gob of legs and feelers with my rubber slipper, and then sat and finished up my sandwich feeling bad.

This little roach affair got me into a theological mood. Saturday mornings are like that. If I'm not involved in the immediate occu-pational therapy of domestic chores, then I forthwith lose myself in an ever-widening spiral of questions about the meaning of life. Take the matter of souls and whether cockroaches have them. It's a touchy subject that cuts to the heart of centuries of religious debate. Buddhists, Hindus, Jains, Druids, Naturists, Animists, and certain cults of Bear, Sky, and Tree worshippers say yes. Muslims, Christians, and Jews tend to equivocate on the subject. Carolyn, obviously, is firm in her belief that they don't. For myself, I'm not sure. I tend to take my cues from old Hawaiians who believed that everything has a soul, including the grasshoppers they'd catch and string on flower stems to broil for snacks. (They'd talk to them first and explain.) Still, I'm not fully convinced one way or the other.

Be that as it may, the now-dispatched roach and his possibly liberated roach soul also got me thinking about the lousy reputation bugs seem to have with nearly everyone. Mention the word "insects" to a local person, for example, and the first thing that probably comes to mind is termites. Both the dry-wood and ground types keep quite a few local people employed as exterminators. Other than those folks, armored with industrial foggers and high-pressure spray cans, everyone else hates termites. And for good reason. Hawai'i has more termites per linear board foot of lumber than anyplace else in the world. Wood is to termites what rice and potatoes are to humans. It is a basal and elementary substance. In search of it, termites gather in great armies and attack the nearest source. When a termite is poisoned by an exterminator — the insect equivalent of dying in battle — it immediately ascends to bug-Valhalla on a wooden ladder that it eats on the way up. For termites, heaven itself is a Mount Everest of untreated posts, joists, studs, planks, and logs.

In Hawai'i, human/termite interactions follow a predictable pattern. First, the termites start shedding their wings into your soup and salad when they are swarming. Usually this happens on clammy, humid nights when the trade winds stop blowing and you are already irritable from the heat. Then, over the next several months — and with some varieties, in a matter of days — the little buggers literally disappear into the woodwork. If you are an optimist, you probably think they have gone next door. What they are actually doing is munching on the walls and beams of your house. One day you see some salt-and-pepper-colored droppings on the tiles in your kitchen. A week later, the refrigerator tilts and starts sinking through the floor. That's when you call the guys with the gas masks.

There are also other troublesome bugs. Mosquitoes, for example. Over the course of numerous backpacking trips through Hawai'i's rain forests and along remote stretches of beach — and even in my own house — I have gotten quite curious about these small, long-beaked, wobble-winged critters. I've always wanted to understand, for instance, how it is that mosquitoes can tell the exact time that a human being is falling asleep. That's the moment they infallibly choose to fly up a nose, squeeze through an eyelid, dive down an open, snoring throat, or embrace the workings of the inner ear.

Scientifically, mosquitoes are hard to study. Consider the research impediments involved simply in figuring out which mosquitoes prefer which kind of environments. Or which type produces the worst itch or the loudest buzz. To properly study these matters, you would have to identify and isolate the various local mosquito species and subspecies and then band and track them with radio transmitters. The other way to accomplish this would be to capture several billion of them, separate them by species, age, and gender, observe their various bite, buzz, and itch-inducing behaviors, sequentially dump each type into the top of a blender, and then analyze the various mosquito extracts that you have now produced.

Obscure insect research of just this type takes place all the time in Hawai'i. Just the other day, for example, I heard about a gent named Eric Jang of the Tropical Fruit and Vegetable Laboratory in Hilo. Jang spends most of his waking hours inserting tiny wires into the hairs on the antennae of Mediterranean fruit flies. It's a hell of a job. The hairs are 0.0005 inch long. The wires being inserted are connected to an oscilloscope, which records nerve impulses. All of this patient and detailed effort is aimed at finding better ways of combating the Medfly, the scourge of our $15-billion agricultural industry. My approach to annihilation and general roachicide — call it the Conan The Barbarian Method — seems more direct, but each to his own.

There are other professional bug killers around also. The State and Federal Departments of Agriculture employ a small army of civil servants who wage full-time all-out war on orange spiny whiteflies, nitidulid beetles, spotted alfalfa aphids, tomato pin-worms, agromyzid leafminers, banana skippers, and horn flies. The Vector Control Division of the Department of Health has its own staff of specialists who deal almost exclusively with *Musca sorbens*, the dog dung fly. Even the U.S. Army has a battalion of bug killers stationed in the Islands simply to fumigate battleships and bivouacs for bedbugs, lice, and cockroaches.

Occasionally we find some out-of-the-ordinary use for insects that causes a momentary reconsideration. Professor Lee Goff, for instance, is a much-in-demand bug man from the University of Hawai'i who also works for the City and County of Honolulu in the Medical Examiner's office. Goff is a "forensic entomologist," one of only 38 or so registered in a world directory. His primary responsibility is to help solve murders by establishing the precise time someone was killed. And how does he do it? "There is a fairly distinct fauna around decomposed remains," reports Goff. What he means is that there are, in Hawai'i, no less than 190 varieties of local mites, spiders, flies, beetles, ants, and wasps that will attack rotting flesh in a certain succession. Once you understand the pecking order and decomposition timetables that are involved, calculating backward to the time someone was done in becomes possible.

Goff's work, though, is the exception. In general, the insects of Hawai'i simply don't seem to merit much respect. Our scorpions, the stinging ones that look like lobsters and live in dry underbrush, our ants — all of the many varieties — and our dog dung maggots just don't get good press. Even our butterflies and moths are largely ignored except for those few that get captured and embalmed in clear plastic paperweights. For the rest, it is my wife's worldview that prevails. The only good ones, so the logic goes, are those that have been properly killed off with bug spray, rubber slippers, fly swatters, genetic splices, or by electrocution from outdoor zappers.

I find this deplorable, not just because insects may have souls, but because they are, unquestionably, the most fully and successfully adapted creatures in Hawai'i. Insects — far more than people — ought to be admired for their intelligent and skillful accommodations to life in general and to the Islands in particular. From the tops of our volcanic mountains down to the salt shores of our seas, insects in Hawai'i consistently show us their resilience and beauty. Instead of stomping them flat on the sidewalk, we should apologize to them for our bad attitudes. We should gaze at them with an unjaundiced eye and admire the complexity of their rituals and the unbridled enthusiasm of their reproductive lust. We should cherish their diversity and fecundity and honor their instincts for survival. At a minimum, we should study their ways and acknowledge — grudgingly if it must be so — their courage and forbearance in the face of human perversity.

None of this comes easily. Insects, after all, call up a primordial repugnance in our own warm-blooded species. Someone, though, must rise to the challenge. The bugs need a champion. They need a publicist and spokesperson. They need an advocate who will relentlessly lobby on their behalf and who will represent their interests with sensitivity, intelligence, and compassion.

All of which — in lieu of lawn mowing, car washing, and leaky faucet fixing — I now declare to be the uppermost priority for the rest of this rapidly disintegrating Saturday and for however many more Saturdays and Sundays it may require. It's a thankless job, but someone has to do it.

*　　*　　*

Let's begin with Orville, who is, in his own way, a symbol of all that is right with Hawai'i's bug world. Technically, Orville is not a true insect at all. He is — along with bees, butterflies, fleas, scorpions, crabs, lobsters, and crayfish — a member of the much larger phylum called Arthropoda. To get right to the scientific point, Orville is an arachnid, which makes him taxonomically distinct from his distant cousins in the classes that contain, to name just a few, grasshoppers (Insecta), centipedes, (Chilopoda), shrimps (Crustacea), and horseshoe crabs (Merostomata). All of these creatures are descended from a simple, segmented annelidlike worm that more or less ruled the world 600 million years ago. And most of them can, for my lay purposes at least, be considered "bugs."

Orville, however, is not just any old bug. He is *Theridion grallitor*, a quarter-inch-long adult male Hawaiian "happy face" spider who is now memorialized in a glossy eight-by-ten color blowup mounted on the wall of my study. The picture was taken by William Mull, one of the most perceptive and productive amateur bug watchers in the Islands. Bill, who is spending his retirement years in a cozy little cottage in the rain forest village of

Volcano, has a keen interest in matters entomological. For years he photographed the colorful creatures that inhabit our smallest local environments. First it was a series on slime molds; then, for a long time, it was the happy face spider. These days he has gridded out a patch of rain forest to study the territorial behaviors of certain flies.

The name Orville, however, has nothing to do with Bill Mull. It barely has anything to do with the happy face spider. I call him Orville in honor of a childhood chum whose athletic nickname was "Spider." Orville Gershon Moskowitz was, in fact, the best shortstop, cleanup hitter, and base-stealer on our south-side-of-Chicago sandlot baseball team when I was twelve years old. Unfortunately, Orville Moskowitz hated his name. He considered it unfit for a kid with the athletic prowess of a power lifter and the temperament of a wolverine. In fact, Spider would regularly mash in the giblets of anyone who called him by his real name. Hence, "Spider."

But back to the happy face. As a member of the class Arachnida, Orville has the same bifurcated build as his better-known cousins, the tarantula and daddy longlegs. From front to rear, there is a bulbous front body called a cephalothorax containing eyes, head, claws, throat, and legs. Behind this is a much larger rear body that is all stomach muscles and digestive juices. Unlike the tarantula, however, Orville's abdomen is hairless. Not only that, he is wearing what looks like a yellow aloha shirt imprinted with a large smiling mouth and two small eyes on top. The design looks remarkably like one of those lapel buttons that says Have A Nice Day.

This, of course, is the kind of clever little subterfuge we have come to expect from the bug world. Insects fool us regularly. Up close, for example, the true mug of the happy face spider is a piece of gruesomeness straight out of a Ridley Scott Gothic science-fiction horror movie. Yellow mandibles dripping with the gooey white remains of something it just ate are waving around and searching for still another meal. Spindly, translucent legs are poised to skitter off should something bigger, including Orville's lovely wife, attack. All in all, Orville looks like a real street fighter.

The happy face spider in my picture, however, is basically unhappy. He is, in fact, a big wimp. Like most native Hawaiian land creatures, he is completely harmless to humans, a fact that in and of itself would disappoint me if I were a spider. Most of the time, the male happy face hangs out under the broad leaves of native plants doing nothing. The markings that make up his false happy face coupled with the green and yellow sunlight filtered through his leaf are his M.O. They are a camouflage. This leaf-shroud also takes the place of the web he is incapable of spinning. Through it, he detects the vibrations of smaller insects that happen to land on his house.

Male happy face spiders also have other problems. After an elaborate communication process full of bobbing, leaf pulling, and strand plucking, Orville, if he's a typical male, will try to mate with the lady happy face spider of his dreams. If he is unsuccess-ful, he will probably get eaten. If he does succeed in mating, then he will probably die soon after anyway. Life, however, goes on. After she has dispensed with Orville, Mrs. Spider settles down to serious motherhood. And here, the happy face spider ascends into its own. Mrs. Spider will guard her silky eggs ferociously and, when they start to hatch, will help each little spiderling break out of its sac. Then, babies close at hand, she will catch a fly or two and feed the little buggers their first meal.

The happy face spider is just one of hundreds of interesting endemic arthropods and insects found in the Islands. There are other peculiar adaptations that should be admired as well. There are stink bugs that have lost their stink and flies that no longer fly. There are oversized dragonflies and giant katydids. There are damselflies that are completely terrestrial and chirpless crickets that walk instead of jump.

My personal favorites, however, are the critters that live on the tops of Mauna Loa and Mauna Kea on the island of Hawai'i. These summits resemble the moon and are ecologically classified as "tundra." Cinder and spatter cones made up of jagged frozen lavas alternate with deep fissures and vents. There are the deep snows of winter and the parched days of summer. In this alpine desert made of stone, except for a few brittle lichens tenaciously clinging to certain rocks, there is no vegetation. There are also no birds, mammals, or reptiles. Because there are no streams, there are virtually no aquatic fauna — no fish, mollusks, or crustaceans. There are, however, bugs. Look closely amidst the fractures, rifts, and vents and you can find tiny native centipedes, several varieties of hunting spiders, a lichen-eating moth, and a few other little curiosities eking out a meager but nonetheless sustainable living in some of the cracks.

One of the most interesting of these mountain dwellers is the *wēkiu* bug, a tiny wingless insect that lives off the death throes of other insects that have been blown up from the humid and fertile forests below 10,000 feet. In fact, tons of organic matter — seeds, pollen, insects, and other debris — swirl up on Hawai'i's thermal currents and settle on the mountains. An unlucky moth or fly that finds itself swept into this airborne planktonic soup and then dropped down on top of Mauna Kea stands a good chance of having the last of its room-temperature body fluids sucked out by a *wēkiu* bug before it actually freezes. The *wēkiu* itself, by virtue of a complex body chemistry, is immune to the cold. It's full of antifreeze. If you were to pick it up with an ungloved hand, writes Sam Gon, an ecologist with The Nature Conservancy's Hawai'i Heritage Program, its proteins would solidify like a hard-boiled egg.

The *wēkiu* is unusual and if you are intent on seeing one you have to be prepared to suffer. First you must struggle your way up to the top of Mauna Loa or Mauna Kea. If you go on foot — the way it ought to be done by anyone who wants to be a member of the Hawaiian Hairshirt Bug Watchers Society — it's something just short of a two-day death march. Once you are up there, the next trick is to stay long enough for your body to adjust to the altitude. Finally, when you are fully acclimatized, you will probably have to spend several days crawling over sharp lava rocks on your hands and knees with your posterior parts freezing in the breeze and your eyes focused straight down like a microscope. All of this edge-of-death and on-the-brink aggravation — which backpackers crave anyway — is worth it because it will eventually lead you to the *wēkiu*.

Other interesting Hawaiian bugs are far more accessible, though, and are recommended for people who are saner, lamer, or simply less discerning about the bug oddities they want to observe. For sheer ubiquity, for example, you might want to inspect some of the members of the genus *Drosophila*. The best way to do this is to take a mango or banana or avocado, put it on the ground, kick it around a little bit, and then let it ripen. Let it ripen, in fact, until it becomes a mushy glob of rat-chewed, gecko-gnawed, bird-pecked fruit sludge. Then pull up a lawn chair, strip off your clothes, smear some sunblock on your normally unexposed parts, snap the top off of one of those cans of beer in your cooler, and sit quietly nearby to watch. If they aren't there already, several squadrons of tiny winged things will soon zoom in on the crud in front of you. The flies are drosophilids, also known as pomace flies or vinegar gnats.

These flies make great research subjects. One reason is that there are millions of them. Another is that they have giant chromosomes that are easily viewed and manipulated in laboratory experiments. Still another reason is that Hawai'i has the greatest diversity of *Drosophila* species in the world. More than 500 have been described and an estimated 500 more are awaiting discovery. Conceivably, you may just find a new one while you are sitting there guzzling down beer. You would then have the honor of naming it *Drosophila adleri* after the person who gave you all this free advice.

Be warned, however. This kind of concentrated bug watching also takes extreme amounts of patience and great attention to detail. If you are used to bigger, faster events — the Chicago Bears versus the Washington Redskins, for example — then the exhilaration of seeing a pack of drosophilids swarming over some rotten fruit may not be for you.

If your mind does start to wander, reach over, grab another beer, and give serious consideration to the idea that our local drosophilids may soon yield a major refinement of some of Charles Darwin's theories of evolution. The reasoning goes like this:

In 1859, Darwin argued that the destiny of any given species is determined by the natural selection process that occurs when a line of creatures responds to new or changed environmental conditions (i.e., available habitat, natural enemies, climate, and food supply). "Natural selection" essentially involves survival of the fittest. Those individuals that adapt best — those that are smarter, stronger, or quicker in the evolutionary sweepstakes game — get to mate and continue their own genes. Those that are less capable get left behind in the dust. Being a product of the Victorian era in England, however, Charles didn't consider the fundamental power of sex — at least not publicly. Sex was not a subject for discussion at the time. And here's where the *Drosophila* come in.

What more experienced bugmen and bugwomen in Hawai'i have found — with the aid of sensitive microphones — is that the flies most prone to survival are not necessarily the healthiest, sprightliest, or most powerful. Rather, they are the best lovers. Male flies, depending on the particular species, communicate their intentions to sexually active females in an astounding variety of ways. Some vibrate their stomach muscles to create certain acoustical patterns. Others beat their wings. Still others do an exotic fly dance in front of their intended or spray certain pheromones around to attract them.

This last method, by the way — the emission of perfumes — is well documented in a piece of research the title of which caught my fancy when I was browsing through the accumulated insect titles at our local library. The study, by Lorna Arita and Kenneth Kaneshiro, is called "Structure and Function of the Rectal Epithelium and Anal Glands During Mating Behavior in the Mediterranean Fruit Fly Male." Perfumes aside, it is important to remember that all of these various forms of message sending are aimed at one thing: the exact same thing that Spider Moskowitz and I and the rest of our hormonally hyped-up peers spent most of our free time lying about when we weren't playing baseball.

Back, however, to the *Drosophila*. Once a male fly finishes his courting ritual it's now up to the lady to make her own moves. Some females — particularly those in older, larger, and more established fly populations like those found on the Island of Kaua'i — are incredibly picky. They fuss and fidget, primp, act coy, put out various types of come-hither signals, and then tell nine out of ten guys to buzz off. Others — the ones on geologically newer islands like Maui and Hawai'i — are more wanton. They'll grab the first beachboy *Drosophila* that comes along strumming his stomach muscles regardless of the fact that his music may be the tonal equivalent of cat screeching.

All of these sexual antics begin to suggest that evolutionary trends, at least with certain species, may have as much to do with courtship and mating as they do with scrounging food and out-foxing enemies. In other words, the old Darwinian law of natural selection may not be nearly as immutable as most of us think. Fruit fly research in Hawai'i is still in its infancy. Given enough time — and the right microscopes, stethoscopes, and procto-scopes — ever more will be revealed.

"Big deal and so what," I hear you muttering under your breath. What does any of this stuff really mean? Conservatively estimated, after all, there are at least one and a half quintillion (1,500,000,000,000,000,000) individual bugs in the world that break down into approximately (and also very conservatively) three million species worldwide. Another three million may still be buzzing around incognito. Diversity is a feature of these critters. J. B. S. Haldane once noted that God "is inordinately fond of beetles," of which there are more than 350,000 species. Lots of these interesting bugs live in places like Indiana, Russia, Greenland, and Morocco. So what makes Hawai'i special?

The answer is isolation. Because Hawai'i is more or less 2,000 miles away from any other large land mass, our insects have developed in peculiar ways. Talk to one of our real bug junkies — people like Bill Mull, Eric Jang, Kenneth Kaneshiro, or others — and they'll start to fill your ears with a lot of insect trivia. Get them gabbing long enough and certain themes will start to emerge: dis-persal and adaptive radiation, for example, or flightlessness, endemicity, speciation, and loss of competitiveness. These con-cepts are critical to understanding evolutionary history in Hawai'i. They may also offer important insights into the problems that beset people who visit here (the tourists), people who move here (the *malihini*), people who were born here (the *kama'āina*), and the people who were here first (the Hawaiians).

Take dispersal and speciation. Insects were probably the very first land creatures to arrive in the Hawaiian Islands. Altogether, there are an estimated 10,000 species of insects here. This includes 3,000 types of beetles, 1,500 flies, 1,500 wasps and bees, 1,500 moths and butterflies, 1,000 true bugs, 1,000 leafhoppers and scale insects, and another 1,000 crickets, lacewings, grasshoppers, and barklice — and 98% of all of these are found no place else on earth. It is also reckoned that this same 98% are descended from a root stock of fewer than 150 species.

How those original ancestors got here used to be a matter of great debate. A few biologists and geographers believed that the flora and fauna here were a living confirmation of some kind of preexisting land bridge or mid-Pacific continent. Even as late as 1940, Carl Skottsberg, a distinguished botanist, wrote that the natural history of Hawai'i "...can be understood only under the supposition that considerable changes have occurred in the distribution of land and sea, making it possible for plants and animals to travel over land between regions now separated by deep water."

Elwood Zimmerman, a prodigious scholar and chronicler of Hawaiian bugs, disagreed strongly. "I believe that those biologists who 'create' continental land in the mid-Pacific to enable them to give an interpretation of the distribution of the groups of organisms which they are studying are overlooking the fundamental geologic nature of the mid-Pacific islands." Zimmerman elaborated this and other ideas in a variety of publications. His magnum opus, however, was an annotated, drawing-filled encyclopedia called *Insects of Hawaii* and subtitled, *"A Manual of the Insects of the Hawaiian Islands, including an Enumeration of the Species and Notes on their Origin, Distribution, Hosts, Parasites, etc."* Zimmerman spent more than fifteen years preparing volumes 1 through 9 of this series. Six more were eventually completed by D. Elmo Hardy, Mercedes Delfinado, Kenneth Christiansen, Peter Bellinger, and others after "Zimmie" left the Islands. The books are still a standard reference for local entomologists.

Over time the land-bridge theory fell into disrepute. Mesh nets trolled behind airplanes in the upper atmosphere over Hawai'i and the Pacific Ocean produced a myriad of living insects from

Asia, Polynesia, and America. North and South American insects were discovered in drift logs. Even Zimmerman himself found a living bark beetle in the feathers of an owl that had been blown down from the skies over Fiji.

Not every insect that made it to Hawai'i survived. The vast majority didn't, and those that did changed dramatically as they radiated out to fill available niches. One typical pattern of adaptation involved the loss of flight. As certain winged insects found their way to the Islands, they took up roles and residences that, on their home continents at least, would have been occupied by flightless bugs. Finding niches, nooks, and crannies empty and therefore available, the insects — over successive generations — shed their wings and changed their life-styles. This occurred among quite a few members of the beetle family but also to various moths, grasshoppers, and lacewings.

Many of these adaptations led to diverse species lines. For instance, certain sap-sucking planthoppers on the islands of Maui, O'ahu, and Moloka'i now have large bulging eyes and bold camouflage colorations. Colors differ according to habitats. On the island of Hawai'i, however, just a few miles of open ocean away, three related species have gone underground, lost their sight, color, and wings, and now live exclusively off roots of the native 'ōhi'a trees hanging down in lava tubes 30 feet below the surface. From a bug's perspective, notes entomologist and spelunker Francis G. Howarth, each of the major Hawaiian Islands is like a minicontinent with seemingly independent lines of evolution. "It is as if a variety of teams have played the same game with the same rules — but with different players on each island." Where the same species has colonized two separate Islands, however, "it's as if the same game has been played by the same player — but with different rules."

As with the plant and bird life in Hawai'i, the evolution of its insect biota took place over many millennia. Successful colonizations might have occurred at intervals of hundreds — if not thousands — of years. Once humans arrived on the scene, however, the pace picked up. Whole new families of insects came with the Polynesians (roughly A.D. 500), with Western traders, whalers, and missionaries (early 1800s), and later still with the arrival of Chinese, Japanese, Portuguese, and Filipino laborers (mid and late 1800s). With the advent of mass air travel in the 1940s, the rate of insect introductions increased dramatically, particularly during the Vietnam war when Hawai'i was a rest zone for GIs and a port of entry for immigrants and refugees. One study counted 287 accidental arthropod introductions (an average of nineteen per year) between 1962 and 1976.

In the distant past, many of these fortuitous visitors became well-adapted citizens of the archipelago. A few evolved into unique and comely Island characters. The Kamehameha butterfly, for example, is a delightful little beauty looking something like a Monarch (and named for a local one) that lives out its days quietly fluttering around the native shrubs and trees of our mountains. There are ten more butterfly species in the Islands; just one other is truly native.

The same is true with moths. There are nearly 1,500 kinds in Hawai'i, most of them ordinary, nondescript little things to which almost no one pays any attention. One family, though — the Sphinx moths — are beefy, flamboyant creatures that emerge from their hiding places in the early evening. The "Fabulous Green Sphinx of Kaua'i" — the rarest of them all — has a wingspan of four inches and is confined to the forests in the Kōke'e and Makaweli areas.

Other insect arrivals have proven less charming and, in some situations, downright ugly. Take ants. Hawai'i has no native ants. When some inevitably arrived in the Islands, they immediately drove a variety of other native ground-dwelling insects to extinction. Particularly predacious were the bigheaded ant, which overran the lowlands, and the even more aggressive Argentine ant, which invaded certain higher elevations. Today, in addition to these two, Hawai'i is also the home of fire ants, carpenter ants, crazy ants, and yellow ants, all of which are doing damage to local insect species.

What insect tourism portends for endemic bug populations is disruption, decline, and, to be anthropomorphic, despair. Because the original inhabitants, through adaptation and evolution, have dropped many of their traditional defenses — wings and flight being the most conspicuous example — they are vulnerable in the extreme. Moreover, many of the new species that find their way here from Asia and America — the "exotics" — are aggressive and competitive. When endemic and exotic species collide, the new-comers inevitably seem to win out. The old ones get kicked out of their homes, run out of town, gobbled up, or just plain out-popu-lated by the vigorous new creatures that have drifted, floated, or hitchhiked their way to the Islands.

Nonetheless, at least for now, life on a Hawaiian Island creased with lava flows and shrouded in mysterious cloud forests still offers countless surprises to those who observe such things with a discerning eye. One such astonishment, an insect not much big-ger than the last joint of your little finger, has in fact acquired some habits that could, under the right circumstances, be auc-tioned off to the people who made the *Alien, Aliens,* and *Alien 3* films. This one has educed, elicited, extorted, and evolved itself into something that nobody knew existed. Not, that is, until a mild-mannered local scientist stumbled on it by accident in the mountains above Kona.

At first it was all rumor and innuendo, something passed along as a snippet of idle conversation and then dismissed like a used toothpick at a cocktail party. But many months later, I heard it again. Could it really be? Was this the start of Hawaiian bugdom's long-awaited, full-scale evolutionary uprising? Were we in for revenge and reprisals? Impossible, I thought. But then again, maybe not. My curiosity was aroused. And other instincts as well. After all, here was a story that could — with perseverance and creativity — stretch my chore-avoidance objectives out by several more weekends.

Determined to investigate, I tracked down the scientist, called for an appointment, and launched my investigation....

*   *   *

...all of which led me straight to the Bishop Museum, which is to Island bugophiles what the sacred cities of the Middle East are to Arabs, Christians, and Jews. It is the Jerusalem of arthropodic studies and the Mecca of Insecta. All real Bug People eventually come to the Bishop Museum because it is the cosmological center of the entomological universe. It is Bug Research Central.

Why such superlatives for a bunch of old buildings that have been around for a century but that remain more or less mysterious to most people, even those who live here?

To begin with, there are the specimens. There are bugs of every hue and stripe. There are bugs as big as hubcaps and bugs too small to be seen without microscopes. Bugs that look like psychedelic, iridescent rainbows and bugs that could easily be mistaken for a clod of dirt or a dustball. In fact, miles upon miles of bugs have been dried, pickled, sorted, labeled, pinned into trays, plopped into bottles, and then stacked, ground to ceiling, in large metal cabinets that can slide across several of the museum's largest floors. Most of these are unknown to the public. People simply don't realize they are there. This hidden treasure is one of the largest bug collections in the world. Although no one has actually counted them, upwards of 13.5 million insects have been desiccated or embalmed with ethyl alcohol and stuck away in the Museum's back rooms.

Then there are the scientists who study these creatures. The Bishop Museum's Department of Entomology boasts, depending on its current portfolio of government grants and foundation awards, a staff of some 25 scientists, technicians, and graduate students along with their offices, laboratories, instruments, and libraries. Many of these people are renowned in their field: people like Frank Howarth and Scott Miller. Others are neophytes who, through scientific apprenticeships of one sort or another, will "make their bones" in entomology or any of a dozen entomological subspecialties.

The work these people are involved in comes together in a premier program of research and publication. Roam the corridors of the department and you will find the quiet bustle of a dozen different enterprises in various stages of progress. These include coordinated long-term interdisciplinary projects on evolutionary biology, ten-year studies of beetles and cave arthropods, and the production of thick treatises on insect borers. Researchers are writing monographs on thrips and additional volumes in the *Insects of Hawaii* series. There are constant field studies in and around Hawai'i and, when that kind of money is available, expeditions to far-away places.

Finally, there is the Museum's overall educational program. As in the Smithsonian or any other good museum, there are lectures, seminars, and films for the public. And on the third floor of Pauahi Hall there is a room of exhibits called the Hall of Hawaiian Natural History that synthesizes much of what is important about Hawaiian entomology for the casual visitor. The room contains a variety of oddments illustrating some of the more compelling facts of Hawaiian biogeography. There is a table model of the Hawaiian chain. There is a simulation of life in a lava tube and a diorama of early Hawaiian civilization that includes a back-bred, freeze-dried "poi" dog. There is a glass case containing the bones of an extinct ibis and another with a stuffed goose, the *nēnē*, and some even rarer honeycreepers. There is a silversword plant and a panel with the names, pictures, and biographies of people who did pioneering work in Hawai'i in the natural sciences.

On the far end of one *koa*-paneled wall is the exhibit that interests me. It is called Adaptive Shift, which is the phrase biologists use to describe the long-term changes in habit that occur when an invading species finds particular ecological niches vacant and when there are no natural enemies to discourage the filling of those niches in new ways. This evolutionary modification of behavior is an important principle if you want to understand why so many local animals and plants are endangered.

The insect that is featured here is a larva of the Pug Moth, genus *Eupithecia*. It is a caterpillar. In their final form, *Eupithecia* — and there are eighteen different species — are innocuous, nondescript little moths, mostly mottled brown, that can be found fluttering over any of a number of Hawaiian habitats extending from the subalpine zone to the lowland wet forests. Few are rare. They are, however, unique among the world's inchworms. So far as anyone knows, the Hawaiian caterpillars of this particular group are the only ones on the planet that eat meat. They are ambush predators and carnivores.

The man who discovered this trait is Steve Montgomery, a well-regarded entomologist with a quiet manner and an irrepressible penchant for bugs in general and for local bugs in particular. Montgomery's background and credentials are probably not atypical of those of the Bishop Museum's associated scientists: an early interest in the natural world, lots of time spent outdoors and learning how to carefully record animal and plant observations, summer vacations spent gathering and displaying the birds and insects of his native South Bend and garnering prizes for those collections at the Indiana State Fair. Later, a job doing damselfly research in Oklahoma and a mosquito census in Louisiana, followed by a chance trip to Hawai'i. Eventually, a Ph.D. at the University of Hawai'i and a succession of postgraduate jobs doing various types of entomological research.

I meet with Montgomery at lunchtime in the Bishop Museum's coffee shop. Over the years, I have had numerous opportunities to talk with him in other settings, because in addition to being a respected bugman, Montgomery is also a veteran of several fiery conservation battles. He and some of his colleagues, in fact, helped stave off the introduction of commercially valuable but ecologically dangerous Japanese unagi eels on O'ahu. Off and on he has also worked at the Legislature and has a broad spectrum of knowledge about land, water, and public health matters. Today, however, the topic of discussion is bugs. It is my intention to find out everything I possibly can about carnivorous caterpillars, to report this information to the world in general and to my bug-hating wife and daughters in particular, and to pin this gentleman down as to certain philosophical issues that are still on my mind.

Montgomery, a slim man with long brown hair and a graying beard, looks thinner than I remember him. In fact, he has just returned from a five-month Museum-sponsored collecting trip to the Marquesas in French-speaking Polynesia. Montgomery was lead scientist. The Fatu Hiva Biological Expedition, he tells me, was extremely successful. Conducted on board the research vessel *Aeolus*, it returned to Honolulu with 2,000 specimens and a mountain of ethnographic material about Marquesan plants and insects. Home for less than a week, Montgomery is now trying to gain back the 25 pounds he lost on the trip. "I'm afraid I wasn't a very good sailor," he admits over a double order of barbecued chicken, rice, and vegetables.

During lunch, I turn on my tape recorder and start the interview. The story of the "killer caterpillars" unfolds. In late 1972 Montgomery is rummaging around in a rain forest on a mountain north of Kona on the Big Island doing fieldwork. Specifically, he is looking for drosophilids. The work is painstaking and repetitious. It involves sitting in one place — usually in the mud — for long periods of time. Distractions do occur, however. Montgomery notices a rare lobelia plant nearby with rosette leaves on a slender stalk. He goes over to examine it, and then his gaze drifts down to a particular leaf. On the leaf he happens to see a small, green inchworm holding a fly in its front talons. The fly is half-eaten.

Although Montgomery isn't the excitable sort, his first reaction is something verging on incredulity. Inchworms don't eat flies. In fact, they don't eat anything except leaves. They are vegetarians. Immediately, he presumes that he is dealing with a mentally ill caterpillar. If people can come unglued, why can't bugs? Just maybe he has found the first recorded case of insect psychosis. Then another thought strikes him. Maybe he's the one who's getting demented. Hunting flies in the rain and mud for days at a time can make anyone daffy. Maybe it's time to voluntarily commit himself to the Home for the Environmentally Insane. Presuming the worm is some kind of interesting mutant, however, he deposits the leaf, caterpillar, and attached fly in his collecting bottle and then moves back to the task at hand: finding more drosophilids.

Back in Honolulu, he takes out the collecting bottle, puts it on his desk, and ponders the critter inside. The worm, he notes, looks more or less like any other inchworm. It has a set of talon-tipped legs in front and another in back, five rudimentary and not very functional sets of eyes, and a long, segmented, tubelike body with some occasional hairs sticking out. Overall appearance: something along the lines of a gasoline tanker truck that can bend in the middle.

Over the next several days, Montgomery watches his little beastie, fully expecting it to revert to its normal leaf-eating behavior. Nothing happens. And now, little light bulbs start to go off in the middle of Montgomery's cranium. It's the aha! experience, that rare, fortuitous breakthrough that happens once in a scientist's life if he is blessed with the right proportions of curiosity, perseverance, and luck. Montgomery rounds up a stray fly and puts it in the bottle with the caterpillar. This time, the entire murderous little drama unfolds in front of him as he watches in disbelief.

It is a play in three acts. In Act One, Montgomery drops the fly in the bottle and it lands near the inchworm, which is sitting perfectly still. The fly brushes a few of the 200 sensory bristles located along the length of the tanker-truck body, and the worm is alerted. Specifically, the hairs on its rear end trigger a neurological ambush mechanism that causes its front end to rear up.

Act Two commences without an intermission. Anchored firmly to the leaf by its back legs, the worm swings around sideways and grabs the fly with its six claw-tipped front legs. The talons sink into the fly with the strength of industrial grappling hooks. All of the action thus far has taken place in less than one-tenth of a second.

Act Three: the caterpillar begins to feed. With the kind of arthropodic precision and grace that warms a true bugman's heart, it methodically holds the fly and starts to eat chunks of it. When the inchworm is finished, all that is left are a few miscellaneous pieces of leg, wing, and fly gristle.

Ambush, seizure, ingestion. In the everyday natural world where things dismember and eat each other at every meal, this small spectacle is so commonplace as to be virtually meaningless. Montgomery, however, is elated. What he has found, after all, is totally improbable: a mechanically efficient killing and feeding machine that will, in its final molt, become a harmless, banal, nectar-sipping moth that survives on the juices of rotting fruits.

And now, Montgomery starts his own metamorphosis. He winds down most of his drosophilid research and takes up serious worm work. He does endless repetitions of the fly experiment, takes copious notes, photographs his *Eupithecia* from a variety of angles, rears the inchworm to adulthood, and then sends the resulting moth off to "Zimmie" in London for analysis and consultation. Elwood Zimmerman, aging but still in command of his bug-loving faculties, writes back and says: "Find more." That task will take another year. Montgomery puts the word out to scientists at the Museum and in the community at large, and it is one of Montgomery's good friends who finds the second one on Maui. Number three comes some months later from Bill Mull, who discovers it at Poamoho on O'ahu.

As Montgomery explains all this to me between mouthfuls of chicken and rice, more and more questions crop up in my mind. How many varieties of killer caterpillars are there in Hawai'i? What are they like during other phases of their life cycle? Where did they originally come from? When and how did they actually transform into meat eaters? Did they evolve their carnivorous habits here or elsewhere? And what might have prompted the great evolutionary event? Patiently, he wades through my gush of questions and shares what he knows.

A total of twenty species of Hawaiian inchworms have been discovered, he says. Two of them are vegetarians, the rest carnivores. They are also found in dramatically different environments. *Eupithecia orichloris* is green and lives in rain forests. *Eupithecia staurophragma* is brown and craggy and very much resembles the dry twigs it tends to sit on. *Eupithecia craterias* is tan and makes its home at the 5,000-to-7,000-foot levels on Maui and other Islands. In their life cycles, though, all of the caterpillars are more or less the same. Eggs are laid singly or in small clusters of two or three to avoid larval stage cannibalism. After 14 days, the caterpillars hatch and start through their molts. After the fourth molt, they are moths.

As to their evolutionary transformation into connoisseurs of insect flesh, that remains a mystery. When Montgomery was leading the Fatu Hiva expedition in the Marquesas, he spent a good deal of time looking for meat-eating inchworms. Alerted to his discoveries, scientists in other parts of the Pacific have also been on the lookout for ambushing inchworm counterparts. None have turned up. Perhaps, he speculates, an Asian, Pacific, or North or South American connection eventually will be found. For the moment, though, they are uniquely Hawaiian.

"So what's your next step?" I ask him as our meeting draws to a close. His answer is obvious and direct: lots more biogeographical research. He intends to collect and catalog the other species that may be out there, understand their habits, and try to protect the various caterpillar habitats from human encroachments. Montgomery's normally calm demeanor now evaporates as he gives me a frantic minilecture on the need to discover and protect such creatures before they are obliterated by urban and agricultural development.

Lunch and interview over, Montgomery tours me through the corridors of the Entomology Department and introduces some of his colleagues. We briefly chat with researcher Frank Howarth and the general keeper of the bug collection, David Preston.

As we say our goodbyes by the Museum's front entrance I pause and launch one last query. "Tell me, Steve, when all is said and done, when the last worm has turned (so to speak), do you think bugs have souls?" Montgomery gives me a quizzical look, strokes his chin, and thinks for a moment. "I guess I'd have to say that I've seen no evidence one way or another. What about you?"

"Well," I tell him, "I'm getting more and more convinced that they do. It's people I'm not sure about."

"You may be right," he says with a sigh. "You may be right."

* * *

How then shall we appreciate the insects of Hawai'i? Testimonial dinners for some of the more lovable species — the butterflies, for example — might be one way. An official congratulatory resolution from the Mayor citing the happy face spider and the carnivorous caterpillars' extraordinary cleverness above and beyond the genetic call of duty might be another. We might even contemplate the declaration of a Be Nice To Mosquitoes Week sponsored by the Blood Bank or an official dog dung fly poster contest managed by the Hawaiian Humane Society. The possibilities are endless.

But all of these are token bureaucratic gestures. The real need is the reinstatement of a more equitable political status for Hawai'i's bugs. We're talking about your basic bug rights. Bugs need the right to assemble, the right to privacy, and the freedom to pursue bug happiness without being mindlessly squashed, swatted, zapped, poisoned, or flicked off into oblivion like pieces of dandruff. This means sacrifice. Each of us must stand ready to redress some of bugdom's collective discomfort even if it means sacrificing some of our own. And for my part, this begins with a grassroots approach in the little wilderness of our own backyard in Mānoa Valley.

The yard I am referring to contains, among other things, our fabled avocado tree, a few weed-tangled flowers, and a small but perennially unmowed stretch of crabgrass. This you already know. It also contains a hollow-tiled compost pile in which the detritus of the rest of the yard is poured. In the yard there is also a brown and yellow cat. The cat doesn't belong to me. In fact, he doesn't belong to anyone except himself. He lives under some rotting lumber in our neighbor's yard and considers our place to be a part of his. Like all cats, he refuses to acknowledge the little things that mark a "civilized" man's sense of dominion over nature. Things like zoning laws, fences, property lines, hedges, and border shrubs. As everyone knows, cats — even the most domesticated of house cats — never define themselves as pets. They are bosses. And this cat in particular is the Big Boss of the neighborhood. He is, in fact, one of the wildest, scroungiest, ugliest, and meanest cats I've ever seen. When I step into MY yard, he stares at me with the yellow, fevered eyes of a jungle creature, as if I were stepping into HIS yard. He also hisses at me with the same sound that I imagine werewolves make when they are about to tear out your throat, as if MY presence were an intrusion into HIS territory. So be it. Over time, through trial and mutual terror, we have come to terms. We share. It is OUR yard.

But questions arise, particularly on a Saturday afternoon when I am busy shirking yardwork. What, for example, does this cat eat? For a long time I didn't have the foggiest idea. Not, that is, until I noticed that a pair of mynah birds were noisily nesting near our deck. Their courtship produced two chicks that promptly got eaten by the cat-from-hell. I know this because I found their heads and portions of their wings, feet, and shoulders lying on the grass one morning. Other bird pieces have also shown up from time to time: chunks of Mejiros, the Japanese White-eye; bits of sparrows and cardinals; leftover doves; and half-chewed pigeon carcasses. I presume that some of the relatives of these birds were smart enough to vacate the premises when Cat was around. The slower ones became cat food.

So be it. That is the way of the world, and there's no sense getting sentimental about it until it directly confronts you in the form of shark, bear, alligator, insurance salesman, or tax collector. Still, the issue of cat food invoked other gastronomical concerns, the next one being the matter of bird food. I started to watch more attentively, and eventually the answer to that mystery came clear as well. Pigeons and doves deal mostly in seeds. White-eyes seem to favor flowers. Mynahs, however, will eat damn near anything, including lizards — which just happen to dwell in great abundance at our place. Working my way down the local evolutionary ladder, I now started taking serious notice of the geckos, chameleonlike anoles, and skinks that also call our place their own. And what, might you ask, do they eat? You guessed it: bugs.

As Edward Hoagland once noted in an essay about turtles and frogs, it is not an enviable role to be the staff of life. That, however, is precisely what the bugs in my backyard are. Take the compost pile, which I have spent a considerable amount of time turning, tending, and proudly contemplating. As heaps of decaying matter go, it's a pretty decent pile that carries lots of rewards for those who are patient. It produces a fair amount of mulchy dirt and a certain amount of good fortune. By good fortune I mean staying connected, however thinly in these weird urbanized environs, to the turning of the seasons and the trembling of the earth.

The current boodle of compost — more than a year old now — is made up of humongous amounts of avocado leaves and grass cuttings, a steady flow of peelings and cuttings from the kitchen, and an occasional purchased bag of chicken manure. It is a solid, workmanlike compost pile that, like any synergistic creation, generates its own heat and energy, an energy that also supports an entire little ecosystem.

Studying this mess you see the wonders of life itself in a nearly self-contained microcosm 4 feet high, 4 deep, and 4 wide.

Earthworms revel in the rotting leaves. Slugs move slowly through the wet materials extracting the nutrients they need. Anoles stealthily creep through the dry stuff on the top. Two mice who the kids named Gus and Jack also hang out there eating everything they can. Birds periodically visit the pile. And the devil-cat, bless his wicked little soul, keeps a peripheral but nonetheless supervisory eye over the whole scene.

Turn over a few layers of leaves and grass, however, and the staff of life — which is also the stuff of life — becomes readily apparent. My compost pile is, in fact, a wilderness preserve for bugs. It contains, either in the pile or near it, thrips, mites, spiders, ants, bees, carpenter bees, scorpions, wasps, roaches, beetles, stem borers, earwigs, mosquitoes, fruit flies, house flies, dog flies, ladybugs, grasshoppers, leafhoppers, centipedes, millipedes, and crickets. These are only a few of the species that have taken up residence in and around the pile. They are, however, my comrades and, for the moment at least, full and free citizens of the town of Bugville, Hawai'i, USA.

Carolyn thinks all of this compost watching is slightly eccentric. She refuses to come near me or the pile when I'm of a mood to examine it or pontificate about it. She explains it to the children as "dad's strange hobby." For myself, though, it's a sanctuary of sorts. I watch this pile ascend and descend and I see the bug population go through its successions. Birth, growth, death, and decay come to its denizens as they do all things. I see feast, famine, and war. I see insect populations breed and spawn and mature and move through the cycles of their time just like us. For the most part I leave the pile and its residents alone. Oh, I turn it periodically, and spade out a little bit of earth-matter from the bottom, but mostly I let it sit. Rain alternates with sun. Clouds come and go. The pile does its thing. So too with the cat, the mynah birds, the green anoles, the insects, and all the other kinds of biological matter that are somewhere down near the base of the whole system.

And what, you ask, is the point? And I answer, softly as can be: souls. Not just bug souls but all souls, including human souls, that collectively make up something larger and that somehow get touched by the rhythms and cycles in ways too subtle to understand by the instruments of science or the dogmas of religion. Periodically I do clean the whole mess out, spread its rich, loamy alloy around the gingers and roses, and let the bugs, cats, birds, and lizards scatter and fend for themselves. Then I start the pile over again and help it grow. Each time, however, I observe the wriggling lives within and am reminded of the powerful weave of life on these Islands: because compost and bugs speak to essentials, because they are life. And because matter, in the final analysis, matters. The rest is simply detail.

4

Totem Fish

I may not agree with your bumper sticker, but I will defend to the death your right to stick it.

men's room wall, Merchant's Cafe,
Seattle, Washington

OUR FAMILY TREE, AS EXPLAINED TO ME BY MY PARENTS and grandparents when I was very young, is actually a rather puny, scraggly, and thin-limbed bush. Judging by the existing anthropological evidence of my brothers and myself, I would guess that very late in history my people still retained certain traits that are now more commonly associated with barbarians and troglodytes. Be that as it may, those few generations that are actually known are remembered as ordinary and nondescript people of general central European descent. Basically, they were mongrels, a mix of races, religions, and ethnicities that ultimately ended up as Catholics and Jews on proximate sides of the Austro-Hungarian border. Most were peasants, storekeepers, traders, and small-town artisans. A few, if childhood stories are to be believed, became locally prominent as gamblers, spendthrifts, and horse thieves. The vast majority went to their graves with no lasting claim to anything even remotely resembling money or fame.

Perhaps the most illustrious person in our contemporary lineage was my grandfather Oscar, an Austrian conscript who deserted from a telegraph wire installation unit in the Kaiser's army in 1917. Having had three mules shot out from under him during the First War-to-End-All-Wars, he simply decided that fighting was no longer an appropriate thing to do. According to my grandmother, Theresa Adler, he also missed her cooking and his weekly poker games. So he walked away from the mutilated corpse of the last mule and didn't stop until he got home.

A quarter century later his son — my father — undertook his own clandestine escape from Hitler, decamped from Europe, made his way to America under a forged passport, married my mother (also an immigrant), and settled in Kentucky, where I was born. Later he arranged for Oscar and Theresa's escape and tried to get others out as well. Most of the members of my parents' immediate clans — including my maternal grandparents — never made it. They died at Auschwitz and Bergen-Belsen. The few remaining survivors in our family — other than my parents — dispersed to places like Oregon, Israel, and Ireland, where they became respectable and appreciative citizens.

This is our contemporary history. Somewhere in the farther and murkier reaches of our past, however, an otherwise unknown member of our clan carrying the genes of Celts, Jews, and Mongols in his veins somehow came to be named "Adler," which is the German word for eagle. Whether this name was bequeathed or, as I suspect, merely appropriated as a convenient alias, we Adlers no longer know. What we do know is that the eagle became — and still remains — the patron animal of our family. In effect, it's our totem.

Even today, hanging above our dining room table there is a large color print of an American Bald Eagle swiveling his mean little beak around and glaring at the photographer who snapped his image. That glare eventually found its way into the calendar of the Sierra Club. Now reprinted and framed, that snarling head faces us each morning and evening as we gather around the communal table for food and conversation. Adorning it are two wild eagle feathers Corey and I picked up along the banks of a remote salmon stream northeast of Seldovia, Alaska, while we were fishing. The older girls understand, I think, what the photo, its gracing feathers, and the animal itself stand for. Someday the youngest will too.

Totemism can be viewed in many ways. In American culture when the idea does occur, it is generally viewed as archaic, inappropriate, and slightly weird. Often it is simply trivialized. Animals become "mascots" for teams or are incorporated into business logos. A more traditional view, however, holds the totem as an integral manifestation of cultural and family self-consciousness. Totems were — and still are, in some cases — the connective tissue that threads together the human, animal, and spirit worlds. The ancient Hawaiians called them *'aumākua*, their personal ancestor gods who inhabited certain animals or plants or rocks that guarded — and were in turn guarded by — succeeding family generations. An *'aumakua* might be an ocean creature — the manta ray, shark, or squirrelfish — or it might be an *'ō'ō* bird or a *milo* tree. For many contemporary Hawaiians, as with many current-day Micronesians, Eskimos, and Aborigines, personal totemism is still a living practice.

Whatever their form, totems are traditionally a family or clan affair and, in many cases, linked to rites of passage; that is, to the initiation of young adults into full maturity and societal responsibilities. In many American Indian cultures, for example, it was requisite for a teenager to step out of society and out of the human world at least once before assuming the normal responsibilities of adulthood. Alone in the woods, the desert, or the mountains, the young person searched for a special song, a secret name, or a personal spirit. Usually, these came in the form of an animal or plant native to that region that would, forever more, command special attention and respect. It became the source of his or her "power." Such cultures, says wilderness poet Gary Snyder, honored the man or woman who had visited other realms.

If all of this talk of totems and spirits seems oddly out of place in a twentieth-century Hawai'i in which many people are preoccupied with foreign investment, real property values, visitor counts, and East-West trade balances, consider the strange turns of events in which the entire populace of our state was invited to help select a totem fish to represent all of us who by luck or chance happen to live here.

* * *

In 1979 when Peter Apo returned to Hawai'i after several years of working in the California music business, there was no way he could have anticipated the fierce political storms that would cloud him in controversy a mere five years later. Peter — a waterman, fisherman, and all-around expert on ocean affairs — is also a true native son of the Wai'anae coast. He grew up in and around the water, believes strongly in our maritime future, and wants to raise everyone's consciousness about the sea a few notches higher. To implement his visions, Peter started a seaside outdoor education program for the Kamehameha Schools, helped revitalize the sport of canoe paddling, and then ran for a seat in the State House of Representatives. He won handily.

Like every freshman legislator, he was immediately besieged by all manner of lobbyists seeking a special vote here, a friendly nod there, or just a simple favor for someone's uncle's favorite cause. Peter calmly threaded his way through all the log rolling and pork barreling of his first session, kept his constituents relatively happy, and even managed to win a few important rounds on the Hawaiian rights front. Then, in his second session, serious controversy caught up with him. Political scandal? Kickbacks? Shady, under-the-table dealings with the syndicate? No, none of these. Instead, conflict wore the benign face of a fish.

What some lesser soul might have called "The Late Great Hawaiian State Fish Fry" began humbly enough and with the best of intentions. One day Mark Markrich, a Sunday columnist for the local newspaper, marched into Apo's office at the State Capitol and laid out an idea that went like this. Hawai'i has an official State bird — the nēnē. It has a State flower — the hibiscus. It has a State tree — the kukui. It has a State mammal — the humpback whale; a State anthem — "Hawai'i Pono'ī," and a State motto — "Ua mau ke ea o ka 'āina i ka pono," which means "the life of the land is preserved by righteousness." What Hawai'i doesn't have, Markrich pointed out, is a State fish. Moreover, Hawai'i is historically and culturally linked to the sea and is the only state completely surrounded by it. Markrich talked to Apo, and several days later Apo introduced an official legislative resolution calling for the naming of an official State fish.

At first, the idea was dismissed as child's play and a diversion from more serious matters, but then, as if guided by some greater force, it gathered momentum. Bipartisan support was generated and a political — oh — fishing expedition started to evolve. The bill that emerged from the smoke-filled back rooms of the Capitol building on Beretania Street called for staff members at the Waikīkī Aquarium and students at the University of Hawai'i's Marine Options Program to poll people on all Islands, primarily schoolchildren, and to report back to the legislature on which particular fish would be most appropriate. Three criteria were to be used in the selection process. First, it was suggested that any critter chosen needed to be native to Hawaiian waters. Second, the State fish had to be culturally important. Third, the fish needed to be easily seen in its natural habitat. Apo's legislation cleared the House and then the Senate, but not without some grumbles from his colleagues. A few legislators still thought the entire matter was insignificant and not worthy of the great body's time. Others pushed for particular favorites. Apo rose up like the ghost of Daniel Webster and defended the matter both on the floor of the House and in the press.

"My feeling is that as a State we don't pay enough attention to our ocean resources," argued Apo in a newspaper interview. "From an economic standpoint, our value system is all screwed up. Our system of rules and regulations is designed to react to threats to our fishing industry but we give little thought to the protection of marine life. The selection of a State fish is basically a consciousness-raising mechanism." Apo's opponents muttered under their breaths. A stupid idea, some legislators thought, but we'll give the new guy what he wants just to get him out of our hair.

So the great contest was on. Eight nominees were chosen from an initial list of twenty-six eligible fish by the committee that had been set in place to implement the selection process. They were the *manini* or convict tang (*Acanthurus triostegus*), the *'āweoweo* or bigeye squirrelfish (*Heteropriacanthus cruentatus*), the *lauwili-wili* or longnosed butterflyfish (*Forcipiger longirostris*), the *kūmū* or red goatfish (*Parupeneus porphyreus*), the *kala* or unicornfish (*Naso unicornis*), the *uhu uliuli* or parrotfish (*Scarus perspicilla-tus*), the *humuhumunukunukuāpua'a* or bluntnosed triggerfish (*Rhinecanthus rectangulus*), and the *hīnālea* or saddle-back wrasse (*Thalassoma duperrey*). All eight were Hawaiian reef fish. All eight were more or less small, harmless little things, and all eight commonly could be found in Hawaiian waters despite the overfishing of recent years.

Immediately, there were howls of protest. Why, demanded deep sea fishing enthusiasts, wasn't the Pacific blue marlin included? The marlin, after all, brings tourists to the Islands and dollars into the State's bank accounts through internationally famous tournaments. And what about the *'ahi* and *aku*, growled the commercial fishermen? Both of these large, free-ranging tuna are prized by everyone — as *sashimi*, fish steaks, and "*aku* belly" soup. Shouldn't one of these magnificent pelagic water animals be acknowledged as our foremost finny friend? An even more direct opinion was voiced by Mark Suiso, a Sea Grant extension agent who works in Apo's district on the Wai'anae coast and who viewed the entire affair with disdain.

"The way this contest is set up," Suiso told me as we glutted ourselves with breakfast at the Tasty Broiler one morning, "we are going to end up voting for the wimpiest fish in the sea." Suiso, a man of strong appetites, has tousled, sandy-colored hair and a gangling, irreverent, opinionated manner. He is also as knowledgeable about the ocean environment of Hawai'i as anyone else and maybe a little more so. Suiso's current maritime passion calls for him to spend most of his days and nights teaching Wai'anae fishermen how to catch and render down sharks for food, leather, and fun. Critters like the 10-foot whitetipped reef shark that is known to dine on the overhanging arms and legs of surfers. Or their larger and even nastier-tempered cousins, the tiger sharks. Tiger sharks grow to 18 feet in length and eat the surfboards along with the surfers. "Belts," Suiso said. "We could be exporting genuine, made-in-Hawai'i tiger-shark belts that would be the envy of every pants-wearing male in the world."

In Mark's crystal ball, sharkcatching will eventually become a major business around the State. "In fact," argued Suiso as he swallowed his tenth pancake of the morning, "sharks are important culturally." He then explained how there were good sharks and bad sharks, how the shark, or *manō*, was important to many

Hawaiians, how certain people were thought to be born with the spirit of the shark in them. The *ali'i*, Hawai'i's royalty, used to put to sea in twin-hulled canoes and catch and even ride sharks bare-backed just for the fun of it, he went on, sometimes using slaves captured in raids as bait. Not very sporting, I thought to myself, but then each culture has its own ways (mine having some of the strangest).

Mark, however, was not telling me all this for the sake of breakfast conversation. The long and the short of it was that Suiso wanted the State fish to be something with a little more authority to it than a butterflyfish. Sharks would do nicely. "What about the blue shark or the brown sandbar shark? Or how about the hammerhead? They're a bit on the small side, 12 feet or so, but they at least would tell the world that Hawai'i is a place to be reckoned with."

Suiso's gorge was rising even as we gobbled down the last of our eggs and pancakes. "Otherwise," he growled at me, "instead of a serious, no-nonsense State fish we are going to end up with some insignificant little reef fish that is less than a foot long and that nobody cares about anyway. It's a real crime. An outrage against all of us who take fishing seriously."

Suiso was clearly upset — and representative, I presumed, of the solitary, opinionated, and hard-working men and women who supply all of us white-collar types with the basic ingredients of our *mahimahi* sandwiches. So I asked him what he thought should be done. A write-in campaign, he suggested. "Flood the buggers with shark nominations," he said as he smeared half a jar of jelly on his last piece of toast. "We'll mount a genuine, grass-roots political campaign the likes of which no one in Hawai'i has seen for years." I agreed to consider his ideas and asked him to pass the jelly. And there, for a short while, the matter sat.

*   *   *

Suiso's proposition rattled around in the back of my brain over the next day or so even as the State fish contest revved into second gear. I asked Carolyn and the kids to give it some thought, which they all agreed to do. Meanwhile, the *Advertiser* and the *Star-Bulletin* featured separate front-page stories on the State fish question, and letters to the editor starting pouring in with opinions. TV and radio time was generously donated to promote the idea of the contest, and the Waikīkī Aquarium worked hard to turn the selection process into a meaningful political event. In fact, one Friday evening the Aquarium held a campaign rally upon which was visited some of the fiercest lobbying to be seen in these parts since the 1950s Statehood question. That, you may remember, was when most but not all of the local political establishment decided it was time to be a "proper" part of the Union rather than a second-hand territory barnacled onto the west end of Los Angeles.

In any case, several hundred people showed up at the Aquarium to exercise their democratic prerogative and, in the finest of American traditions, do a bit of armtwisting and leverpulling for their favorite creature. The eight major fish candidates were ably represented by large walking, talking papier-mâché models inside of which were human voices. Cub Scout Pack 42 from Maryknoll Grade School immediately rallied around the *hīnālea*, who appropriately bowed and bobbed to the accolades. Mr. or Ms. *Manini* — I've never quite figured out how this business of gendering a fish really works — mumbled about a "scandalous attempt to discredit me by my opponents." Meanwhile, State Representative David Hagino, a friend of Apo's, had forged a strong alliance with the *kala*, and Rear Admiral Clyde Robbins, U.S. Coast Guard, was accused of being in the pocket of the goatfish (presuming goatfish have pockets).

As the evening wore on, the oratory grew fierce. An impassioned plea for their patron fish, the *humuhumunukunukuāpua'a*, was delivered by members of the Waikīkī Swim Club. The *humuhumunukunukuāpua'a*, to the dismay of many, seemed to be carrying the day; in at least one major exit poll, in fact, it appeared to be garnering local sentiments 2 to 1. Moreover, the *humuhumu* had managed to acquire the support of both John Craven, the State's top marine affairs expert, and the eternally loquacious Neil Abercrombie. Abercrombie and Craven, it should be noted, are both possessed of mighty and powerful intellects along with large lung capacities and razor-sharp tongues honed to a fine edge on lesser matters than the choosing of a totem fish. Both men have also been known to filibuster their ideas when rational argument failed. But despite Craven and Abercrombie, a minor resistance movement was still in force. At the end of the evening Leighton Taylor, the energetic and ever-optimistic director of the Aquarium, was still holding out for the long-nosed butterflyfish.

Meanwhile, back on the home front, opinions were equally divided. Discussions ranged from crabs, octopuses, and moray eels to South American piranhas, which are occasionally discarded into Hawai'i's freshwater streams by disenchanted pet owners. Nonetheless, Carolyn seemed inclined toward a sympathy vote for the squirrelfish just because nobody else seemed to like it. Corey, on the other hand, favored the parrotfish because of its striking colors. "I like 'em," she said with an air of artistic authority in her voice, "and that's that!" Dana and Kelly — obviously influenced by the Cub Scouts from Maryknoll — loudly endorsed the saddle-back wrasse. They mailed their ballots in and the matter seemed to be closed. At least for them.

A few days later I decided that the time had come for me to cast my vote. Suiso's lament was still swimming through the backchannels of my cranium. Down on the seafloor of my brain, however, deep in a veritable kelp bed of creative possibilities, a small idea had taken root. I knew my little notion wouldn't entirely satisfy Suiso, but it might just represent a small step for fishdom, a larger one for the State, and a really big one away from the growing political tangle surrounding the eight reef fish nominees. Why not go straight to the top with it, get my own little campaign organized before Craven and Abercrombie and any other political heavyweights knew what was going on, and — simultaneously — strike a blow for a more thoughtful and representative State totem? I spent a few days doing some research and then trundled down to the governor's chambers to have a chat with The Man himself.

The governor's office sits in an alcove on the fifth floor of the

Capitol building overlooking the State Library, City Hall, 'Iolani Palace, and the Supreme Court. A properly powerful confluence of buildings for a matter as weighty as this, I thought to myself. I found the right room, ignored the small sign on the door instructing me to knock, and marched in with my notes and papers. "Can I help you?" said a musical voice. "My name is Dr. P. S. Adler," I announced, figuring that titles might help me out a little bit here. "I want to register my vote for the State fish contest." A whiff of perfume spiked up my nostrils. "I'm Fay," the Governor's subassistant to the assistant secretary said sweetly. Fay, whom I judged to be about 19 years old, was concentrating 100% of her attention on fixing her nails, as if they were the key to the Governor's political future. The Gov, it turned out, was off on the Windward side of the island pumping hands and kissing babies at a fund-raiser. Fay had been parked in his office to answer the phone. My campaign, I decided, would start with her.

"And which fish do you want to vote for?" she asked without looking up.

"None of the ones on your list," I said, noticing the clipboard on the side of her desk. Fay looked up at me. I stared straight into her large and liquid eyes. "Well, do you have a write-in candidate then?"

"Megamouth," I replied.

"I beg your pardon?!" she said, suddenly wary and obviously offended.

"No, not you," I apologized. "Megamouth the fish." And then, ever so patiently, I began to explain my choice even as Fay turned her attention to the small bottle of apple-blossom polish sitting before her and to the waiting nail on her right pinky.

*   *   *

What I told Fay was the story of a fish — a fish, let it be said, that might have come straight out of Jules Verne's *20,000 Leagues Under the Sea*; a fish that should rightfully inhabit McGelligots Pool and the strange imaginings of Dr. Seuss; a fish that no fisherperson ever dreamed of catching nor would have wanted to, given knowledge of it.

Back in November of 1976 a Navy research vessel was wandering around some 25 miles off the Windward side of O'ahu conducting a variety of oceangoing experiments. Preparing to heave to in 500 feet of water one morning, the navy noticed that something had fouled the anchor lines of their ship. What they pulled up caused the scrubs on board and, later, the entire scientific community of Hawai'i, to consider anew the strange manner of beasts that lie below our paltry ships. It was a new or at least hitherto unknown kind of fish; a shark, but a shark like no one had seen before. Fifteen feet long, definitely a male, and weighing in at a flabby 1,653 pounds, the creature turned out to be not just a new species, but a new genus and family as well. The navy was astounded. Not even the Russians had one of these!

Paul Struhsaker of the National Marine Fisheries Service and Leighton Taylor of the Waikīkī Aquarium immediately took charge in a civilian sort of way. They were later joined by shark experts John McCosker of San Francisco's Steinhart Aquarium and Leonard Compagno of San Francisco State University. The animal was disentangled from the anchor lines into which it had blundered overnight and suffocated. It was pulled on board, rushed to the Hawaii Tuna Packers plant in Honolulu, and iced down like a giant mullet. The next day Taylor named the creature "Megamouth" because of its flexible, 4-foot maw; its large, rubbery lips; and its 236 small and distinctly uncharacteristic and unsharklike teeth. Early evidence, Taylor noted after a cursory inspection, suggested that Megamouth lived at great depths and could produce bioluminescence. In other words, this shark carried its own light bulbs. It probably fed on small sea life and would not, he noted, be tempted by any kind of run-of-the mill baited hook. Nor by legs or surfboards. The great beast was then preserved, cut open, systematically surveyed, and micro- and macro-scopically inspected from stem to stern.

In the 4 years following Megamouth's discovery, other discoveries came to light, particularly inside Megamouth's mouth. A never-before-seen-or-heard-of species of marine tapeworm was found down in the bottom of its gut. The tapeworm was named

Mixodigma leptaleum. Megamouth itself was given a proper scientific name for both his genus and species: *Megachasma pelagios.* Speeches were given and an article was written for the Proceedings of the California Academy of Sciences. Megamouth quickly became the darling of the ichthyological community both here and on the mainland.

Even as I explained all this I could see Fay's interest reaching the end of its tether. "Do you think my nails would look better in mauve or salmon?" she asked, holding her digits out in front of her. And then, without waiting for a response, she took a bottle of nail polish remover from her desk and started saturating a piece of cotton preparatory to swabbing the also-ran hue. Apple blossom was definitely out.

The discovery of Megamouth, I continued without losing stride, raised interesting questions. How was it, for example, that a new kind of fish this size could be found so close to shore and in relatively shallow waters and yet be totally unknown to sportsmen and commercial fishers — or, in fact, to anyone? Was Megamouth really a deep-water creature that had wandered in toward shore, as its anatomy suggested? How did Megamouth really feed? Did it actually attract its food with small lights and sieve down whatever came its way, or did its lighting system perform some reproductive function? Was Megamouth a "local" fish found only in Hawai'i or was it more widespread? More important, was this particular one a fluke, some kind of a mutant, or was it genuinely a kind of animal new to us? Finally, whatever it was, how many more Megamouths might actually be down there mucking around in the murk waiting for navy boats to heave an anchor out?

Taylor, McCosker, Compagno, and Struhsaker speculated away. Then, on November 29, 1984, a second Megamouth was pulled out of the sea. This time a commercial fishing boat cruising 5-1/2 miles off Catalina Island near Los Angeles trolled one up by accident. As luck would have it, a California Fish and Game officer was on board and he immediately suspected what they had caught. The new fish, also a 15-foot, 1-ton male, was alive when it was netted and brought on board but died shortly after. Like its Hawaiian cousin, the second Megamouth was rushed to port; it was iced down in the parking lot of the Natural History Museum of Los Angeles. Leighton Taylor, hearing in Honolulu about the catch, leaped up in the air behind his desk, gave a guttural shout of primal ecstasy, and immediately jumped on a plane headed for L.A.

Megamouth no. 2 confirmed the family name. When MM no. 1 was the only one of its kind known there was always the nagging possibility that it might have been a freak of nature. Taylor had argued otherwise, of course, because MM no. 1's internal anatomy appeared normal and properly sharklike. Nonetheless, the Los Angeles fish proved conclusively that the first one was no mutant. Moreover, MM no. 2 extended the fish's range and corroborated much of what had been discovered from its pickled cousin in Hawai'i.

As I brought my story to a close, Fay sat there, mouth agape, eyes fixed straight ahead at her nails. I stowed the sheaf of notes I had been discoursing from back into my briefcase and closed the latch.

"Dr. Oddler," she said with a slight touch of impatience, "why don't you just sign on the dotted line for the fish you want and I'll make sure that it gets included in the vote." She passed me the clipboard with a pad of slips attached, being careful not to smear the polish on her repainted nails.

I tore one off, wrote M E G A M O U T H in letters bigger than anything John Hancock or Patrick Henry ever produced, signed my name, and handed her the paper. I then asked if she had any opinions about the fish contest.

"I have a guppy named Herbert," she said. "I think guppies would be a totally awesome State fish." I noticed that she was already starting to apply nail polish remover to her left hand.

"Nice meeting you, Fay," I said as I closed the door and left.

*   *   *

And so my vote was cast. I called Suiso the next day to tell him the news. From my perspective, I said, a vote for Megamouth was a vote for fairness, justice, and a new and entirely more progressive order in Hawai'i. Suiso seemed to think otherwise. "Look,

Adler," he grumbled, "Megamouth is just a big, slobby plankton eater. So what if he's rare? Nobody cares about anything like that except the pinheads from the University. I mean Megamouth is interesting but he's just not the right symbol for the State of Hawai'i." I considered his comments and said, "So who is?" "*Carcharodon carcharius*," he said. "That's who my vote goes for!" Old LumpJaws himself. Benchley's Bomber. The Great White Shark that occasionally enters Hawaiian waters just for the pure fun of terrorizing those few local fishermen who happen to see him. "What I like about the Great White," said Suiso with a deviant laugh, "is that they've been eating Californians recently. That makes them the perfect symbol for us. What a message we'll be sending out!"

Over the next week, starting with the *A*'s (Arlo A. Adler) in my address book, I methodically began calling everyone I know to exhort their participation in the fish contest. A vote for Megamouth, I told them in no uncertain terms, was a vote for a cleaner, sounder, fairer, and decidedly more Godly Hawai'i. The Hawai'i of the future. A twenty-first-century Hawai'i in which the natural order has been restored, and strange and interesting creatures that fit nowhere else (strange creatures like me, I emphasized) have a home. "A fish like Megamouth deserves a megavote," I said. And if you absolutely cannot find a place in your heart for old blubber-lips, I added, then at least consider my deviant friend's candidate, the Great White Shark. After calling the last person in my black book (a brief acquaintance from long ago by the name of Otto K. P. Zabrinskiby), I settled back to watch the results.

* * *

A month later, the great State fish contest came to a decisive and — from my perspective — disappointing close. Fanning out around the Islands to collect the opinions of our schoolchildren, the staff of the Aquarium and the University of Hawai'i Marine Options Program collected 60,191 votes, many of them from adults. With the final tallies in, the *humuhumunukunukuāpua'a* had won a resounding victory — 16,577 votes had been cast for this 9-inch triggerfish; its nearest competitor, the convict tang, had a mere 8,742. Voting had been hot and heavy on O'ahu, but ballots had also been received from places as far away as New York, Massachusetts, Texas, and Maine. Why foreigners should have been allowed to express an opinion on an important matter like this was beyond me; however, those were the rules. Above and beyond the eight official reef fish, many other write-ins had been received as well. At least a small handful of spirited stalwarts had lobbied hard for the Portuguese man-of-war and a few kindred souls (probably friends of Suiso's) had cast their roll of the dice on the poisonous sea snake that once in a rare while frequents our parts. Down at the bottom of the list, however, all alone but not totally forgotten, sat one vote apiece for Megamouth and the Great White Shark.

And so it was that the *humuhumunukunukuāpua'a*, the common, weed-eating, piggy-faced triggerfish, came to be selected by the populace as the totem fish of Hawai'i. A fitting symbol, perhaps, for a population slowly declining into cuteness and yuppyism. And a far cry, be it noted, from any of the more ferocious, interesting, or gastronomically acceptable symbols Suiso and I and others had wanted. Edward Hosaka, in his classic work *Shore Fishing In Hawai'i*, described the *humuhumu* this way: "Body elliptic, compressed; skin rough to touch and leathery; mouth small, with thick lips, a single row of sharp, notched incisor-like teeth in each jaw.... Edible qualities: the flesh is moderately firm and is liked by some, but in general, it is considered a poor quality fish...."

Bear in mind when you see the *humuhumu* plastered on T-shirts and bumper stickers that the Hawaiians themselves do not seem to hold this creature in very high regard. An old, white-haired Hawaiian man I met on a beach practicing with his throw net once told me so. And here, as he explained it to me, is how the ancients used to prepare *humuhumu*.

"What you do, brah," he said as we squatted on our haunches picking rocks and cigarette butts out of his net, "is you go catch yourself one nice-size *humuhumu*. Den you make a good beach fire, da kine from driftwood an old dried seaweeds you find round da high water line. Den you let da fire burn down and make nice hot coals and den you *hemo* your *humuhumu* and split 'em half-half. Li dis," he said with a flourish of his hand. "Den you take out da guts and pin 'em down on one board. Den stand 'em up about 2 feet away from da fire," he continued. "Den you wait. Maybe drink a few beers. Maybe wait a little longer. In fact, brah, you wait until you stay real hungry. When da *humuhumu* meat turn all brown, you throw away da fish and eat da board."

Benjamin Franklin, so it is said, once tried vainly to convince the people of his time that they had chosen poorly when it came to our national bird. Franklin, bless his kite-flying, key-jingling, lightning-addled soul, had lobbied for the wild American turkey, the bird that he believed best exemplified the indomitability of the American spirit. Moreover, said Franklin, the wild turkey is the cagiest and tastiest fowl in all of North America.

The rest of the United States, of course, disagreed. They sided with the Bald Eagle. "Any country that would choose a featherless, fish-eating, carrion-gobbling bird like the eagle is doomed to eventually become what it symbolizes," he is reputed to have said in a fit of sour grapes. I forgive him. I would even go so far as to say that the theory he espoused is probably correct, offensive as his particular example is to us Adlers. And thus it is with Hawai'i 200 hundred years later. The *humuhumunukunukuāpua'a* is now an official State totem and we, the tax-paying public, are the sucker-fish that let far more significant and noble creatures like Megamouth and the Great White Shark slip off the hook and back into inglorious obscurity.

5

Persistence

When the last individual of a race of living things breathes no more, another heaven and another earth must pass before such a one can be again.

William Beebe

O N THE DESK IN THE OFFICE where I spend most of my working hours, there's a dinosaur — or, to be exact, a plesiosaur, a sea lizard that lived approximately 250 million years ago. This particular animal is a 10-inch replica made of hard, cobalt-blue rubber that I bought at a store in Ala Moana Shopping Center. If the emerging science of genetic engineering ever makes it remotely possible, I intend to get a real plesiosaur for my office and train him to handle some of the more vexing people that come my way. He would sit next to me with his elongated 50-foot body filling my necessarily remodeled work space, showing off his four imposing flippers, and — attached at the business end of a snaky neck — a mouth full of fangs capable of grabbing, holding, and then compacting a small safe. Indeed, a live plesiosaur would give my usual work day that little extra element of excitement that's been lacking the past few years.

Such is not to be, of course. Real plesiosaurs haven't been around since the late Paleozoic. And few of us get offices big enough to put one in. So for the time being, at least, I'm stuck with a dinky blue model that is tucked between my Scotch tape dispenser and a chipped coffee cup full of pencils. I keep the little monster on my desk for two reasons.

First, there is the essential wonderment that an animal like this lived at all and that it breathed and bred in the same general atmosphere in which I do those things today. I am amazed that it existed and even more amazed that it survived for millions of years. In proper perspective, we would rightfully have to acknowledge that the plesiosaur and its cousins made up one of the greatest and longest running shows on earth.

And that gives rise to a second reason, namely extinction. Extinction stories interest me. I believe, in fact, that extinctions are worthy of far more attention than we normally give them. They are, in fact, good yarns that often have intricate plots, copious amounts of sex and violence, and moments of true and high tragedy. In addition to being quintessential drama, however, extinction stories are also excellent mind food. They instruct us by focusing our attention on some of life's bigger questions including the ultimate value that we place on life in general and on lives other than our own in particular.

Consider, for example, the following incidents, the first of which is chronicled in Peter Matthiessen's masterful book, *Wildlife in America*.

In the summer of 1844 and under the explicit direction of scientists, a rowboat carrying fourteen sailors pulled up on the shores of Eldey, a cold and rocky island due west of Cape Reykjanes, Iceland. As their boat touched shore, a pair of curious land birds, blinking in the sunlight, waddled up to two of the sailors — Sigour Isleffson and Jon Brandsonn — who immediately clubbed them to death. The two sailors then found a single egg of this species, which they casually smashed as well. The skins of the birds — flightless, penguinlike creatures once common to the seacoasts of northern Europe — were eventually sold to a Reykjavik taxidermist for nine pounds and, still later, turned over to a collector of stuffed animals.

This brutality might have gone unnoticed by historians and natural scientists but for one fact. It was, so far as anyone knows, the last time the garefowl, or Great Auk, was ever seen alive. The killing of the Auks, Matthiessen tells us, was not as we might first suppose an indiscriminate act attributable only to the loutishness and ignorance of nineteenth-century seamen; to the contrary. Persistently hunted for its meat, oil, and feathers, the Great Auk had been in decline for centuries. With its disappearance from

European waters its value changed, however. By the middle of the 1800s, the last auk had become a scientific curiosity. Isleffson and Brandsonn were simply bounty hunters.

Ten thousand miles of water separate Iceland from Hawai'i, but the connecting thread, in terms of eyewitness accounts of disappearing wildlife, is stronger than might be presumed initially. Take Laysan Island, an uninhabited Hawai'i atoll situated in the Leeward chain 900 miles northwest of Kaua'i between Maro Reef and the Northampton Banks. Oval and only 50 feet above sea level at its highest point, the Island is — and as long as anyone can remember always has been — a salt-encrusted chunk of coral rock a mile and a half long and three-quarters of a mile wide with a large lagoon in the center. Laysan is today what all eight of the inhabitable Hawaiian Islands will eventually become: a more or less waterless, weathered, and seldom-visited remnant of former volcanic glory.

Laysan might have spent the twentieth century as nothing more than an isolated way station visited by occasional fishermen, but for one thing. Some enterprising traveler realized that the atoll contained commercially valuable guano deposits. In a few short years, guano — known as birddoo to most of us — became the basis for a small but highly exploitative mining industry in the early 1900s. A group called the North Pacific Phosphate and Fertilizer Company was formed, and a small work force soon set about digging the stuff up and shipping it off to the plantations and farms of O'ahu, Maui, and Kaua'i. Disruptive as this probably was to the atoll's ecology, the North Pacific Phosphate and Fertilizer Company ultimately made a far costlier mistake. Someone introduced rabbits to the Island, perhaps as a source of fresh meat. Within 2 years, its thin strands of vegetation were gone. Very quickly, the flightless Laysan Rail, the *loulu* palm, and the native sandalwood all disappeared. Then another extinction occurred, this time witnessed by a team of scientists from the Bishop Museum's 1923 Tanager Expedition. The last three Laysan honeycreepers were seen and photographed; the following day they were found dead, killed by a sandstorm that swept the denuded Island. The photographs of the corpses are available for all to see at the Bishop Museum.

Contemplate these extinctions for a moment. The death, not just of an individual animal, but of an entire line of creatures; the passage in which a grand biological experiment, a confluence of blood, bone, and tissue, winds down. Century after century there is growth, adaptation, and survival. Then, a great diminishing — and finally the last one or two of a kind. Perhaps the obscure disappearance of these animals is observed. Or perhaps not. And then the creatures are gone and all possibilities of replication and continuity are severed forever. "We have come," says poet James Dickey in a verse on extinction, "to the end of this kind of vision of heaven." In his poem, the very last wolverine and the very last eagle sit high in a tree in the spare arctic dawn, the great northern lights shimmering above as the animals instinctively cling to life. There is fear and, on the far side of fear, a hollow whisper. "Lord, let me die, but not die out." The lines of the poem, like the animals, dissolve into silence.

Poems aside, I would have these extinctions be different if I could. For myself, I'd prefer endings to remember; wilder, fiercer, and more memorable conclusions with some moments of genuine spite and hate; endings that stir up comprehensible and, for me at least, more familiar emotions. I want endings that have a little revenge in them; endings that would at least make the five o'clock news. In my vision, the last two auks — and it could just as well be the last two Laysan honeycreepers — go down like seventeenth-century samurai warriors; like a ditch full of Marines at Guadalcanal; like the Jews at Masada.

Take the situation with the auks and replay it this way. The two sailors approach with clubs in their hands. The birds hunker down, their short claws outstretched, their eyes fearful and angry instead of blinking and dumb. Sigour Isleffson and Jon Brandsonn hesitate for a moment, not used to encountering resistance. The garefowls leap into action. One goes for Isleffson's face and in the frenzied attack, human flesh and avian feathers mingle. The air is filled with shrieks and screams. The auk's death comes at the end of Isleffson's club, but Isleffson's face is torn and bleeding from the struggle. The other auk guards the last remaining egg. Brandsonn chokes up on his stick. The auk jumps for him, and only at the last minute does

Brandsonn move quickly enough to avoid having his throat torn open. The last auk ducks, weaves, and snaps. She lunges for Brandsonn and Brandsonn screams in pain. Eventually, the auk goes down. The egg is smashed, but Brandsonn has lost an eye. Maybe both of them. Are accounts balanced? Is guilt lessened? Not really, but at least the scales of justice aren't quite so lopsided.

So the first of many modern-day queries surfaces. How, in an age when death is routinized, does one contemplate the end of a line of creatures millions of years old? What does the death of an animal or plant line really mean anyway? Does it make any difference over the long run? In the short run? And faced with the constant threat of our own extinction in some nuclear shoot-out or by slow asphyxiation from our own effluents and emissions, can we really be expected to care about the accidental or intentional killing of "lesser" beings like birds?

To be sure, the auks of Eldey and the honeycreepers of Laysan are bit players in a larger and more ominous melodrama that is being acted out on a global scale. Currently reckoned, there are probably four to five million species of animals and plants left on planet Earth. Fifteen to 20% of these — about 400,000 species — will become extinct in the next twenty years. Many, if not most, of these extinctions will be tropical and semitropical plants and invertebrates that have not even been officially discovered, described, and cataloged. And at least a small percentage of these will be animals and plants that would have been potentially beneficial to humans as food and medicine.

The forces propelling these future deaths are well known. Most will be caused by clear-cutting forests, draining swamps, altering waterways, filling in lakes and ponds, leveling mountains, and releasing vast amounts of poisons into the biosphere. Much of this deterioration will be insidious. It will affect plants, insects, fish, snails, reptiles, and other organisms that are out of our general line of sight and therefore outside of our personal bubbles of consciousness — and conscience. Occasionally, the degradation will spiral back into our existence in some dramatic form like the mercury deaths at Minamata or the radiation released from Chernobyl. For the most part, however, we will not see the impacts until it is too late.

Admittedly, altering this trajectory of death is difficult. It means, in the final analysis, dramatically shifting our personal and collective thinking about nature, the value of life, and the limits to growth. It also requires better qualitative and quantitative understandings of ecosystems that have already been degraded and that must be more aggressively insulated from deleterious influences. In this regard, sea islands are vulnerable in the extreme, their biotic systems among the most defenseless in the world. And here, the Hawaiian archipelago serves as a textbook example of how species come and go.

In its prehuman isolation, over millions of years, Hawai'i originated some of the strangest and most beautiful biological permutations ever known. The initial Hawaiian settlers were seeds and spores, immigrants that arrived by air and by sea, clinging to the underside of drift logs or blown here by the high Pacific winds. Once a basic flora developed to capture the sun's energy, insects, birds, and mammals were able to establish toeholds.

Over hundreds, sometimes thousands, of generations, changes occurred among the colonizers. Species radiated out to fill available niches. Concurrently, features changed to adapt to new conditions or needs. Inevitably, species spawned subspecies that ultimately came to look and act sufficiently different from their parent stock to be considered altogether different creatures. The blunt bill of a seed-eating finch, for example, curved downward, enabling it to obtain particular types of nectars and survive in greater numbers. Certain insects lost their wings. Small clumps of shrubs turned into trees and then into canopies of trees. The seeds of a few plants blew up the slopes of windswept mountains where they adapted to volcanic ash. Other plants lost their protective thorns or took on new and vibrant colors to accommodate new habitats.

Intricate twists and turns down various genetic corridors led to the extraordinarily diverse flora and fauna that, even in its currently degraded condition, is still to be admired in Hawai'i today. But, from an ever so slightly different angle, sanctuaries are also prisons. In evolutionary terms, the gradual endemicity that occurs on islands is more often than not a one-way voyage. Once certain changes take place there is no turning back. In the mazeways of evolution, adaptations and distributions are specific. Most creatures cannot re-adapt when some new and threatening force suddenly makes its presence felt. Hence extinction.

In Hawai'i, the dynamics of these deaths are readily available for study. Hawai'i, in fact, has the sad distinction of ranking first in the United States in the number of both extinct and endangered birds. A case in point is *Loxioides bailleui* — the *palila* — a cousin of the late and lamented Laysan honeycreeper. Roughly 6 inches long with a short, stubby bill and yellow-gray coloration, the *palila* is found only on the island of Hawai'i. At one time it was common above the 5,000-foot elevation on the Big Island and could be sighted in the mountains above the Kona and Hāmākua coasts. Today, its habitat is restricted to a thin belt of *māmane* forest girdling Mauna Kea at mid-altitude. Both the *māmane* and the *palila* are dying, a result of intrusions by goats and feral sheep. In a precarious, tenuous balance, the *palila* is dependent on the *māmane*'s green seed pods, which have been decimated. Estimates vary, but there are now probably fewer than 4,000 birds left.

The *palila* is not alone. Nowhere on earth have so many uncommonly diverse creatures been destroyed in so short a period of time as in Hawai'i. Since Captain Cook's arrival in the Islands in 1778, at least 256 plants found no place else in the world have disappeared along with twenty-four species and subspecies of native birds. Actual extinctions include the Hawaiian Rail; the O'ahu, Hawai'i, and Moloka'i ō'ō; the Lana'i Thrush and Creeper; the O'ahu *nuku pu'u*; the grosbeak finch and greater *koa* finch, both from Hawai'i; the *'akialoa*, *'amakihi*, black *mamo*, and many others. And in the grim contemporary "who's who" of avifauna, almost every major Island has added to the current endangered species list: the Maui parrotbill; the Kaua'i *nuku pu'u*; the Moloka'i *'i'iwi*; the *Lāna'i 'apapane*; the Laysan Finch; the Nihoa Millerbird. These are the rare ones, the ones on the edge. So diverse and pressured is birdlife here that an entirely new and unknown genus and species in the honeycreeper family, *Melamprosops phaeosoma*, was discovered in the Hāna rain forest in 1973 and immediately added to the official roster.

Although the death or near-death of each line of animals is a story in itself, the causes of this collective decline in Hawai'i go back at least a thousand years, long before the advent of Westernization. It is well known, for example, that the Polynesians who first settled the Islands altered the alluvial valleys and rain forests for their own agricultural purposes. Pigs, dogs, and rats — all predators in their own ways — came with the Hawaiians from the Marquesas and Tahiti. Certain wild birds were hunted intensively for their feathers. New trees like the *kukui* — the candlenut tree — were intentionally planted and surely displaced other native forest plants. Nonetheless, the Polynesian tradition of living closely with one's surroundings prevailed. Various plants and animals disappeared, but the Islands, especially in the uplands, remained isolated, self-contained, and ecologically healthy.

Once Hawai'i was opened to the rest of the world, however, a true tidal wave of devastation began, one that washed across the chain, destroying dozens of local plant, bird, and insect species and at least two native mammals. Exploitation of nature and a perverse philosophy of "social Darwinism" advocating the survival of the fittest were dominant themes in nineteenth-century Western thinking. Animal introductions, both accidental and intentional, included two additional species of rats; everyday varieties of cattle, goats, and sheep; the mongoose; mosquitoes; and several species of predatory snails.

Human depredations were just as bad. Lowland and upland forests alike were raided to satisfy an insatiable market for sandalwood. Habitats were destroyed to make way for sugar and pineapple plantations. Natural watercourses were diverted, hillsides carved away, and lagoons and fishponds filled in. And with the twentieth century came another storm of changes, this one driven by rapid population growth, urbanization, and industrial tourism. The legacy of those forces is what exists today: an ever-expanding sprawl of highways, hotels, housing tracts, and other human developments.

Conservation in general and the preservation of wild birds in particular must be thought of as a science of diminishing possibilities. Even modest levels of success involve all-out efforts aimed at protecting natural communities, controlling adjacent human populations, limiting industrial and agricultural encroachments, and checking new biological colonizers. Today, in the face of so many threats to Hawai'i's physical and cultural environments, the life or death of one or two more kinds of animals may seem almost insignificant, a near irrelevancy. Amidst all this gloom and doom, however, there is one Hawaiian creature that, so far as extinction stories go, falls into the "victory snatched from the jaws of defeat" category. The account of this particular creature should be an inspiration for the work that is still to be done. And the closest place to see it just happens to be a few miles from our house.

* * *

It's a blistering, intensely bright Sunday afternoon and I should have my head examined for this. We are on a trip to the one place that any resident of Hawai'i with a lick of sense is most likely to shun on a hot day. I'm talking about that neon gumbo and human maelstrom that makes up the nearest thing we have to a Hawaiian-style Sodom and Gomorrah: Waikīkī. I jostle, elbow, and crowbar our old Size-6 Ford Pinto into a Size-3 parking stall ten blocks from where we want to be and then, lathered up from driving and parking, stare out at the urban inferno that awaits us.

Our specific destination is the Honolulu Zoo, a green and shaded oasis at the end of Kalākaua Avenue. After that, we're going to a nearby beach. To get to both these places, we need to survive Waikīkī, which has — today at least — the hottest set of pavements in the world. Our main objective is to visit the cage of a certain rare bird. An odd place, one thinks, to find an endangered species. A bit like looking for traditional Hawaiian foods at the hotel snack bar. Nonetheless, off we go.

Surrounding me as I climb out of the car is a pack of cackling and distracted children who, if my instincts as a social scientist are at all correct, are not really children at all, but five aliens disguised as ferocious, supremely self-confident miniature humans, disguised, to be even more specific, as our daughters and their closest friends in the entire world, the Ogimi kids. Unquestionably, we are an expeditionary force with which to be reckoned.

On point as we push our way down the street are the preteen forward artillery observers, Tricia Ogimi and Corey Adler. They are walking along with two sets of headphones tethered to one Walkman. They consider themselves officers and gentlewomen and are disdaining any type of contact with the inferior enlisted grades that are five steps behind them. As it happens, two of these lower-order grunts are holding hands and skipping over certain lines and spots in the sidewalk that only they can divine as being poison snakes and boiling peanut butter. These enlisted types are Dana Adler and Tricia's younger sister Michelle.

Directly behind them and marching to her own drummer — in fact, in her very own parade — is our secret weapon, Kelly Adler, known to the others as "The Terminator." Finally, at the very end of the line is the quartermaster corps, consisting of Carolyn and myself carrying a full complement of swimsuits, masks, flippers, snorkels, towels, shirts, shorts, pants, spare underwear, toys, food, water, and sunblock. Nosily, the kids race out in front, cleaving through knots of pedestrians like the prow of a boat, scattering tourists and locals alike. At last, we pass through the main entrance of the zoo and stroll out into the sunshine past the monkeys, giraffes, camels, alligators, and tigers. The kids are enthralled with everything, including the more free-ranging animals that live in and around the edges of the main cages. These are the crypto-zoans, the bottom-dwellers and general hangers-on of the zoo's weird ecosystem. The freeloaders include fat, white pigeons that mate in front of the hot dog stand; a screaming peacock sitting on a branch by the hippo pond; quick, bold, sneaky little sparrows that snatch away breadcrumbs and popcorn from the large cats, who aren't supposed to have them anyway; and dozens of broody roosters and chickens with fluffy chicks all scratching out the best living they know how considering there isn't an authentic barnyard within several miles of the place. Spongers and goldbrickers, all of them. I suspect they are tolerated because they become food for the meat-eaters when they expire on the zoo's grounds.

Past a row of cages holding the imported, exotic birds, past the Burmese binturong, the Asian small-clawed otter, and the North American puma, we find the birds we are looking for in a large open area enclosed by a waist-high cyclone fence. The girls immediately pull out two sacks of stale bread and sprinkle crumbs on the other side of the fence. Two of the birds take notice, then more. Soon a large part of the flock of some twenty-five are carefully munching a free lunch out of our hands. The birds seem hungry but act as if they are doing us a favor. They have long, snaky necks (not unlike my plesiosaur in some respects) with small heads, beady eyes, and black beaks that pluck the chunks of bread from our fingers, never once mistaking flesh for food. The pecking order here demonstrates why the term has become so widely used. Older, more mature birds chase away the younger and more impulsive ones. Males bite at females. A few loners stand by themselves on the edge of the crowd. Yet, all in all, they are an orderly, well-mannered group. Heads rotate and pivot, inspecting the food before they eat it. There is a low, raspy honking as they feed from our hands. All of the birds that so choose come away with at least a modest midday snack.

The birds we are visiting are *nēnē*, the Hawaiian goose, official State bird. *Branta sandvicensis* is normally a resident of the upland forests along with the endemic owl (*pueo*), the Hawaiian crow (*'alalā*), and the Hawaiian hawk (*'io*). In the wild its muted call sometimes resembles the mooing of a lost calf. It can fly, but awkwardly. It lives off berries and soft plants, and spends most of its life innocently grubbing about amidst the sparse vegetation of our alpine areas.

On first viewing, this particular gaggle looks anything but endangered. They are sleek, well fed, content, and thoroughly used to people like us gawking and clucking at them. They look healthy and plump, as if they were all ready to march forthwith into the frying pans and broiling racks of Kentucky Fried Chicken. In fact, I can visualize these birds cleaned, dressed, trussed up with meat thermometers, cooked slowly to a golden brown, and then served with cranberries, stuffing, and plum pudding.

If this seems harsh and uncivil treatment for a bird high on the endangered species list, it is at least historically accurate. Captain Cook is reputed to have enjoyed a *nēnē* for Christmas dinner on his ill-fated visit to Hawai'i. I can easily imagine this stalwart, lonely seaman seized with a lust for something distinctively English. The expedition has finally come to Kealakekua Bay. The ship's larders are out of salt pork, fresh vegetables, rum, and ale. It is the day before Christmas, and Cook is homesick and miserable. He sits in his cabin on the *Resolution*, trying hard to concentrate on the business of being an explorer, but his heart is not in it. There are no Christmas trees, no presents, no sweet waifs caroling in the snow. He looks down at the table that has been set and sees a bowl of gray, three-day-old *poi*; a small slab of bony, stinking fish; a few fire-hardened sweet potatoes, and a glass of tepid, slightly fermented coconut milk. "Enough," he yells, sweeping it all off the table. "I want goose!" Cook's cook runs out, paddles off in a longboat, and returns with a *nēnē*. For a few bent nails and rusting scraps of iron, the Captain gets his bird from some obliging Hawaiians, unaware that in the very near future his own goose will be cooked and ceremonially deboned by these very same people.

If the low road to *nēnē* appreciation is an unimaginative and straight-line thoroughfare through the human stomach, the high road has more scenic and interesting detours. The *nēnē* is one of those evolutionary oddities that testifies to the powerful relationship between geography and biology. Tough, strong, and handsome in a goosely way, it is a first cousin of the Canada Goose that migrates across much of North America. Blown off course in the distant past, in Hawai'i it has adapted to the rigors of sparsely vegetated volcanic mountains. It thrives on the waterless lava lands of Maui and the Big Island, and bones found in sand dunes tell us that they once lived on other Islands as well. Both the webbed feet, which have evolved into rock-grasping claws, and the buff coloration around the cheeks and neck are local specializations.

Nēnē have a powerful homing instinct. Adult birds usually return to the same nesting area year after year to brood. Under normal conditions, female *nēnē* build their nests in November and lay clutches of two to five eggs, which hatch in about a month. Both young goslings and molting adults are flightless and therefore vulnerable. Stuck on the ground, they are at the mercy of predators and, in former times at least, hunters.

The plight of the *nēnē* first captured the public's attention in 1945. Paul Baldwin, an ornithologist with a wide-ranging interest in local birdlife, studied the *nēnē*'s diminishing habitat and distribution and estimated a population of fewer than 50 birds confined to a 1,150-square-mile tract on the Big Island. In the latter half of the eighteenth century, reckoned Baldwin, there were probably 25,000 birds living on the slopes of Mauna Loa, Mauna Kea, Hualālai, and Haleakalā. By the turn of the century, however, the *nēnē* was clearly in decline. Much of the upland forests had been slashed and cut back for agriculture, and the mongoose, goat, dog, and cat had all been allowed to proliferate. The toll on generations of young goslings was enormous. To make matters worse, the *nēnē* were also hunted for sport, flushed alive for pets, and, at one point, commercially exploited for meat.

George C. Munro in his *Birds of Hawai'i* stated that *nēnē* were commonly captured by Hawaiians for food when the geese were molting. Never, however, did Hawaiians hunt the *nēnē* with the greed and brutality of Westerners. Throughout the late 1800s, traders, settlers, and ships' crews took thousands of birds, many of them salted down and sent by clipper ships to California for hungry forty-niners. If this seems unduly harsh and exploitative, it fits in perfectly with the times. The era of indigenous Hawaiian autonomy was coming to an end. Demographically and culturally the Hawaiians themselves were in decline, victims of intrusions by diseased sailors and Bible-thumping missionaries. "Civilization" was descending on an island chain blessed with clear waters, pristine weather, a vibrant human culture, and one of the most diverse animal and plant populations known on Earth.

The *nēnē* dwindled. A few noteworthy attempts at salvaging and restoring flocks were started as early as 1823, but the decline continued. Artificial propagation was tried in both England and France at specialized laboratories, and in England there was limited success. Nonetheless, based on his own research and collecting, Munro (1960, p. 42), the "dean of Hawaiian birdlife," was pessimistic.

> We hunted this goose in December 1891 on the
> rough lava flow of 1801, down nearly to sea level,
> and up the side of the mountain on the Huehue ranch
> to about 2,200 feet elevation. It was open shooting
> season and a party of hunters went over ground at the
> higher elevation where we had taken specimens a
> few days before. They found a nest with four eggs,
> caught two very young chicks and shot a young bird
> nearly full grown. It pained us to kill specimens at a
> time when the birds had young but the few we killed
> were as nothing compared to the numbers the hunters
> would shoot of this unwary bird.

In 1911 the hunting of *nēnē* was legally banned by the Territorial Board of Agriculture and Forestry. Yet the serious task of saving it from total extinction didn't get started until the 1950s. By that time, the wild goose population was down to thirteen birds, all in captivity. The *nēnē* was clearly headed for extinction. Then came Harold Shipman. Cattle rancher, Hilo businessman, and conservationist all rolled into one, Shipman had started breeding *nēnē* in 1918 with a pair of donated birds and, over the next thirty years, had produced a respectable flock. As with other amateur naturalists throughout history, Shipman's determined effort was fraught with setbacks. Some of his birds were given away to start experimental breeding programs on other Islands, most of which failed. Four pairs of *nēnē* went to a rancher on Moloka'i but were released into the wild too soon. Six others were given to a wealthy philanthropist on O'ahu and were never heard from again. At least three geese were sent to a plantation manager on Lāna'i and were probably eaten by laborers shortly after their release. In the meantime, some of Shipman's Hilo flock escaped and others were killed in the tidal wave of 1946.

Yet a few survived. In 1949 a territorial breeding and research station was established on the slopes of Mauna Kea at Pōhakuloa. By the mid-1950s, thanks largely to breeding pairs donated by Shipman, the efforts of both the Board of Commissioners of Agriculture at Pōhakuloa and the Severn Wildlife Trust in England had produced strong hatching programs. In 1958 the U.S. Fish and

Wildlife Service provided funds for further *nēnē* management, bringing together a full complement of private, State, and Federal restoration efforts. By 1963, with help from across another ocean, an English gander named Kamehameha had sired some 200 offspring. Fifty *nēnē* were flown back from England to restock a virtually nonexistent Maui population. In 1972, still more birds were released on Mauna Kea, Mauna Loa, and Hualālai, and in 1975 — nearly a century after its near annihilation — the *nēnē* was finally admitted to the U.S. official list of endangered species.

Today, the *nēnē's* future seems more secure, although it is far from assured. About 900 birds exist in the wild and another twenty breeding pairs are in captivity. The breeding programs in England and at Pōhakuloa have produced at least 1,600 birds, and local and Federal wildlife officials continue to manage the species intensively. Yet the presence of a stable and secure wild goose population is not just a function of numbers. *Nēnē* habitat areas continue to be jeopardized by feral goats and pigs, by the introduction of exotic plant species, and by commercial land developments. The rat, mongoose, dog, and cat also continue to take their toll. Finally, the *nēnē's* own reproductive rates seem to work against them, and mortality is still high. Breeding pairs do not typically lay many eggs nor do all of them hatch. Of those that do, many chicks do not live to become fledglings.

If the *nēnē's* collective hold on life is tenuous, at least in terms of overall numbers, one would never know it by visiting the zoo. Here, on the large, grassy knoll they occupy, the *nēnē* seem only passively interested in anything at all, including tying on the midday nose-bag. Pigeons, sparrows, mynah birds, and peacocks compete for the morsels of bread strewn about by visitors. An old cracker thrown into the air brings down several squadrons of different kinds of winged critters all intent on being first in line for some grub. Each outstretched hand creates a flurried, feathered scrambling that lasts to the precise moment the bread bags are empty. Through it all, the *nēnē* prefer to peck and preen themselves. Occasionally they deem it diplomatic to visit the visitors and to accept a proffered gift of wadded-up dough, more out of obligation than need, it seems. A goose looks up at me, black beak searching and nibbling, gazing out from eyes that seem to me to reveal a sluggish and smug complacency. The same look, in fact, that I once saw in the eyes of caged birds in a commercial chicken slaughtering operation that produced 10,000 fryers a month in Jefferson County, Missouri.

Under the best of circumstances it is impossible to tell how a *nēnē* bird might be feeling about life in general and about its own existence in particular. At the zoo, they do not appear to be feeling much of anything. Yet, given their history, perhaps deep down there is still some recessive and biological spark of willpower left, waiting for an opportune moment to emerge. Maybe one of these birds will be the Spartacus or Che Guevera of goosedom, a *nēnē* revolutionary who will lead his or her fellow goslings over the fence to freedom. Once they make their wholesale jailbreak, they'll head for the hills. Up Kapahulu and across Wai'alae Avenue, up St. Louis Drive and on into the Ko'olau Mountains and the sweet streams of O'ahu's watersheds. Once there, they'll settle down to the real matter at hand: revenge against every dog, cat, human, and mongoose that ever did them a bad turn.

In the most truthful corners of my own existence I know this will never happen. Chalk it up to small ravings brought on by the midday heat of Waikīkī and the gnawing realization that the wild Hawaiian goose is doomed. Cooked. Done for. Possibly, the spirit of persistence has deserted this species just as it may one day, sooner than we think, desert us. In my heart of hearts I fear that there's less to this bird than first meets the eye.

* * *

Christmas time. Four of us have donned our hiking duds and hauled ourselves off to Maui to spend the holiday inside Haleakalā crater. It is 10,000 feet up, deliciously cold, and totally removed from the hordes of shoppers that are stampeding through the stores of Honolulu. In a religious tradition with roots far older than Christianity, Haleakalā is the "house of the sun," the mountaintop where Māui the demigod-trickster snared the sun in a fishnet to slow it down in its rush across the sky. Hale-a-ka-lā, resonant name for a resonant mountain; a great, mysterious, vibrating symphony of stone; a reputed power spot; a living biological laboratory; a geological treasure trove.

Carolyn and I and our old friends Ramon and Elaine will spend two days inside the crater, hike ten miles downhill through a great rent in the side of the mountain called Kaupō Gap, regroup at sea level, and then walk and hitch our way to the town of Hāna near the Seven Pools. From there, we'll fly out on a commercial carrier that runs ten-seater Cessnas. A magnificent getaway into below-freezing temperatures and the stark moonscape that the mountain presents in the winter. We register and get our camping permits at the National Park Service headquarters and then thumb a ride to the summit with a long-haired night watchman who works at the telescopes at the top. There, we pay a brief visit to the ranger who runs this mountain and then descend down Sliding Sands Trail into the bowl of the crater.

Having last erupted in 1790, the volcano, for all practical purposes, is extinct, although geologists, covering their bets, prefer to say "dormant." It could erupt again. Three thousand feet deep, seven and a half miles long, and two and a half miles across, the crater has three distinct environments: a barren, windswept tundra at the summit; a dry, desertlike caldera floor; and in a windward gap at its lowest elevations, a deep, lush rain forest. Moving down Sliding Sands Trail toward the crater's bottom we are headed in the general direction of Hōlua cabin, which brings us into the vicinity of the silversword.

The Haleakalā silversword, *Argyroxiphium sandwicense*, is a famous yuccalike member of the sunflower family that migrated in the long distant past to the top of Maui's highest mountain, where it ekes out a highly evolved living in volcanic cinders and ash. Not unlike the century plant of the American Southwest, it is a stunning creation with lustrous, daggerlike leaves covered with fuzzy silver down. In the exceptional brightness and dryness of the crater it grows five to eight feet tall, and at the end of a life cycle that can extend to twenty years, it produces — one time only — hundreds of purple flowers. It scatters seeds about and then dies. Like so many other endemic animals and plants in Hawai'i, it is highly endangered but is slowly returning as the goat eradication program takes hold.

In the late afternoon, we pitch our tents near a water tank by Hōlua cabin and then set off for a half-mile jaunt around Silversword Loop, a side trail off the main route across Haleakalā crater. Inside this loop are several dozen plants in various stages of growth and decay. The red lava flow that forms their bed doesn't appear to have the slightest bit of nutrient: no soil, moisture, or shade. And yet little slopes and crannies lined with volcanic ash somehow provide just the right combination of conditions for these otherworldly creations.

In this miniaturized forest of silverswords there are also the leavings of ancient human involvements: piles of stones, markers, and rock platforms that once formed a Hawaiian *heiau* — a temple. Taken all together, the silverswords and stones look like part of some strange space colony, the remnants of a former civilization on a planet in some other solar system. When I mention this, Ramon remarks that it's us two-legged beings with opposable thumbs and oversized brains that seem out of place.

The next day we are up and off on a west-to-east march through the crater that takes us a few thousand feet lower in elevation and into a new ecosystem. We hoof our way across a spider web of trails, over old cinder cones and rocky sloughs, up small hillocks, and down into valleys of ash and pebbles. By the time we reach Palikū — the cabin at the head of Kaupō Gap — we are at the fringe of a moist forest with tall *māmane* and *'ōhi'a* trees, thick grasses and ferns, and shrubs of quivering *'ōlapa*. Constructed of wood, cement, and tin, Palikū is a stout little cabin nestled down at the base of Haleakalā's east wall at the top of the gap. It sleeps fifteen but we pitch tents in a clearing a few hundred yards away.

During a spectral sunset Elaine hears a distinctive honking, calls to the rest of us, and points up toward the east wall of the crater. Six birds that look like miniature pterodactyls glide and circle in large ellipses. Contrary to what I have been told, they are not awkward flyers at all. They move in unison as they fan the air, the tips of their wings stretched out to feel the currents and updrafts, necks bent and craned forward, feet tucked in. They drop down, swoop up again, and then finally, in the dim, gloomy light, land about 20 feet away in a clump of grass just outside my line of vision. Two minutes later, having stayed in the same spot, I hear a *nēnē* swishing through the grass toward me. As the bird comes closer there are soft honks and squawks, little goose quackings that carry a certain ring of contentment. This particular *nēnē* seems to be returning home from a hard day at work and looking forward to his easy chair, an extra dry martini, and the evening paper. Or maybe it's Mrs. *Nēnē* who's coming home from work. In fact the bird I hear approaching turns out to be a pair, waddling through the grass not in the least disturbed by the dozen or so campers and hikers hanging out in the general vicinity of their nesting area. Because of this, I immediately presume that these *nēnē* are approachable like their sisters and brothers at the zoo.

I'm wrong. I stand as still as I possibly can and the two of them walk by me. If they are aware of me they don't show it. They are about 4 feet away and infinitely more wary and intelligent-looking than their Honolulu cousins. When I shift my weight from one foot to the other, a twig cracks. Startled, the bird closest to me turns and lunges, tries to peck me, and then leaps into the tall grass and disappears.

Not precisely like my imaginary auks clawing Isleffson and Brandsonn on Eldey, but close enough. The last thing I see is a pair of feathered rear ends scuttling into the underbrush, tails raised like flags. I break into laughter and Carolyn comes over and asks me what's so funny. It pleases me no end to see these birds close up, I explain. I like seeing them flying in formation here in the far and desolate reaches of an obscure volcano in the middle of a remote island chain. Moreover, I like their alertness, that innate wariness and caution that true wild creatures have. And most of all, I like the idea that the last of the *nēnē* are not doomed to live out their lives on a regimen of bread and peanuts in a barred prison somewhere between the otters and the monkeys on the outskirts of Waikīkī.

It is impossible for me to credit these *nēnē* birds with the kind of intelligence it takes to weigh alternatives and make conscious, willful decisions. In my anthropomorphic fantasies, I want to believe that the *nēnē* birds have survived because of their cellular spark, a kind of collective urge to persist, buried in their chromosomes, transmuted across several spare, lean, and not very pleasant generations, and now flowering like wind-blown seeds after a heavy rain. I want to believe that survival is not just a question of being the fittest or wisest or best adapted but that it also involves willpower.

Maybe this driving, inner push to persevere is a real and tangible thing that will one day be found under the probing eyes of nuclear microscopes and laser-powered body-scanners — instruments so powerful that they can track the inner life of atoms and take pictures of your thoughts. Maybe eventually every home will have one. Or perhaps it will be some graduate student studying molecular biology or genetics who finds the secret "it" buried in the eggs and sperm of a few white rats — some new type of molecular object that fuels collective as well as individual survival instincts in times of stress. Perhaps it is a kind of battery-run life clock stuck on the underside of an odd gene at the farthest end of a single chromosome. Suddenly, the human future may begin to look very different as our notions of the past and of order change.

But conversely, perhaps there is nothing more to all this than sensible management, something Americans pride themselves on and at which they do occasionally excel. Maybe this insistence on survival is a purely human affair in which credit for biological ingenuity does not belong with the *nēnē*, but to George Munro, Harold Shipman, scientists at the University, and a few hard-working men and women employed by the national parks and various fish and wildlife services. Maybe it's human genes that have saved the day, not those of the *nēnē*. Maybe it's good old American (and English) organization and know-how, or correct wildlife management and the intelligent administration of private, State, and Federal dollars, the public lobbying of conservation groups, and a bit of well-directed pork barrel money squeezed out of some hidden pocket in the budget of the Department of the Interior. In the tortured, uncharted world of cause and effect, the *nēnē*'s presence on the planet may be due to some cigar-chomping politician in a baggy suit who agreed, twenty years ago, to throw a few grants and jobs in the general vicinity of Hawai'i in exchange for a new airport in Fatback, Louisiana.

At Palikū we see the geese one more time. In the early morning, Carolyn and I crawl out of our tent and walk the fifty or so yards needed to get a bucket of water for general tooth brushing, tea brewing, and oatmeal mixing. Halfway, we hear honks and turn back toward our tent in time to see two birds flying off from a nest close to where we slept. There is no playful circling and gliding now. The *nēnē* take off like fully loaded B-52 bombers, a lumbering, upward lift-off in the general direction of north along the wall of the crater; soon they are out of sight. I'm thinking of trying to find the nest. I'd like to see it. Carolyn suggests I leave it alone. Enough just to see the birds, she says, suspecting that I'll blunder around and cause unintended harm to eggs and home. And she is right. The thought of some uninvited alien giant poking around and rummaging through our house in Honolulu looking for Corey, Dana, and Kelly puts it all in perspective.

* * *

What of the *nēnē*'s future? Does it all end happily with the salvaging of a species and the restoration of *nēnē* populations in a few of our more protected places? Unfortunately, not so. Recently, research and management specialists from the State Department of Land and Natural Resources, the U.S. Fish and Wildlife Service, and the National Park Service met to discuss and coordinate their work and to issue a status report. Although it was generally agreed that the *nēnē* is no longer in imminent danger of extinction, our wild goose population is far from self-sustaining. Mortality rates continue to be high. This means that group releases in both old and new habitat areas will be required for the foreseeable future and that under current conditions, regular restocking is essential.

Their report suggested, moreover, that the current upland *nēnē* areas on Maui and Hawai'i may not by themselves support self-replicating goose populations even if the number of wild birds in Haleakalā and Volcanoes National Park increases dramatically.

Fossil evidence on several Islands suggests that the *nēnē*'s natural range may in the past have included lowland areas, especially during the breeding and molting seasons. Like the Canada Goose, the *nēnē* was probably a local migrator making periodic journeys between lowland areas and the uplands of Haleakalā, Mauna Loa, and Mauna Kea. Despite the inbreeding and genetic bottlenecks of the past, the experts say that there appears to be sufficient variability in the current *nēnē* gene pool to allow for adaptation to new lowland habitats. All of which probably means that for the *nēnē* to survive and again become self-perpetuating, new and different habitat areas must be opened up. Protection of Hawai'i's alpine regions may not guarantee a healthy, breeding *nēnē* population. To that end, the report offers a variety of other recommendations and next steps.

First, clear out predators like the mongoose as quickly as possible; meanwhile, reintroduce the *nēnē* to the mongoose-free islands of Kaua'i and Lāna'i. Second, spend some money to develop a better "genetic plan" for captive breeders and prepare a *nēnē* population model that can take account of stocking and mortality rates. Third, train *nēnē* to avoid feral dogs and pigs. And, finally but not last in order of importance, develop and implement nesting and postnesting programs in lowland areas like the Ka'ū Desert that will provide and utilize better knowledge of *nēnē* migrations and fertility rates.

With or without these actions, it appears that the *nēnē* will continue its collective grip on earthly existence even if that grip remains tenuous. Life will be a struggle but the odds of continuation are, at least for the moment, better than even — better, in any case, than they were in 1950. The *nēnē* can rest assured that a few scientists, philanthropists, conservationists, and government officials are really concerned about them. Not that the birds at the zoo or even the somewhat wilder ones in Haleakalā seem to care. All of them are perfectly oblivious to the battles being waged in their name.

Efforts to preserve disappearing animals and plants occur for many reasons. For some people, the preservation of threatened species is an intellectual imperative, a rational commitment to ensuring basic ecological health through continued biological diversity. Other people wish to reaffirm continuities with the past. Perhaps it's a moral or sentimental matter. They sense the loss of the world as they know it and are filled with dread or nostalgia. They cannot imagine a world diminished. They cannot bear the thought of such deaths.

The protection of the *nēnē* could fall into either of these categories, but I can also imagine that preservation may ultimately depend on some determination of utility. Maybe that same graduate student studying molecular biology, or the one at the microscope next to her or him, will be the person destined to discover an extract from the *nēnē* that prolongs life, cures cancer, eliminates warts, grows hair on bald people, and replaces Geritol, Ex-Lax, and Preparation H. Or maybe some cross-bred variation will be developed that is smart enough to pilot spaceships, take giant steps for mankind, and report back to earth for additional duties. For those who object to conservation for its own fuzzy-headed sake, new practical uses like these may just breathe a few more years of life into the *nēnē*.

All of which has its momentary importance, but which doesn't excite me. Preserving lives — bug lives, fish lives, bird lives, and other lives — is more than an exercise in pragmatism. Humans, I once read, are worth a little less than fifteen dollars on the open market if you render a person down to his or her trace elements. Luckily, most of us don't appraise people in these terms. It would be too absurd. Where in such a calculus, after all, would we put tonight's sunset, the piano sonata that is playing on the radio, or the cooing of a baby son or daughter? What is the value of the things we cannot count now or cannot see yet because they are waiting unborn around the corner?

Somewhere beyond the year 2000, in the potentially dark days to come, I can envision a well-guarded room in a newly built forty-story chrome and concrete Business and Technology Administration Building on the campus of the University of Hawai'i. All but one of the building's forty floors will be occupied by a single multi-billion-gigabyte computer capable of holding and analyzing all known data about living things in the State of Hawai'i. Only the basement will be reserved for humans.

Inside this room there will be a wall-to-wall plastic map with overlays of statistics, matrices, and graphs plotting various "quality of life" trajectories. Unfortunately, every index and S-curve will be sloping downward. Gathered together in this underground chamber and swept up in learned conference will be a group of scientists, technicians, and government factotums wearing green eyeshades. Several of these people will be engaged in studying just how many animals and plants are left in Hawai'i. They may not have to count very high.

If I can, I intend to be present at this meeting to report on my own sideways study of survival and persistence. Being in foreign territory, I'll arm myself with the antiquated writings of Whitman, Emerson, and Muir and then, true to that tradition, I'll do everything I can to be a general pain in the neck. If nothing else, I'll simply hurl epithets and sing old labor union songs at them just to disrupt the flow of their deadly charts and numbers.

Once I get the attention of all these bean counters, though, I'll try to remind them of Beebe's analogy of animals and plants as natural masterpieces that are made once and never again. Perhaps a few people in the room will listen. Undoubtedly, I'll have to work hard to convince them that there were other reasons for saving the *nēnē* that had nothing to do with economics. I'll cross that bridge when I get to it.

For now, I take personal pleasure in the fact that Hawai'i still has room for a few odd creatures that, as far as I can figure, have absolutely no redeeming commercial value.

6

On Makapu'u Point

*Among the snakes there is a legend that
there was a mama and papa snake in
the Garden of Eden and they were cor-
rupted by humans.*

Leonard L. Levinson

S UNDAY MORNING. WE COULD BE SLEEPING IN, or ordering pancakes, or reading the Sunday funnies. Instead, for the third
weekend in a row, five of us — Carolyn, her 63-year-old
father Tetsui, myself, and two other people we know only casually
— are threading our way up a narrow, mile-and-a-half trail that
leads to the lighthouse and Coast Guard station at the top of
Makapu'u Point. One misstep could lead to a fall of several hundred feet onto some very large and jagged black rocks protruding
from an always treacherous shore break. Body recovery in this area
is generally considered out of the question.

Our slow, careful walk along the crumbling cliffs of O'ahu's
eastern coastline is also more dangerous because it is 4:30 a.m.,
and in the predawn dark we are carrying, among other things,
binoculars, telescopes, cameras, hats, small coolers, sweaters, and
shorts. I also have a pocketknife, jacket, sunscreen, rain poncho,
several cans of beer, and a copy of Thoreau's *Walden*. Off to our
right, the sea is spectral. Glints of phosphorescence faintly sparkle
up from below. Whitecaps are flattened by the mist. In the gloom
of the early hours stones and rocks are purple bumps to be avoid-
ed. Vines cross the trail trying to tangle our feet. It is still night
when we arrive at the peak of the bluff. We find a good spot and
nestle in; soon there is a soft glow to the east and a growing crimson cast on the land. Then a long, gentle dawn erupts as the sun
ascends the horizon. With daybreak the wind comes up, an on-

shore breeze steadily stiffening. Good weather: windy, cloudless, exceptionally clear. East by southeast down the archipelago's spine, three islands come into view. Moloka'i's west end is the closest. Behind that, the rounder and softer features of another mass, probably Lāna'i. Beyond that, in the distance, Maui.

But we didn't trudge up this chunk of rock just to scan pale islands in a pink sunrise. We have other business; whale business, to be exact. Somewhere out beyond Makapu'u Point one of God's most beautiful and graceful creations is steaming through the water at several knots per hour following O'ahu's offshore currents. She (or, just as likely, he) is *Megaptera novaeangliae*, the humpback whale, 40 feet long, 35 tons, gray and black with a white underside. We are the welcoming committee.

From a close-up view I once got while crossing the Moloka'i Channel, this whale is well worth welcoming. She has the prettiest front flippers in all of whaledom, 12 to 14 feet long on the average, white and scalloped on the edges. She is both a "rorqual" and a "baleen;" rorqual because she belongs to a group of whales with dorsal fins, baleen meaning she takes food in through large strainers. The humpback has no teeth. She feeds on anchovies, small shrimps, and plankton. Like most other whales, even the maligned and mostly misnamed "killer whale," she is graceful, playful, and intelligent. Her brain weighs eleven pounds and functions very much like human gray matter. She bears live young, is sociable, communicates, and seems to feel joy and pain.

Her physiology, feeding and reproductive habits, breathing and diving routines, even the evolutionary course she has taken from a prehistoric landlubber, have all been studied extensively. It is documented, for example, that she is a slow swimmer, that she can stay underwater for seven minutes between breaths, that she mates chest-to-chest while rising upward to the surface at great speed, that gestation takes ten to fourteen months, and that she typically has close to half a ton of barnacles clinging to her hide. That humpbacks talk with each other (possibly through songs) seems to be clear. What they say is a mystery.

All of which gives us an ostensible reason for being here: to learn more about them. It's a volunteer effort to help Dr. Edward

Shallenberger with his winter humpback whale count. He wants to find out how many are returning, to estimate how many there are in the Hawaiian populations, and to establish, in at least a crude sort of way, how many are left on earth. Shallenberger and other Hawai'i biologists ask dozens of questions about the whales but the bottom line is numbers. That's where we come in. The five of us can count to a hundred (using each other's fingers and toes), and we have signed on as official O'ahu whale watchers.

There are other reasons as well — a day in the sun and, now that my bug, fish, and goose research is finished, yet another opportunity to parry those odious and never-ending chores around the house. It's also a chance to see a part of the Island we don't get to very often and, in between observing the whales and taking in the exceptionally lovely scenery, an opportunity to read, think, and drink a can of ice-cold beer in the shade of a fine tree I've spied on the way.

Naturally, there are trade-offs. To get to all this relaxation, I've had to indenture myself to Shallenberger as a serious amateur whale watcher and concerned not-for-credit student of marine and coastal affairs. In the spirit of the thing, I've brought along a small tribe of people who are crazed with the idea of counting whales. Tom Sawyer never had it so easy. Everyone wants to glimpse a whale. Being on a spit of land well removed from the highways and tourways of the rest of our crowded Island is an added bonus for them. As for me, this quiet, peaceful, windswept rock is a perfect place to fiddle away my time as well as Shallenberger's.

Anthropomorphically speaking, I'd guess that the whales are a little like the five of us in this regard: they seem to gravitate toward places that people shun or cannot reach. They like privacy and solitude and their reasons for being here require it. These whales are part of a small northern humpback population that migrates between Hawai'i and the Arctic each year. They are a "kama'āina" species. They've been around a long time and are permanent, regular visitors. In the fall when the ice pack thickens and the krill supply dwindles, they start their 2,000-mile journey. Arriving here, they hug the Islands tight, rising and sounding, singing and feeding, and finally, in the warm blue waters off

Maui, Lāna'i, and Kaho'olawe, give birth to their young. Summers in the Arctic, winters in the tropics. Good taste.

Their unregulated travel, however, drives scientists crazy. Technical people want things understood in an orderly and sequential way. Randomness makes them nuts. Their hair falls out, their eyes get bad, and their teeth start to rot. But there are other reasons for wanting this count. The specialists need to find out what they can about the whales because what they already know frightens them. Other Pacific whales — finback, bowhead, blue, and sperm — have been in serious trouble for some time. Some are still hunted legally and probably illegally as well. Shot out of the water by harpoons with explosives attached to the barbs, their bodies are snatched by factory ships and rendered into lipstick, cold cream, poultry feed, lubricating oil, and pet food. Humpbacks are "legally protected" by international law, and their numbers seem to be increasing slightly. Nonetheless, scientists from the National Marine Fisheries Service in Honolulu and the West Coast Whale Research Foundation in Vancouver estimate there are probably no more than 3,000 left in the population that returns to Hawai'i each year.

It's an hour and a half after sunup and the heat is rising. We peel off jackets, shirts, and long pants. Once in a while birds flit in front of us or off to the side: shearwaters, frigatebirds, terns, and noddies nesting in and around the cliffs. Beyond us we can see Makapu'u Beach and the first hang gliders of the day. About 50 yards above us are three concrete bunkers; squat, ominous-looking gun emplacements left over from World War II. They are dark and dank affairs, little Stonehenges with spikes of cactus growing through the gun ports. Inside, the bunkers are trashed with beer cans, cigarette butts, and empty cans that once held Spam, beans, and Vienna sausage.

Back to the watching. Two and a half hours now and nary a glimpse. We've been watching the water keenly for three weekends and seen nothing. I'm trying to approach this activity in a disciplined and philosophical way, the way good old inspiring Henry David Thoreau would. The way he sat and watched the comings and goings of loons at Walden Pond, turning each and every observation into a penetrating insight on man and nature whether he saw anything or not. But I'm still at square one. Learning to sit. My own personal version of Za-Zen. Trying to fix my attention on the constant emptiness of the ocean. Trying to keep my mind and senses from straying too far, or my control center from shutting down.

In the first hours of today's whale watch, the waiting is a clean, slow rolling of time, an Island yoga, playing with the edges of perception and reveling in the elements themselves. Meditating on the wind that is blowing in my face, letting my eyes roam and peel off in obscure directions, and allowing them to be fully directed by the play of foam and surf, everything seems the same. But slowly, things change.

I watch the to-ing and fro-ing of the waves for those stray movements that would indicate whales. There aren't any. After a while, the image of what I am doing begins to rattle back through my skull and bounce around in strange ways. Binoculars are stuck to my face, an 8 X 30 power-extension turning my eyeballs into stalks and the rest of me into some weird kind of whale-watching insect. I'm like a voyeur hoping for a peep, prying and probing, waiting to sneak a look, maybe even see the whales Doing It. The constant, steady rhythms of the water are lulling. But time moves at a slower and slower pace and it becomes harder and harder to shrug off the irritation that stabs at me when I think that all this might be pointless. There are moments of simple, total, incredibly relaxed watching. And, increasingly, there are others in which I am fighting off massive boredom.

Frustration eventually becomes insidious and soon I realize that I am no longer paying attention. If a white whale swam by in front of me with a neon sign on its back saying Eat at Moby's Chowder House, I'd probably miss it. My attention span has diminished to the level of that of a hyperactive kindergarten class. I want to watch the hang gliders circling through the air like a bunch of buzzards. I force myself back to whales. Then I see a boat. I look for more of them. I watch birds. I see a cloud on the far horizon that looks vaguely menacing, a little like Corey, Dana, and Kelly when they are about to get into it with Carolyn, me, or each other. I notice cracks in the rock in front of me and start to watch an ant hauling a chunk of something off to an anthole. I start thinking about ants. My skills as a whale watcher have now plummeted off the grid completely. By rights, Shallenberger should fire me.

But just about then, Tetsui wanders over and relieves me. It's my turn to take a long break under the large *kiawe* tree. Thoreau beckons me to the gentle, self-contained universe he made for himself at Walden Pond near Concord, Massachusetts. The shade of the tree needs to be studied firsthand. That semi-tough-looking little cloud bears at least a few minutes more of concentrated daydreaming. And over and beyond these agendas, I can hear faint little voices coming from the Budweiser cans inside the cooler, a call of the wild, a niggling but essential reminder that Sundays are, indeed, handed to us by a force greater than the National Football League.

* * *

As most people know from one of the few high school literature classes that didn't put them to sleep, Thoreau was the original American beatnik, a hippie and nonconformist who railed against the Establishment of his time, went to jail for antiwar activities, and was, during his tenure at Walden Pond, plain and simple, a drop-out. I've always viewed Thoreau — along with Tom Paine — as one of America's most important dissenters, an outstanding and much to be admired fly in the ointment. Born in 1817, the son of a pencil manufacturer, he grew up in and around Concord. At Harvard University he influenced (and was influenced by) Emerson, Channing, and other transcendentalists. Not unlike some of today's intellectuals, the transcendentalists believed that knowledge of reality could and should be derived from intuitive sources rather than from objective and analytical fact-finding. Always a dreamer, Thoreau was also restless. His travels carried him around New England, out of which came his first book: *A Week on the Concord and Merrimack Rivers*. Like all his others (including *Walden*), it didn't sell. Perhaps in a mood to settle down, Thoreau — according to some biographers — then spent several years unsuccessfully wooing various females in the Ralph Waldo Emerson household. These intelligent and iron-willed ladies of New England all rejected him. Till the end of his days, he remained a bachelor.

In 1845, perhaps on the rebound from one of the Emerson women, Henry activated an idea that had been brewing for some time. He moved to a small cabin on the shore of Walden Pond. Henry was not the recluse and hermit history has made of him. During his time at Walden he sallied back and forth into town at least once a week, spent days at the Emersons' house, and kept up a fairly active schedule of lectures and meetings. Nonetheless, his days in the cabin between 1845 and 1847 would become the basis for his most remembered works, including the great "On Civil Disobedience." At other times in his life he would be a pencil maker in his father's factory, a teacher, a private tutor, and a magazine salesman. Always, it seems, Thoreau struggled to make ends meet — financially, emotionally, and spiritually. The ends never quite came together. Today, it is his Walden experience we remember best, but in his own time, neither the book nor the man were much appreciated.

Rereading *Walden* these many years later I have been trying to think through what Thoreau's musings might mean to us in Hawai'i. Thoreau himself refers to "the Chinese and Sandwich Islanders," saying the focus of his writings is on New Englanders and is not for us outlanders living in the provinces. Probably nothing more than a contrived bit of exotica on Hank's part, but the question remains. Does a wonderfully original North American nature book written by a transcendentalist have anything at all to offer those of us who live on a small Island state in the middle of the Pacific more than a hundred years later?

Walden is a chronicle of two years spent in the woods outside of what is today metropolitan Boston. Even at the time it was a comfortably settled region of America, full of rich farms and smug, prosperous towns. The outskirts of Boston were wilderness enough for Henry, however. There was the pond itself, stands of reasonably thick forests with deer, woodchucks, and badgers, and just enough open space to put down some plots of vegetables. So Thoreau more or less disappeared from Concord's public view, unencumbered by worldly possessions and ready to undertake his grand experiment in living a simplified life. He built a cabin, planted a bean field, went for long walks, and wrote about everything that happened. It's a simple regimen, one I keep thinking I'll replicate here in Hawai'i. Maybe in the rain forests of Kohala, down in the desert near South Point, or off in the "Wild West" district of Puna south of Hilo.

But back to *Walden*. What Henry gave us was a series of thoughts and insights on human nature and on men and women coming to grips with nature as a state of pristine awareness. He also explored the inherent and now nearly universally ignored need to live in harmony with one's surroundings. Thoreau seems to have struggled mightily with these themes and with his own impulses and offers us different and sometimes contradictory thinking.

Most of the time this "self-appointed inspector of snowstorms" is in near rapture over drops of water sparkling on a spider web or a patch of wild flowers growing outside his cabin. All of this is "nature." From Thoreau's viewpoint, nature is a state of purity, a sweet and sublime condition that humans began falling away from about the time monkeys first started walking upright. Henry means to recover it.

Thus he gives us situation after situation in which he demonstrates how easy it is for a person like himself to live in perfect harmony and contentment with his surroundings — all of which he would have us emulate and copy. Nature, for Henry, must always be written in capital letters: not nature, but N A T U R E, as if it were the name of another country or planet. Take Henry fresh out of the tub: "Sometimes, in a summer morning, having taken my accustomed bath, I sat in my sunny doorway from sunrise till noon, rapt in a revery, amidst the pines and hickories and sumachs...." Who would dare disagree and say that raptures and reveries are not to be explored and treasured? On the other hand, how many of us ever get to hang around in the trees until noon? Who wouldn't feel closer to nature lounging about naked on our *lānais* on a Tuesday morning with a cup of coffee? Most employers and personnel managers, however, believe Nature means getting your buns to work at 8:00 a.m. sharp.

Or take another of Henry's observations: "I rejoice that there are owls. Let them do the idiotic hooting for men. It is a sound admirably suited to swamps and twilight woods which no day illustrates, suggesting a vast and undeveloped nature which men have not recognized." Again, Henry talks good sense. I'd certainly prefer to have more *pueo* — our native owls — in the neighborhood and fewer people. Fate, however, has dealt me a different hand. One of my neighbors, a guy with large sons and two truculent pit bulls, views all birds as free protein supplements for his dogs. And as if that weren't enough, I've recently learned of a City and County ordinance that forbids hooting (owl or human) above 45 decibels between 9:00 at night and 8:00 in the morning.

And then there is Henry ruminating on bad weather: "There was never yet such a storm but it was Aeolian music to a healthy and innocent ear. Nothing can rightly compel a simple and brave man to a vulgar sadness." Now here's where Thoreau and I truly part company. I've spent a number of exceptionally miserable nights in storms on top of Mauna Loa, in Hālawa Valley on Moloka'i, and once in our old house in Kāne'ohe when a leaky roof and a blown-out window dumped dozens of gallons of cold rainwater into my immediate environs. My sadness at such moments goes beyond the vulgar. It becomes homicidal and dangerous to the health of people like Henry David. The last thing I need when I am wet and wretched with my only roof caving in is someone talking about "Aeolian music."

Despite Thoreau's romantic, sugar-coated view of the natural world, however, I recognize the essential purity of his motives. Not only are his ideas decent and important, they are inspirational. Certainly none are more powerful than his reason for going to Walden in the first place:

> I went to the woods because I wished to live deliberately, to front only the essential facts of life, and see if I could not learn what it had to teach, and not when I came to die, discover that I had not lived. I did not wish to live what was not life, living is so dear, nor did I wish to practice resignation, unless it was quite necessary. I wanted to live deep and suck out all the marrow of life, to live sturdily and Spartan-like as to

> put to rout all that was not life, to cut a broad swath
> and shave close, to drive life into a corner, and
> reduce it to its lowest terms, and, if it proved to be
> mean, why then to get the whole and genuine mean-
> ness of it, and publish its meanness to the world; or if
> it were sublime, to know it by experience, and be
> able to give a true account of it in my next excursion.

This, I want to believe, is the real Thoreau, an odd and benignly impractical man who takes his philosophizing seriously: a man who wants to sink completely into his immediate environment to know it totally and completely and who then wants to report back to the rest of us on what we are missing. Thoreau didn't heave off on a spring vacation in Nepal to figure out who he was. No EST seminars, Outward Bound experiences, or humanistic psychology courses would have satisfied him. Nor would Henry have bought into much of the pap spooned out by famous gurus who argue that the only thing that counts is being responsible to yourself.

Henry's way was different. Not unlike certain friends of mine who years ago decided to live their lives in the coastal forests of Puna on the Big Island, Thoreau consciously buried himself on the periphery of his own little community. Once there, he made himself comfortable in a meager sort of way and then set out to know precisely what was around him — the animals, the plants, the weather, and the pond. Henry argued that you can't know the big picture without getting down and groveling in the everyday particulars of your own neighborhood. For him, nature never meant escape. Nature is the ground you walk on and the things that surround you as you go about the business of living. Nature is inside you.

And that is what Thoreau has to do with us in Hawai'i whether he knew it or not. If we take Henry at his word, it means coming to grips with the genuine sublimity of this place as well as the mean and dirty details. It means concerning ourselves with what makes Hawai'i *HAWAI'I* and not Boise, Idaho, or Cleveland, Ohio. First, we need some basic bioregional knowledge. How many of us, for example, have any idea at all where our electrical energy comes from? Or where our toilet water goes after we flush

a few gallons down that little hole? Or the names and histories of
the weeds that grow in our front yards? Or what the land under
our house was like 100 years ago and who used it and for what?
Or what lies up the hill in the mountains of O'ahu beyond the end
of the housing tracts?

How many of us know about Hawaiian trees? Or how green and
yellow Mejiros from Asia got here? Who knows anything at all
these days about flowers and watersheds, why Orville-the-Spider
has a "happy face" painted on his topside, why there are hardly
any land snails left, and why 95% of the *mahimahi* we eat doesn't
come from here? Who knows where golden plovers roost at night,
or the different types of bananas and tangerines and where they
grow, or where you can find a decent breadfruit tree, or why earthquakes happen? Who but Civil Defense and the TV weathermen
know how storms, even "Aeolian" ones, form and wash Hawai'i
down with periodic hurricanes, or why Waikīkī will probably be
under four feet of water in another few hundred years? If some
twentieth-century Henry were to take himself down to 'A'ala Park
in the heart of Honolulu for a year — and 'A'ala would probably
be as good a place as any — you can bet we'd have reports on
such things.

In *Walden* Henry is also a reporter, but first and foremost, he is a
philosopher beating away at the larger questions surrounding our
existence. Who are we? What are we here for? How should we
live? The same irritating, complicated problems bothered Plato,
Jesus, Mohammed, and the Buddha. At Walden Pond, however,
Thoreau had plenty of time to read, think, and ponder matters.
"Time is but the stream I go fishing in. I drink at it; but while I drink
I see the sandy bottom and detect how shallow it is. Its thin current
slides away but eternity remains." And what is eternity? The eternity he sees in the stream is nature's own rifeness, an inexhaustible
vigor and unexplainable pulse of wild energy in which humans are
no better or worse than any other creature and in which all things
are interconnected.

What, then, are we to make of a strange, bearded man who tells
us to wade out into the stream of time and fish up a flapping, wriggling creature called "wildness"? Do you take it home and clean it

or do you throw it back once you've caught it? If you do take it home, what do you eat? And what if Henry were still alive and in Hawai'i? Would his mosaic of nature still be majestic and grand after several years on crowded O'ahu? Would Henry fall victim to "Polynesian paralysis"? Or worse yet, "Rat Race in Paradise": house, job, two cars, yard work, traffic, termite problems? What, in particular, would he tell us about whale watching here on Makapu'u rock?

Unquestionably, he would delight in the setting of Makapu'u Point: the sheer cliffs and blustering wind, the sun, sea, and sky. I also suspect he'd find this to be a wonderfully useless activity and a perfect complement to his theory of simplification. Henry would like sitting around jawing about philosophy and anything else that happened to crop up. Indeed, Henry would probably be able to sit around for two or three days at a crack without moving a muscle, his concentration unfazed by the humble things that disturb the rest of us, like heat rash, sunburn, and mosquito bites in unreachable places. He wouldn't worry about the mortgage and the kids' braces. Undoubtedly he'd gaze at the waves, his senses totally tuned, keeping watch faithfully and religiously. And where my thoughts waddle off into the twisted corridors of my own mental junk yard, Henry's simple observations probably would carve out some powerful new wrinkle in an already penetrating philosophy of nature. I can see Henry and me sitting here together talking past each other. "Hey, Henry, it sure as hell is hot up here. Help yourself to one of those cold Buds from the cooler." And Henry would give me a sad, transcendental look and say: "Ah, Peter, time is the stream I go drinking in."

So very quickly, I suspect, Henry and I would need to adjourn from this whale-watching business for some serious discussion and disagreement. Because the more I reread Henry David Thoreau, the more I try to fit his ideas to Hawai'i, the more the suspicion gnaws at me that Henry really didn't have the last word on wildness; that even Henry himself didn't always fully believe what he wrote; and that, in the final analysis, his notion about nature was at the time — and is now even more so — only a small part of the real story.

* * *

I go back on whale duty in the heat of the early afternoon. The five of us have kept a decent vigil going since sunup — eight hours of looking and we've seen nothing that even mistakenly might resemble a flipper, fluke, or fin. With the sun straight overhead, the hues of the water are flattened to a steel gray-blue with glare exploding out in all directions. The few shrubs around me are wilted and drooping in the heat. Just like us.

I stare at the mesmerizing interplay of currents off to the right of Rabbit Island. Waves casting shadows are deceiving. Wave or not-wave, which is it? The farther out I look the more difficult it is to distinguish shadows from substance. Given the difficulties of spotting the humpbacks, I start to manufacture thoughts on how it might be if we actually saw a few whales and started counting them for Shallenberger. I imagine sitting just like this watching a particular spot and puzzling over something that looks like it may be a "not-wave." I'd crane my neck, look again, scratch my head, and then clarity would break loose like hell's own horde of thunderbolts! Suddenly, that "something" I'd be seeing would become clearly and unmistakably different. I imagine it would take a moment or two to register. Then I'd yell "There!" Carolyn would come racing back from one direction, Tetsui from another, and we'd all swivel our necks around like spectators at Wimbledon pointing to the same place.

And there they'd be, a small pod chugging across the cove straight out from the cliff. One moment there would be nothing but the movement of current and spray. The next moment something black would break the surface and wheel through the surf. Then more forms would appear, and then others. If my wish were granted we'd see a large pod or maybe several small pods together, with mothers and calves in the middle and maybe a few big bull whales outriding on the flanks. We'd see them rising and plunging and sounding and spouting. Then they would move in closer to shore and we'd begin picking out individuals and describing them. All of us would be counting and writing and jumping up and down and squealing with excitement. And by the late afternoon, we would have it all down on paper with photos for proof. We'd have counted hundreds of whales and seen the entire

Hawaiian tribal humpback nation gathered here from all parts of the Pacific for their own festive purposes and for the sake of Ed Shallenberger's receding hair and worry-induced ulcers.

All of which certainly will not happen today, nor tomorrow. Or ever. The whales, if they come, will be in small groups. If we're lucky, we'll see one or two. We'll see the spoutings for sure, little geysers and fountains off in the distance and maybe one or two will break the surface and we'll note the time and place and write it all down like the good whale accountants we're supposed to be. Then Shallenberger will study the record of our glimpses and extrapolate it, massage it in a variety of ways, feed it in with information from other lookouts, and make an annual estimate. The objective, as a friend once said about physicians, is to improve the odds on the guesses they make to better than even. For the moment, though, there is nothing to do but imagine what a sighting might look like, because this third and final weekend of whale watching is drawing to a close and so far the only thing we have to show for our efforts are exceptionally good-looking suntans that are bad for you anyway.

So the hours drag on and all of my grand ideas about sighting whales remain vast conjectures with no basis in truth. Reality is the constant, empty sloshing of the water, an eternity of currents flowing around this lighthouse. My question now is what lies beyond Makapu'u Point? If there are whales out there, they are traveling other courses. Perhaps lookouts posted on Maui and Lāna'i are having better luck. Perhaps the whales are bypassing O'ahu this year and heading straight for their breeding grounds in the shallows off Maui. Or perhaps they simply aren't coming back anymore. This idea leads to darker, more fearsome thoughts and a simple wondering at the power of the unknown to instill fear — and curiosity. If Henry were here, I think he'd understand.

* * *

Unquestionably, Thoreau was a complicated man. In fact, his writings reveal many different Thoreaus. The one most of us remember, the one we look for in *Walden*, is Henry the naturalist, an astute observer and superb commentator on nature's rhythms. Rereading him all these years later, however, I see other Thoreaus as well; little, lesser Henrys that I never noticed before and now can safely bring up without having an English teacher flunk me for insolence. Not that Thoreau hasn't been worked over and properly criticized by various wilderness writers and literary types; anyone interested in some especially good Thoreau nit-picking should read Edward Abbey's *Down the River* and George Sibley's *Part of a Winter*. Now it's my turn.

To begin with — just for the sake of a starting point — there is Thoreau's tendency to tell everyone else what to do. Throughout *Walden* and many of his other writings, he is an insufferable sermonizer and an advice-giving prude. Much of his advice, moreover, is bad. Take the following (which Carolyn and I have discussed and found to be especially useless): "The generative energy which, when we are loose, dissipates and makes us unclean, when we are continent invigorates and inspires us. Chastity is the flowering of man...." And even when Henry's advice is good it is too often offered in the unctuous and self-congratulatory tone of undertakers and Sunday school teachers. Nobody — but NOBODY — I know would actually put up with the man or his homilies for more than a minute.

So that's one Thoreau, a kind of nineteenth-century Ann Landers who has lots of thoughts on what might constitute the high and low roads of life and who did not shrink from telling us which one to take. Next we have Henry the scrooge, a penny-pinching, miserly CPA-type, backing up his incessant and sanctimonious opinions with endless budgets and trial balances. Presuming always that his readers are passionately interested in the details of his meager financial life, Henry gives us a blow-by-blow of every nickel and dime he spent building a cabin, feeding himself, and raising a couple of acres of beans. Henry is extraordinarily proud of his ability to come out on top. Thus we learn that he spent $28.12 for secondhand boards and window glass, nails, caulk, bricks, and two casks of lime that turned out to be more than he needed. Then we find out that for eight months he earned $13.34 doing day labor and carpentry and spent $8.74 of it to feed himself, leaving a surplus of $4.60. If you have a hard time sleeping at night, all of this makes for good reading.

Thoreau, however, takes his financial reports seriously and wrings out infinite philosophical consequences. Gleefully, he reminds us that you and I are capable of this kind of economy if we are willing to live close to nature. Doing what, you might ask? Why, growing beans of course! Subsistence farming. Something every real farmer the world over is trying desperately to avoid. Henry, though, sees dirt farming as one of the higher rungs on life's ladder to heaven.

How, then, does he behave when he finally stumbles across a genuine, no-nonsense American peasant living a mile from Walden Pond? Not very well, I'm afraid. In fact, Thoreau becomes downright rude. Out for a walk he encounters a less than aeolian storm and takes shelter at the home of the Fields family, who offer him tea and hospitality. Mr. Fields is an authentic blue-collar type, an immigrant Irishman with lots of children living on the thin edge of poverty. To Thoreau, he represents "man fallen from nature's grace." So what does Henry do? Gives him a lecture, of course. "...I purposely talked to him [Fields] as if he were a philosopher, or desired to be one. I should be glad if all the meadows on the earth were left in a wild state, if that were the consequence of men's beginning to redeem themselves. A man will not need to study history to find out what is best for his own culture. But alas! the culture of an Irishman is an enterprise to be undertaken with a sort of moral bog hoe." Moral bog hoe? More like using a twelve-ton pile driver to put in a thumb tack. Henry works poor Mr. and Mrs. Fields around as if they were mutant bugs, examining them, dissecting them, and finally pickling them in his own moral formaldehyde. And in a final parting shot, he suggests that these weird specimens, along with all of their cone-headed, runny-nosed children, should take off for the woods like himself instead of toughing it out on the dirt farm. "If he and his family would live simply, they might all go a-huckleberrying in the summer for their amusement."

Henry handles his own small farming successes somewhat differently, of course. These he attributes to thrift and good sense and to the boundless generosity of the land. Henry believes he is in full accord with nature's inherent game plan. He can't describe precisely what it is but he likes it. Moreover, ruminating on it always puts him in a good mood. Henry clearly prefers life's sweeter side, those aspects of nature that allow him time to think and write. And when he writes about nature's kinder side, he is at his genuine best. There is always, for Henry, a worshipping reverence for what life gives, including a profound respect for animals and plants, an appreciation of nature as gift and a willingness to give back. Indeed, hoeing around in his bean field, Henry is happy to let every squirrel, woodchuck, and grasshopper in Massachusetts have a few of his beans, something no farmer I've ever heard of would actually do. He blesses the sun and rain, the glorious days of summer, the trees and clouds, the clods of earth under his feet. He extols the moods of the seasons and tries, whenever he can, to live life morally, simply, honestly, and in harmony with the outdoor universe he loves so much.

Thoreau's love for nature, however, does not include people. And here we have still another Henry. In many ways, I like this Henry. At one time or another in the course of a few chapters — and more concisely than I could have managed it — Henry grumpily shows us all of the kinds of people he dislikes and gives good, well-reasoned logic for his opinions. Put simply, this Henry is the village crank. Included on his transcendental hit list are grocers, tailors, saloon keepers, store proprietors, students, professors, writers, publishers, bankers, architects, and post office workers. And, in more generic terms, the Irish, the English, the Spanish, and almost all Americans. In fact, Henry doesn't seem to have liked anyone very much with the possible exception of Mrs. Ralph W. Emerson.

The problem with all of these folks, says Henry, is pretension. They are, from his point of view, unnecessarily "civilized," meaning they eat too much, overdress, pursue the wrong kinds of goals, and spend too much time trying to make themselves comfortable. Like the Fields family, they have fallen from the straight and narrow path that Henry would have them travel. He thinks they are fops, fools, or slobs. Though it is easy, a century later, to fault him for his peevish prejudices, one must also keep in mind Thoreau's self-proclaimed role as philosopher and critic. It is the business of such people to be difficult and Thoreau ran true to form.

Still, Henry's basic message is that simplicity, or natural living, offers all of us riches beyond our wildest imaginations; that is, a state of rapturous and mystical oneness with the world that occurs when human life is pared down to its most common denominators. Like Rousseau, Thoreau believed the lion and lamb can lie down together in the shade of a tree without fear. Most of *Walden* is written in this vein and is a simple, clear discussion of nature's basic goodness and humanity's nasty habits and unrealized mystic capacities. There are, however, occasional glimmers of something different, something darker and more carnal that even Henry could not avoid facing.

After the rainstorm and his little chat with the Fields family Henry strolls back to his cabin by the pond. On the way, something very un-Henry-like happens.

> As I came home through the woods with my string of fish trailing my pole, it being now quite dark, I caught a glimpse of a woodchuck stealing across my path, and felt a strange thrill of savage delight, and was strongly tempted to seize and devour him raw; not that I was hungry then, except for that wildness which he represented. Once or twice, however, while I lived at the pond, I found myself ranging the woods like a half-starved hound, with a strange abandonment, seeking some kind of venison which I might devour, and no morsel could have been so savage for me. The wildest scenes had become unaccountably familiar.

What Henry admits, finally, is this: out there in nature-land, things eat each other; as a result, they don't always inherently get along. Or, as Woody Allen puts it, the lamb may lie down with the lion but he's not going to get a good night's sleep. Nature is more than wildflowers, aeolian storms, and poplars swaying in the wind. Nature also has teeth, stingers, barbs, beaks, claws, talons, and a fierce and constant obsession with digestion. Nature, at a primary level at least, means eating and getting eaten. That chestnut-breasted Shama thrush with a song in her heart is a lovely thing to listen to but is also a flying piece of meat. Even Henry himself is nothing but worm food, a matter easy to acknowledge intellectually but rather more difficult at the implementation level. But here, finally, after a hundred pages of worshipping nature's benign and munificent ways, we at last have a more truthful Henry: Henry the hungry, Henry the closet carnivore of Walden Woods, Henry in search of lamb chops, hot dogs, and cheeseburgers.

But as quickly as this pungent little thought penetrates Thoreau's brain, it is immediately drowned in the usual philosophical soup he has concocted for himself and then covered with rationalizations and high-minded denials. Henry, in fact, is a more-or-less vegetarian who thinks meat, tea, coffee, and music are intoxicants. He really can't stand the idea that nature is messy and that a woodchuck with his guts torn out by a hungry human is just as much a part of the scheme of things as an aeolian storm cloud drifting across a pink and orange sunset. And this is precisely where I think Henry went wrong and did us all a big disservice — because, in fact, the same syrupy views of nature that Henry exhausts at Walden have led us down the primrose path of mindless devastation in Hawai'i. Henry is in love with the concept of paradise. It's the old Garden of Eden business all over again. Yes, the same one that got us in trouble the first time when God left the gate open and a snake crawled in.

The problem with Henry David Thoreau was that he loved the idea of nature much more than nature itself. And when the time came to own up to old Mother N.'s grim side, to the side that involves killing and death, he faltered. He backed down and left us with the transcendentalist equivalent of Walt Disney stories in which Bambi and Thumper go to Massachusetts.

We have been victimized by this same thinking here. Hawai'i as a "paradise" is vastly different from Hawai'i as an actual place, and anyone who has lived here awhile knows it. Yes, we have palm trees, white beaches, rare and beautiful birds, lovely, shaded mountains, and even a few pristine forests with wild and exotic animals found nowhere else. But we also have carpetbagging *haoles* from California and greedy businessmen from Japan, and, as a result, any number of legitimately angry Hawaiians who do not go a-huckleberrying for their amusement on Saturday nights.

All of which and whom, at least for purposes of argument, I consider to be a part of nature and far more dangerous than tidal waves, hurricanes, earthquakes, Portuguese men-of-war, and moray eels.

The problem with paradise as a metaphor is that it presupposes and builds on the idea of harmony: perfect consonance. But paradise, when we try to implement that idea, creates enormous problems. Because it is an extreme notion, genuine conflicts must inevitably get treated as abstract philosophical disagreements. Carried further, our landscapes — both mental and physical — are purged of diversity. We start giving nature little haircuts to trim off the rough edges and end up with cement patios that have one old tortured and persecuted Japanese bonsai plant left as a decoration. When it is safe and sanitized and when all dangers have been eliminated, nature loses something fundamental.

Once I took a group of kids on a twenty-four-day wilderness expedition that included five days in outrigger canoes along the south Kona Coast. After paddling hard for two days, we camped at Okoe Bay and fished, ate, swam, and luxuriated in the sun and surf. It was as close to paradise as you can get. On our second night there, several people wanted to go night diving. So off we plunged, four of us decked out in snorkels, masks, flippers, flashlights, and spears, a full moon above us, the water engulfing us, warm, gentle, and languid. We slid into the surf and followed the floor of the bay out to a drop-off by a reef and there we dived. As long as we were diving along shallow, sandy bottom, everything seemed fine and under control; in fact, adventurous and exciting in a logical, knowable, and relatively sensible environment. In deep water, maybe 30 or 40 feet on the outside of the reef, my calm evaporated. All of a sudden, I was afraid. Not abstract fear, the kind you have when you think about war and cancer, but a bone-numbing, spine-tingling, hair-raising, eye-straining, pants-wetting paranoia that something out there was waiting for me in particular. Something big, gray, and fiercely hungry with row after row of serrated teeth just waiting to rip into a chunk of fresh, raw, warm-blooded me. I could feel the near panic in myself, and I could feel it in the others.

What occurred to me later, and now again after rereading Thoreau, is that this is what is missing from most of *Walden* and from most nature writing in general — that special sensation of being a part of and inside the food chain. Not on top of the triangle or outside it in some neat ecological organization chart, but IN it, where things feed on you just as much as you feed on them. Where the business of survival is a two-way street. Where all beings, including human beings, are wary and cautious and constantly sensitive to the possibility of death.

What is missing in most of our notions about Hawai'i, and from the safe little world Thoreau made for himself at Walden Pond, is true win-lose conflict, and, in its most extreme form, the terror that accompanies the survival sweepstakes. All wild creatures seem to have a fear of impending disaster until they are domesticated and made comfortable. Terror, or at least wariness, seems to underlie a sharply honed and keenly aware sense of survival. In my mind, these are just as worthy of exploration and consideration as pretty yellow butterflies and the fresh smell of pine wafting through a campsite. They may, in fact, be precisely what the last of the whales are experiencing somewhere off Makapu'u Point.

*   *   *

In the afternoon, we see one. Or more exactly, we see the spouting of one some 600 yards off shore, a low, broad puffing of water vapors that is unmistakably cetacean in origin. We all zoom in with our binoculars, cameras, and telescopes. A few minutes later we see a second blow, then the black form of a cartwheeling dorsal fin, a momentary flash of tail flukes, and then nothing. All of us scan the water with renewed energy, loading more film, committing the essential facts to our notebooks. The sight of this solitary whale rising and plunging off O'ahu is etched in my memory and the lethargy of the day is broken. I gaze out again, hoping and wishing for another one.

Even one whale, however, is enough to satisfy my vague discontent and fear that the whales may not be coming back this year. There are other whales out there as well. I'm sure of it.

Whales are social creatures and travel together at this time of year. There are probably a few pregnant females, mothers, young calves, and bulls wending their way back to the traditional safety of the Islands.

Another hour passes and it is now late afternoon. The sun arches down in the west. The shadows we cast on Makapu'u rock get longer and still we keep watch, gazing off into the wild, darkening yonder looking for humpbacks, looking for evidence for Shallenberger, and always, it seems, looking for something else. Not just these big, wet, mammalian bodies plunging and hurling through the sea but some larger portent and meaning that the whales might give us. In the setting sun, the ocean chop starts to calm. Seabirds flit around again. The last hang gliders of the day circle back to their perches. The air turns cooler, tingling the skin. It is quieter and softer, a seascape again painted in pastels.

And now, once more, I think of Henry David, of his critical probing and his deep abiding compassion for the natural world outside his cabin. Edward Abbey says that for the better part of a century Thoreau's ghost and the ghost of his writing have lingered over American thinking. So why not here as well? Hawai'i could use his help. The beauty is diminishing and the land and water are getting foul. So why shouldn't his ghost be here, haunting, taunting, and forcing us to confront our unspoken assumptions?

I suppose that if Henry were actually present, my own puny debate with him would quickly be settled. Our quarrel with the world is basically the same. In fact, my respect for the man and his writings far outweighs any differences I might raise for the sheer fun of heckling him. Between us, there would be questions of emphasis and degree, but not, when it came down to it, of ends. Yes, Henry and I would be in agreement on many things, not the least of which is that the world is going to hell in a handbasket. Too many hustlers, politicians, get-rich-quickers, social service con men, and forever-on-the-payroll bureaucrats. Too much flash-in-the-pan and not enough that is solid and foundational for the future.

Henry, then, is one of my heroes. I think of him as a fearless, temperamental, and highly astute agitator who argued with every bit of his being that we must return to fundamentals. He was the man who said "No!," a man who marched off to the woods when most others were lining up in front of draft boards, factories, and literary teas saying "Yes." He was an intellectual smart aleck who liked to poke holes in the prevailing balloons of his time and who, in his own thinking, truly believed in spontaneous relations between man and nature.

So what would Henry say if he were here? He'd tell us what we all know intuitively but seem paralyzed to do anything about: that there are too many people, houses, and cars in Hawai'i, and too much traffic, noise, and congestion. He'd dislike this insane tendency of crowding into Honolulu and huddling up against big money and big politics. Crimps off our mental and moral growth, he'd say; makes people edgy and uncomfortable. The first thing he'd advise is "disperse and spread out." Give each other a little more elbowroom, physically, intellectually, emotionally.

Next, he'd tell us to plant more trees and vegetables. Get our hands dirty. Plant and harvest and relearn the work of tending and nurturing our food. Diversify our agriculture and keep every last little strand of wilderness in as clean and pure a shape as is possible. And while we are at it, he'd say, stop emulating the industrial and technological termite colonies that America and Japan seem destined to become. Let's develop our own more graceful and functional way of Island living, one that does not foul our own nests.

Henry's big message would be to simplify everything: the questions we ask, the things we do for a living, the thoughts we think, the way we pass the time, and, most of all, the way we interact with the natural world. Thoreau was a voice for preservation, not just of wilderness per se, but of those things that are simple and good in our own nature. He'd ask us to slow down, look around, and relish life the way any six-year-old would instinctively, by taking joy from our surroundings and exploring them with gusto. He'd have us teach our children a different set of values. He'd have us all be a little more playful, a little more critical and sharp-eyed, and a little more comfortable with our solitude.

On the subject of economics, he'd certainly have us stop raiding California's redwood trees for pole houses, siding, and shingles.

He'd have us refuse the purchase of goods grown in other countries by multinational corporations that keep the laboring classes of those places chained to cycles of poverty. He'd tell us to learn to live quieter, less desperate, and more salient lives, to think deeply and broadly about the day-by-day, moment-by-moment consequences of what we do. He'd have us all be a bit more spiritual — not religious, necessarily — simply a bit more reverent when we are in the presence of great forces — like the whales.

He'd appreciate and encourage this strange effort of learning to sit and observe, learning to watch, learning to stay put and stay alert to the health of our Islands. He'd insist that we slow down and celebrate our own luck — and the luck of the whales — at being alive. And when the time came for action, when the conversation had reached its inevitable two-in-the-morning end, he'd have us all march downtown and raise holy hell at the Japanese consulate, the State Capitol, and the Federal Building. Henry would be delighted to picket and confront the State's politicians — and dismayed at the suggestion of some of my friends that we all nail our signs to stout 2-by-4s.

If I asked (and probably even if I didn't), it's likely that Henry would tell us that one of God's purposes for whales is precisely what we have been doing. They are here to be watched. Not simply counted and examined as abstractions but genuinely looked at and observed until we know just how close we are to them as co-inhabitants of the same biosphere. Whales, he might say, are a part of the stream of things too, maybe even an integral part because they live IN it while we humans just come visiting a few times a year. If life is a river and Hawai'i is one of its tributaries, then it behooves us to get our feet wet, to wade a little deeper into the water and see what's there; to worship the stream and rejoice in its presence; to mark, through the annual return of the whales, the passage of a year and nature's inexplicable continuity.

Finally, I think Henry would say that the whales are the quintessence of all that is beautiful and free yet kindred in spirit to those of us caught up in this century's transitions. And our work, the work that must eventually be done, is to watch them carefully, to protect their numbers and help them increase, to welcome them back each year, to look deeply at their wild beauty and wild intelligence, and to gather, in our rare glimpses, a feeling of renewal.

Henry David Thoreau was a nasty, difficult, and irresistible man who argued for wildness, wilderness, and wild nature to anyone who would listen. More often than not, nobody did. To the bitter end, he was freedom loving, obstreperous, and sarcastic. In 1860 while out counting growth rings on tree stumps, so it is said, Henry caught a cold. Bronchitis, he was told; it persisted, weakened him, slowed him down, but never truly stopped him. Then, later, it became clear that he had tuberculosis. His dying was painful but didn't seem to affect his brain and tongue. When he was on his deathbed with family and friends gathered around, an aunt reputedly asked him if he had made his peace with God. "I did not know that we had ever quarreled," he said.

On May 6, 1862, Henry entered the deepest stream of all, the final river, the one everyone must swim alone. Muttering to the world in general about "moose" and "Indians," dreaming a sick man's dreams, he nonetheless seemed to glimpse something the rest of us on this side of the current can't see. "Now comes good sailing," he whispered to his sister, and moments later he died. Perplexing us, tantalizing us, stinging us with his ideas, he left the world a little richer than he found it. And Sam Staples, the jailkeeper during Henry's 1846 civil disobedience, noted that he "never saw a man dying with so much pleasure and peace."

Thoreau's accomplishments in *Walden* are more widely appreciated today than in his own time. Henry went to the woods beyond Concord and after two years of grubbing around came back with a vision. In his own irritating and complicated way he founded the American conservation movement and mixed it with Western and Eastern insights. Like many of today's pop psychologists, Henry was fond of quoting Oriental wisdom as a way of sharpening his vision. But he would have denied that his vision was a special gift. It's available to us all, he'd argue, waiting to be called into play. "The light which puts out our eyes is darkness to us. Only that day dawns to which we are awake. There is more day to dawn. The sun is but a morning star." Thus he ended *Walden*.

* * *

Late in the day we pack our equipment and shuffle down to the cars waiting at the trailhead. The shore is bathed in that soft and radiant glow that occurs only when light is refracted and reflected by water. The ocean is calm as a sleeping baby. The lighthouse is amber and orange in the fading light. Beyond Makapu'u Point seabirds wing across the sky. I pause and look out over the ocean. Carolyn sees a spouting close to shore. And then another one, and then several. She shows me the whales. She slips her hand in mine, I give it a squeeze, and then I hug and kiss her. Her lips are cool and salty. "What a magnificent day," she says. Then we turn and walk down the trail that looks exactly like a beautiful river running down the side of Makapu'u Point.

7

Aloha! Keep Out!

A white explorer in Africa, anxious to press ahead with his journey, paid his porters for a series of forced marches. But they, almost within reach of their destination, set down their bundles and refused to budge. No amount of extra payment would convince them otherwise. They said they had to wait for their souls to catch up.

Bruce Chatwin

I SQUINT AT THE PURPLE OUTLINE OF THE HILLS and at the moon, which is starting to descend. The sky is filled with stars, the air cool and fresh from an overnight rain. There are scents: a plumeria tree in full bloom; cut grass lying in the pasture; the rich, farmy smell of horses and cows grazing nearby. In the distance a dog yowls. It is 4:30 a.m. Shivering, I step back inside to get everyone up.

The borrowed house we are staying in is on a hill overlooking the town of Waimea; it is a perfect base camp for a vacation made up of various day trips to Kona and Kawaihae for fishing, to the summit of Mauna Kea to see the telescopes, and to the town of Hāwī to visit in-laws and attend the annual O-Bon dance they help organize each year at the local Buddhist temple. There is also swimming at Hāpuna Beach and hiking in Waipi'o and Pololū valleys. And today, an expedition to the other side of the Island: a long drive to Puna to visit Kele, a very special person I haven't seen for a while, and to show his small farm and orchard to the kids.

Carolyn moves through the kitchen making coffee and packing sandwiches. In the bedroom, Corey, Dana, and Kelly are snuggled under several thick blankets. As gently as I can, I rouse them out of their slumber, which is a bit like messing with bears. The cubs kick and snarl while I get them to brush their teeth and use the bathroom and then put them into some clothes. Eventually, Carolyn and I stuff them, one by one, into the back seat of the car,

153

where our three little bears immediately tangle themselves up in a snoring heap and go back into hibernation.

We creep out of the driveway, travel east through the center of Waimea, turn left at the fork, and head out toward the middle of the Big Island.

The Saddle Road takes us over a lonely ribbon of pavement that traverses some of the most spectacular scenery in Hawai'i. Maybe even in the entire world. I drive slowly. Despite the darkness, I savor the hills and open highway, the fresh Big Island air, and the coffee Carolyn pours us from the thermos. We cross miles of open rangeland, bearing steadily east toward the archipelago's largest mountains, Mauna Loa and Mauna Kea. The sky to the west is dark. Slowly, a low band on the horizon turns pink, joined by orange, red, and crimson. And then, in the full dawn, the entire world is bathed in a soft rose and mauve light.

The tires hiss over the damp asphalt, and in the rhythmic turning of the wheels, I think about Kele, remembering when we both worked for Hawaii Bound, a wilderness school here on the Big Island. A strange and compelling man, Kele; a haole with a Hawaiian name that means "murky and swampy." He is a friend I esteem and with whom I share some abiding memories, though I still don't really understand him even after fifteen years. Much can be said about him, but he remains a hard man to describe. He is a former park ranger and wilderness instructor; a hunter, fisherman, and carpenter; a homesteader, farmer, would-be scholar, a shy recluse; and marijuana grower; a procrastinator, dreamer, ascetic, and — like Henry David Thoreau was — a stern, uncompromising political activist and a bit of a crank. But he is also someone and something more that I can't quite put my finger on, something that is symbolized by the district of Puna, the place where he lives.

Driving into the ascending sun, I turn various thoughts over in my mind. Some seem vaguely connected. I think of plantations and Puna, of Kele's farm and of farmers in general. I think about old Hawai'i and food growing and society and alienation. "That the Hawaiian man was primarily a planter," say Craighill and Elizabeth Handy in Native Planters in Old Hawaii, "is indicated by the fact that the initiation that every boy went through, be he chief or commoner, was a dedication to Lono, the rain and harvest god."

Today's accounts of old Hawai'i are largely histories of the highborn, the *ali'i*, passed on through chants, featherwork, hula, and the tales of gods and chiefs. Of the *maka'āinana* — the Hawaiian commoners — less remains. The old agricultural and fishing folkways have been obscured and much knowledge lost, but some Hawaiians still live by it, and some of them, as well as the Handys and other ethnologists, have carefully codified and preserved what remains of the lore that sustained, according to some bold estimates, a population of more than a million people. The harvests of these hard-working folks included hundreds of strains of taro, sweet potato, breadfruit, banana, coconut, yam, arrowroot, sugarcane, bamboo, paper mulberry, and gourd. There were ample numbers of domesticated chickens, pigs, and dogs. And, of course, great numbers of fish and shellfish nurtured in fish ponds. The Hawaiian farmer and his counterpart on the ocean knew the seasons of the moon, the ways of plants and animals, the movement of tides and winds, and the arts of pollinating plants by hand.

In ancient Puna, as elsewhere in Polynesia, the sanctity of these farming traditions was fundamental. Much of the land from Cape Kumukahi to the upsweeping slopes of Mauna Loa was forested. Intermittently, great stretches of the earth would be scorched by the lava flows issuing from Kīlauea and Mauna Loa. The planters would move to other locations in Puna. They dispersed their houses, built their taro patches, enriched the fields, worshipped their gods, and passed the traditions of the land and sea on from parent to child.

Within these larger harmonies, however, the Hawaiians surely suffered the same troubles that have harrowed all known societies since the dawn of time and that afflict us no less today. As always, there were people who did not fit in. Some were declared *mō ka piko* (lit., "to cut the naval cord") and became exiles from family and kin group. For aiding and abetting a sorcerer, for theft or the breaking of religious laws, or for simply not conforming to the body politic, a few individuals — as in all cultures in all times — were cast out to live or die according to their own resources.

There were also the *kauwā*, the untouchables of the Hawaiian social system. For an *ali'i*, or chief, to be in the vicinity of a *kauwā* was to suffer defilement. Stories handed down on the Big Island from generation to generation say that the *kauwā* were actually the first settlers. Probably, they came from the Marquesas. It is said, in fact, that the original *kauwā* fought hard against the Tahitian invaders that came centuries later. Defeated in battle, they were segregated into reservations and enslaved.

Regardless of origin, the *kauwā* were not viewed as human beings. In the ceremonies of certain *kāhuna*, for example, they were material for sacrifice. The Hawaiian historians E. S. Craighill Handy and Mary Kawena Pukui said in their book *The Polynesian Family System in Ka'u, Hawai'i*, that a *kahuna* went near the border of the *kauwā* land and selected a man "as one might select a fowl in a barnyard." A *kauwā* could not refuse. And if he was not instantly put to death for the ritual at hand, he might be given an elongated gourd called a "garland of waiting" to wear around his neck. Said Handy and Pukui: "To say to one that his ancestor had worn the *'olo* gourd, was the equivalent of saying that he was a person of no consequence."

In Puna, along with other exiles and low-castes, the *kauwā* probably lived like fugitives furtively hiding away in caves by the sea or in the mountains. It is a matter of conjecture, for there is no written record to tell us what special qualities the people of ancient Puna, rich or poor, might have had. Looking at the harsh landforms created by the youngest volcanoes in Hawai'i, however, I can see that a land of immensely wet forests and hot, sulfurous rocks might not be the most attractive of places for farmers, fishers, priests, and warriors secure in their place in society. And it does not take much more imagining to speculate that Puna may always have been a place for people who were different — people in trouble, people on the run.

In many ways, that is still the situation today, and I want my kids to understand this before … before it all changes.

Corey stirs in the back seat; then Dana and Kelly do too. I turn, steal a quick glance, and contemplate the wonderful differences among them. Corey is the oldest, outgoing, fun-loving, and sociable. She truly is a little bear: smart, affectionate, temperamental. A voracious reader and TV junky, she has a bright eye and a creative streak that runs to the artistic. Her comments are astute for a little kid. She is also a little bit lazy and, like me, petulant and peevish when her pride is wounded. Most of the time she is full of stories, riddles, and odd commentaries on the things that she observes. Many of these experiences are secreted away in a diary she started when she was nine. The journal is called "Trips With Me."

Then there's Dana, the middle child. Dana resembles Carolyn. She is reed slim and two hands taller than most kids her age. In the company of strangers, she seems shy — a mistaken impression. She is self-effacing, but like her Capricorn mother, inner-directed and surefooted. Her current preoccupation is cooking and kitchen experimentation: chocolate-covered bananas, ants-on-logs (celery, peanut butter, raisins), and something called tuna-wiggle casserole. She is quieter than the other two and more of a loner, but she also has a will of iron when it counts. Dana is a mountain goat. She is tough and self-disciplined and quite capable of taking care of herself. I would like to be more like her.

Finally, there's Kelly, the human hand grenade. A ball of energy looking for a place to explode. A fun-seeking missile zeroing in on whatever trouble is most readily available. If Kelly were an animal, she'd undoubtedly be an otter. Endlessly nosy, prone to pouting when she is not the center of attention, she is marvelously direct. If she wants to know something or if a random thought enters her mind, nothing will stifle her. She is charming and infuriating and clever with the words and phrases she is absorbing, including the cuss words she has heard from me. With her gift for gab and quick wit, my guess is it's law school and then the White House or the Big House or both.

I think of the three kids and their similarities and differences. How lovely to look at they are. How bright and energetic they seem. And how the things that irritate me most about each of them individually are the same qualities I dislike in myself. What goes around, comes around....

Soon, all three of them are fully awake and complaining and

wondering where we are going and why and what's in it for them. We descend into Hilo, stop briefly to buy a box of fresh buttermilk doughnuts, and then head toward Kurtistown. Later, we make a turn at Kea'au and head south straight toward Kele's house, which is tucked into the forest. Where, if prior arrangements hold true, Kele should be waiting for a day of catching up, of discussion and visiting, of relaxation. "And a canoe ride," I promise the kids, who chatter and eat their doughnuts, indelibly grinding a couple of them into the rented car's velour upholstery.

A few miles outside Pāhoa, I bear left and head toward the sea. Dana asks me how much longer until we get there and I give her the standard answer for all trips: 15 minutes, which might as well be 15 weeks if you're a kid. Eventually, we turn right on a road abutting the ocean and, courtesy of a couple of ruts that look like they were made for bullock carts, we make our way toward Kele's place.

*   *   *

Kele lives at the easternmost edge of the State of Hawai'i. The district of Puna consists of 504 square miles of sloping land extending from the lower reaches of Mauna Loa and Kīlauea volcanoes at one end to the wave-washed shores of the blue Pacific at the other. Human influences aside, most of Puna's geography is made up of geologically recent activity involving Kīlauea's east rift, a continuous fissure of fractured, super-heated rock that extends some 50 miles downslope. Cutting across the entire length of Puna, it is where most of Kīlauea's dramatic flank eruptions take place. Although these are not commonplace, the rift nonetheless dominates the character of the land and, in its own way, the smoldering personality of Puna's inhabitants. Telltale signs of it abound.

Throughout Puna, for example, there are old spatter and cinder cones, ancient lava tubes, and burnt holes in the ground where large trees once stood. Vents and fumaroles can be found steaming away almost any place you might choose to step off the road and walk. People who have lived in Puna a long time take the rift for granted. People from elsewhere are intrigued by it. Some are exploiting it. The only functioning geothermal wells in Hawai'i are located in Puna. Not that far, in fact, from where Kele lives. There is talk of bringing many more wells on-line in the next twenty years and of using undersea cables to deliver the energy they tap to Maui and O'ahu. And there are also rumors that the State wants to bring heavy industries to the Big Island and site them in Puna. Whatever unfolds, the wells are a harbinger of things to come and they make Kele and many of his friends nervous.

Like the great river of energy itself, the land above the rift wears a benign face but harbors a complicated and occasionally fiery temper. There are, to be sure, thick stands of shrubs, woodlands of 'ōhi'a and hau, and lush black-sand shorelines. There are also stretches of land that are uninhabitable. Generally speaking, the heat flowing through the rift is like a slow, meandering stream: every so often, however, the stream floods its banks and spews a bit of boiling magma into someone's backyard. Since 1985, lava has been pouring out of an open vent and flowing down to the ocean, cutting roads, devastating more than a hundred widely dispersed homes, and adding miles of hot new land to Hawai'i.

Most of Puna remains unaffected by this. Life goes on even if you live next to a volcano, and life in Puna is, and always has been, agricultural. The soils that overlie most of Puna's old and abundant lava lands are stable, moderately deep, and well drained. Coupled with a moist climate, they make Puna a good place to grow things. Until a few years ago, this translated into a monolithic plantation-style sugar industry. Today sugar is on its way out and other crops, legal and illegal, have moved in. Small truck farms and orchards of macadamia nuts, bananas, and papayas now dot a landscape that was once an ocean of undulating, rain-swept cane. Planted on some of these farms, or behind them, or tucked off in more remote spots cleared out of the forest and accessible only by pig trails, is the other crop: marijuana. It is the one that keeps much of Puna's cash flow flowing.

Driving through the old plantation towns of Kurtistown, Kea'au, and Pāhoa, one sees part of the transition that this has wrought. Puna is a study in architectural contrasts. Modern pole houses with skylights, solar water heaters, and fancy Swedish toilets mix

along the side of the road with two-room cottages built by plantation workers fifty years ago. These homes, with their tin roofs and
one-hole outhouses, are now occupied by aging Filipino sugar
workers who have retired or been displaced. Inside the newer
homes are the more recent transplants. Many of these are *haole*
retirees from the mainland, people who have chosen to spend
their time in a land without ice and snow shovels.

Traditions mix and blend, and the land itself dictates much of
what we call life-style. Many houses, regardless of their bathroom
decor, have gardens outside full of fresh vegetables and fragrant
flowers. Everyone has fruit and shade trees. Most households have
a horse or two and some chickens or ducks running around their
side yards. Everyone keeps dogs. Drive down any side road in
Puna and you will quickly find a half-dozen snarling mutts trying
to bite your tires as your car kicks gravel and dust in their faces.

Beyond the roads altogether there is still another group of
people who numerically and culturally make up much of what is
unique about Puna, perhaps the true people of the rift lands.
Most of them live on two-, three-, or four-acre patches of land
that they have steadfastly carved out of the forest over the past
ten or fifteen years. These Punans should also be classified as
"new" although they are distinctly different from the other "new"
people in that they are younger, stranger, and — to my way of
thinking — more interesting.

There are also a lot of them. Walk out into the densest part of the
Puna forest and you will probably come across some of them. Walk
out there with some beer and announce a *ho'olaule'a*, a party, and
you will be astounded at how many heads pop out of the bushes.
These people are neighborly in their own way, but they are also a
little bit wild. They value a certain distance between themselves
and each other and a great deal more space between themselves
and mainstream, middle-class Hawai'i. Some burn cinnamon
incense in front of Indian wall hangings. Others go to fundamental-
ist Christian churches. A few appear to be completely rootless and
antisocial; a very small percentage of these, in turn, are heavy-duty,
industrial-strength commercial marijuana growers who have honed
the production, processing, and marketing of grass into its own

covert science. They are responsible for the primary reputation Puna has around the State. Most of the rest of Hawai'i seems to believe Puna is full of dopers, growers, and bandits.

Stereotypes aside, however, most Punans are not dope growers by profession. They may keep a few plants for home consumption or cookie jar income and will surely smoke it if it's offered to them and if it's good stuff. Nonetheless, few of them make their living from weed. In fact, most of these "new" Puna people are respectable, hard-working carpenters, electricians, mechanics, and plumbers who, like my pal Kele, are primarily interested in making their lives self-sufficient. Their goal is to raise as much of their own food as possible with enough left over to sell or trade. This is part of Kele's dream as well. Although he might be considered a bit of an outlaw because of his marijuana arrests, he is more accurately one of Puna's "new age" hardscrabble farmers. He is a bush person: part entrepreneur, part farmer, and part mountain man.

Like Kele, most of the Puna bush people are actually more interested in raising animals and edible (as opposed to smokable) plants. Some are working with bees, rabbits, and chickens. Others are trying their hand at papayas, bananas, or more exotic things like starfruit, cherimoyas, and macadamia nuts. A few are working with milk cows and hogs. All of these people share, beyond a certain "fringe" quality, two things in common: they abhor pesticides and they are absolutely passionate about living in Puna. Other than that, they go their own ways in matters of politics and lifestyle and make their living as best they can.

Most of these folks have sought out Puna. Between 1970 and 1980 Puna's population climbed from 5,000 to 12,000. Most of the immigrants who rolled in during that time were in their mid-twenties to mid-thirties and appeared to be products of the larger American countercultural upheavals that had taken place in the 1960s. The typical newcomer was, if stereotypes harbor even a semblance of truth, a college-educated big-city kid wearing a T-shirt and jeans. He or she was well traveled, iconoclastic, tired of wandering, and eager to put roots down on some of Puna's rich topsoil. To hear it from them, they were idealistic nomads with *Whole Earth Catalog*s looking for stability and new beginnings on the eastern frontier of Hawai'i. Attracted by isolation and cheap land and by the actual possibility of creating a self-sufficient lifestyle, the new Punans quickly became entrenched.

From a slightly different angle all of these earnest young homesteaders appeared to be a horde of dirty hippies. "These are your real crazies," a Hawai'i County government official once told me categorically and with true exasperation. "They've been kicked out of everywhere else. Now we're stuck with them." In any case, the infusion of young, urban "healthier-than-thou" refugees during the 1970s irretrievably changed Puna. Suddenly, old plantation towns began sprouting health food stores and head shops. Gaunt men in beards living on macrobiotic diets made leather belts and tie-dyed T-shirts. Young women who had gone to school in St. Louis or San Jose carried infants on their hip and started growing their own vegetables.

Cultural influences went both ways. Old Japanese men taught blond kids from Los Angeles how to make and repair throw-nets. A few local kids started eating yogurt. Newcomers wearing fringed suede jackets and carrying Buck knives got interested in Hawaiian history, and old-timers with weather-beaten plantation faces started thinking about organic farming. Where the new and the old parted company, however, was in land tenure. The older immigrants — the Japanese, Chinese, and Filipinos — owned theirs outright. They might be cash poor, but they held the deeds to their one or two acres. The newcomers had nothing. Very quickly, the real generational and cultural divide became clear. It was marijuana and the vast revenues it could produce after a few dangerous months of work. For those wandering into Puna with nothing more than a knapsack and some vague ideas about organic farming, grass was the way to get started. Puna's "*paka lōlō*" industry (*paka* meaning "tobacco" or "smoke" and *lōlō* meaning, according to one translation at least, "the eating of brains") quickly replaced sugar as the area's main source of discretionary income.

This is not to say that all of Puna was then made up of pot growers or even of newcomers. Half of the population were still local people who had grown up there — folks whose grandparents were buried in Chinese, Filipino, Japanese, and Hawaiian cemeteries in places like Pohoiki, Kapoho, Mountain View, and Glenwood. But as the Puna Sugar Company declined, so did occupational opportunities. The daughters and sons of the planta- tion — enamored of life in the faster lane — transplanted them- selves to Hilo, Honolulu, and beyond. Into this vacuum came the searchers of the 1960s and 1970s, people looking for serenity, nature, and a slower pace of life. And along with them came an economic resurgence based on marijuana and a prosperity that would inevitably change them as well.

In the local underground economy, fabled pot fortunes were made in the late 1970s and early 1980s. Local merchants noticed it. Hilo car dealers were incredulous when young kids from Puna rolled into the showroom and pulled out a fat wad of $100 bills along with marijuana seeds, old butts and joints, and their house keys. Cars, trucks, and real estate were paid for in cash by smiling longhairs. Puna dope money — possibly to the tune of $150 mil- lion or more a year — paid for groceries, Chevy Blazers, and chunks of good Puna land.

Stories and legends developed: of crazed Vietnam vets guarding their crops with booby-trapped shotguns. Of a kid who flew to Vegas with $100,000 in Puna dope money and doubled his assets three times in a row. Of even bolder growers planting their crops in the middle of Pāhoa or alongside the Volcanoes National Park headquarters. And of one particularly well-organized operation (since busted) that did a $2-million-a-year business operating out of a couple of old greenhouses in the forest.

Within a few years most of these enterprising souls turned legiti- mate. Yes, some still grew, but most became contractors, shop- keepers, or government bureaucrats. Many took out loans, opened businesses, started keeping regular hours, and charged things on credit cards. They continued to live in Puna's boondocks but they also joined Rotary Clubs and formed neighborhood associations. Some of them went into politics. Others became university pro- fessors. Some settled into newly contoured subdivisions or built their little dream houses out in the bush. Almost all of them married and learned to change diapers and take out the garbage like the rest of us. They still smoked dope and they still wore blue jeans and boots but they also now owned lawnmowers and weed whackers.

Today most Punans, new and old, are, from most angles, truly ordinary, hard-working people. Yet, surface respectabilities also mask strong passions. Scratch a successful recent immigrant ("recent" meaning the last twenty years) or one of the new over-65 retirees, or even some of the still older plantation types, and you'll uncover something interesting underneath. For no matter how regular a Punan has gotten, no matter that he or she now owns a brand-new Westinghouse washing machine and a Krups coffee maker, there is still that sense of exclusivity — that shared feeling of living in no-man's-land, of pitching one's tent on the side of a cliff, of being at least a minimalist kind of pioneer on one of the last true Hawaiian frontiers. Puna is indeed different and the people who live there know it and cherish it.

Everything else aside, there is a "last chance" sense to the place, an ambience and atmosphere of "us against the world." Not unlike Alaska, Puna is probably best viewed as a loose-knit confederation of spirited people who have consciously chosen to live out their lives on the edge: on the edge of a volcano, on the edge of the Pacific Ocean — and on the edge, so it sometimes seems, of civilization. Whatever else it may be, Puna is a twentieth-century Sherwood Forest, a refuge for dissenters, dreamers, exiles, outlaws, and crazies who are actually more run-of-the-mill than they admit and who are all growing slightly paunchy as they make a wide turn past 40. Even for those who have plugged their houses into the conveniences of the modern world, it is still the People's Republic of Puna, an elaborate and sometimes mixed-up vision of independence, solitude, and intentional community spiced up with a bit of healthy anarchy.

Much of this may be attributable to the rugged landscape formed by the rift, by the presence of vast stretches of wilderness, and by a population that seems to take true pleasure from rural diversity. Puna's residents place great value on its undeveloped character, on its weather and scenery, on its slow pace, and on its tolerance for human differences. These crosscut age, ethnicity, and income. For some, the Puna life-style means tending a part-time flower business on a half-acre of land to supplement social security checks. For others it is not having any immediate neighbors. For still others it is a combination of hunting, fishing, and farming. And for virtually everyone, it seems, it means a vociferous NO! to industrialization, urbanization, gentrification, touristification, and the kind of general all-purpose middle-class homogenization that seems to be occurring everywhere else these days.

Puna's most contentious activists struggle to describe these feelings. Often as not they announce that they are prepared to fight. For what? "Our life-style. To keep the country *country*. To keep Puna *Puna*!" "The government has plans to turn us into the Pittsburgh of the Pacific," a friend of Kele's once told me over coffee laced with several fingers of whiskey. To prevent this, someone — perhaps Kele's friend himself — once shoved a stick of dynamite into the business end of a large wood chipper that had been set up as part of a commercial logging operation. The chipper was starting to work a stand of native 'ōhi'a trees along the rift. A few years before that, the geothermal plant in Kapoho itself was sabotaged. And before that, in 1970, there were sniper attacks on workers sent down from Hilo to put up telephone poles.

Driving through Puna today, meeting people, talking with the folks who stuck it out during the 1970s, confirms that the views these actions represent are not isolated though the forms of response may be. Yesterday's in-migrants are today's "drawbridge settlers." They have staked out their own little corner of the world, a place that few outsiders seemed interested in fifteen and twenty years ago, and now they want to pull the bridge up and keep the rest of the world out. The world, as always, has other ideas.

On the road between Kea'au and what was once the town of Kalapana, developers have driven bulldozers onto some of Puna's more accessible flat lands and furrowed out the patch-quilt patterns of future housing tracts. These subdivision etchings will probably become bedroom communities housing a workforce that commutes to and from Hilo every day. Most telling of all, however, the town of Pāhoa — just a few miles from the steaming, smoking vents of Kīlauea's recent lava flows — now boasts its own 7-11 convenience store owned by Japanese nationals. Right across the way, in fact, from the older hippie health food store that's been there for more than a decade.

Marijuana is still a lively and viable component of the local Puna worldview. It is more than mystique. For the past several years, State, Federal and local law enforcement officials have been cracking down hard on Puna's growers. In a series of paramilitary campaigns code-named "Green Harvest" and "Operation Sweep," they have descended from the air in helicopters and crashed through the forest in four-wheel-drive land rovers to surprise Puna's *paka lōlō* cultivators. Tons of plants have been confiscated and destroyed and dozens of growers arrested.

Local Punans, the same ones who object to geothermal wells and log chippers, believe the government's current obsession with marijuana eradication is related to its development dreams. "The new County administration wants to make Puna safe for shopping centers and subdivisions," says one of them. "And people who grow or use dope just don't fit in. They simply aren't the boutique, mall, and garden-restaurant type consumers that the developers want to attract."

Whether this is true or not, marijuana continues to be major Puna news. It is not the only issue. Other problems related to ocean mining, papaya irradiation, wildlife protection, and the development of a spaceport and rocket-launch industry in neighboring Ka'ū District also loom large on the political landscape. But in the health food stores and barbershops of Puna as well as out in certain clearings in the forest where rift people sometimes gather to smoke and talk, grass is still an important topic of conversation. And for a few people, including my old friend Kele, it is part of a life-style that is increasingly under siege.

* * *

A recollection.

We are bumping down one of Puna's back roads in Kele's red pickup truck, ostensibly on our way to take a hike. The forest here is called *Wao Kele O Puna* — *wao* meaning inland region and *kele* meaning wet, murky, and lush. The rain forests of Puna. This great shaggy carpet of a jungle, filled with *'ōhi'a* and guava trees, is home to *pueo* and *'io*, the native Hawaiian owl and hawk, and to honeycreepers like the vermilion *'i'iwi* and the crimson *'apapane*. This is one of the main reasons why people like Kele choose to live here: it is wilderness.

Kele is reminiscing about Keoki, his most beloved hunting dog, whose bones now rest someplace in the Kohala Mountains. He tells me about a particularly ferocious pig that Keoki tracked down and that Kele then killed with a bayonet. And about some of his other hunting dogs that were wounded or killed in titanic hog battles. And how he spent four days futilely searching for Keoki. And how much the loss of Keoki, even years later, still grieves him. Eventually, we park the truck and peel off into the woods for our hike.

Two miles down the trail the day's other agenda comes clear. We are here not just for a pleasant morning in the forest. Kele wants to put in some marijuana seedlings he has sprouted at his house and he is now carrying in his day-pack in plastic bags. He asks me if I mind. A host of small fears rise up and nettle my insides. I see a headline reading "Bureaucrat Busted With Puna Dope Dealer" and a detailed article chronicling the unending shame felt by my wife, children, employer, and mother-in-law as they all visit me in jail. Should I turn around and go back? Should I tell him I want nothing to do with this side of his life? The arguments go both ways and one part of me says yes while another says no. As usual, I am ambivalent and give in to the least onerous choice of the moment. I tell Kele that I'm not crazy about doing this, but that as long as I'm observing a bona fide underground pot-planting expedition, I'll treat the whole thing as an ethnographic experience and record it for posterity. All of which leads into a long palaver on politics and some instruction on the art, science, and mechanics of marijuana growing in Puna.

Kele is a small-time grower but he is persistent, reflective and, as in all things, rebellious. Compared to many other aspects of American society, he argues, marijuana is a harmless diversion that brings lots of pleasure, some occasional insight, and a little bit of much-needed tax-free cash to a great many people. As to the other arguments — that marijuana may be addictive, that it may contribute to behavior problems in young people if it is abused, that it may lead to a deterioration of short- and long-term brain function, and that it may have some cumulative dangers as a carcinogen — Kele scoffs. If he had his way, in fact, pot would be legalized and everyone could grow their own to smoke, sell, or give away as they see fit. "Free up grass," he says, "and you start to free yourself and the world."

If that's the case, I ask him, what about the legal risks? He acknowledges them. He knows that police, prosecutors, and the local DEA people don't hold marijuana sellers or even casual dope smokers in high regard. As a matter of fact, I remind him, they think Puna growers are a bunch of troublemakers and drug addicts that are making money off other people's miseries. All of which feeds into Kele's inherent contrariness and immediately raises his hackles.

"That's bullshit," he says. "There's bigger fish to fry, including all those greedy corporate criminals that the downtown guys never seem to bother with ... and besides which," he says after discoursing on the evils of government and big business, "they have to catch me first." Immediately, the headlines flash in front of me again. My liver lurches, trips over my pancreas, and ends up in my throat. In front of Kele, of course, I am Bogart-cool.

We hike for a time and then, at the intersection of what could be any two pig trails in the entire universe, Kele veers left and stalks off into some vines and brambles. I follow and a hundred yards farther we come to a small clearing with half a dozen four-foot marijuana plants. Kele checks them out, runs his fingers over the plants, plucks a few leaves, feels them, smells them, tastes them, and looks around. Then he gives me a smug little smile, as if he's just personally outfoxed the U.S. Congress, the White House, and the Supreme Court on behalf of every bush person in Puna. Which I suppose he has.

"These plants are really interesting," he explains. By "interesting," Kele means they are healthy and valuable. He then goes on to explain some of the details of *paka lōlō* growing. How cannabis prefers loose soil with lots of nitrogen and potassium, a pH of 6.0

or better, and as much sun and water as it can get. He shows me how dope growers prune the tops to force the flow of cannabinol resins into the flowers and then he offers a variety of instructional insights about harvesting. All of which go in one ear and out the other as I'm looking over my shoulder to see if any fuzz or Feds are around.

Kele plants his little seedlings, clears back some encroaching forest, and then packs his things. We hike out the way we came in, clamber into his truck, and drive off.

Back in Honolulu several months later, I get word from a friend that Kele has been busted. Caught red-handed out in the woods, so the story goes, with a bunch of small plants and a few bigger ones worth a thousand dollars. Near the spot, I suspect, where he talked about all those other fish that needed frying.

*   *   *

Another recollection comes to mind. This one is of a very different trip to Kele's place and of a very different side of Kele — and, while we're on the subject, of a different sort of fish that also got fried.

Hawaii Bound base camp manager John Frederick and I have sauntered into Puna to spend a couple of days with our mutual friend. The three of us have walked down the gravel road from Kele's house to the sea carrying masks, fins, snorkels, and spears. It is late afternoon and the water is dark and greasy-looking. We enter the sea over some big slippery boulders and fan out in search of fish.

We are in 15 feet of water, rising and plunging as we hold our breath and hunt. This is meat fishing. Kele has almost no food in his house. He's forgotten to go to the store, which is 15 miles away in Pāhoa and closed anyway. We each poke a few reef fish but it is larger game we are really after. I corner a small *maomao*, a sergeant major, shoot it through the head, rise to the surface, slip it off the spear prongs, and deposit it into my fish bag. I put my face back in the water and out of the lower corner of my mask, I catch a signal from Kele.

He is on the bottom, holding his breath and pointing his spear. A good size *uhu*, a parrotfish, is feeding on a piece of yellow coral 20 feet away. I slowly circle around so that the fish is between us. We start to close our pincer, but my movements are awkward. The fish spots me and bolts for a nearby hole. Kele intercepts it, stalking it around a large coral head. When the fish turns away and reverses, Kele also turns and meets it coming the other way. Again the fish starts to turn, but this time Kele is ready to pounce. He fires and hits.

Just 3 feet away, I see the killing scene as if it were in slow motion. The spear is in Kele's right hand with the surgical rubber that propels the shaft pulled three-quarters of the way up the spear. The muscles in his arm are knotted. He grips the rubber and the spear for what seems like an eternity. Behind the faceplate, I glimpse Kele's eyes. They are fierce, intense, and full of menace as he hunts the fish. He is transfixed. Nothing else matters. The *uhu* turns and there is a single moment in which Kele must take his shot or lose it. It must be precisely right. He releases his grip. I see the spear slide through Kele's hands and enter the fish broadside behind the gills. The parrotfish lunges and thrashes, trying to twist itself off the prongs that have pierced it. Blood and flecks of flesh pour from its wounds clouding the water around us. As we rise to the surface, I look at Kele. His eyes are hooded, his face dark with emotions I cannot fathom.

John and I drag ourselves out of the ocean. Kele is behind gripping the speared fish tightly with one arm, clawing his way up the rocks with the other. Still holding the speared and wriggling fish, Kele walks over to his day-pack, takes out a long, thin-bladed knife, slides the fish off the spear, and quickly kills it by severing the spinal cord behind its head. He looks up at us and suddenly his face relaxes. His eyes soften and he sits down cross-legged on the rocks and cradles the dead fish in his arm — the same way a mother or father would protectively hold a young infant.

Looking directly into its fading eye, he strokes the gleaming, iridescent animal for several minutes and then says to it: "I'm sorry that I killed you." And then he looks up at me and says, "She's beautiful, isn't she?" An hour later, the three of us feast on the lobsterlike white meat that Kele has filleted from the fish's body.

Who is this person? I've been asking the same question for fifteen years. On top of a very complex persona, Kele is a true new-age Punan, with all the contradictions that implies. For example, here is a guy who lives a hermitlike existence most of the year and, within the parameters of that existence, alternates periods of very hard work with long stretches of relaxation and contemplation. Then, every once in a while, something in the newspaper or on the local grapevine grabs his attention and he comes roaring out of the backwoods. Perhaps it's herbicide spraying by the side of the road or geothermal development or new zoning laws or the bulldozing of forest lands. The pattern is the same. He comes up for air, looks around, becomes enraged, writes letters to the newspapers, lambastes a few developers and politicians with threats of class-action lawsuits, and then gets discouraged when civilization refuses to respond to him with charity and understanding. He then retreats to his homestead to fish, hunt, grow weed, read books, and work on his farm.

More seeming contradictions: Kele is a staunch environmentalist, a true believer in free enterprise, and a person who would love, more than anything else in the world, to have his own little school in the woods to help straighten out juvenile delinquents through wilderness experiences and farm life. He is widely read and knowledgeable in amazingly diverse subjects, including the mechanics of volcanoes and watersheds, banana and papaya planting, beekeeping, taro growing, Democratic politics (both national and local), dog raising, general carpentry and stone masonry, *ulua* fishing, soil conservation, pig and goat hunting, canoe building, marijuana cultivation, and the repair and maintenance of old army jeeps. He asks everyone for advice and then laughs at most of it. He instinctively distrusts anything connected with cities but loves to visit them. And in his heart of hearts, he abhors any kind of authority but thinks he wouldn't mind working for the government if he could get himself elected or appointed.

When I think of Kele I picture a friend with whom I've shared some exceptional experiences and from whom I've learned a great deal. The picture also includes ambiguity and complexity and a kind of untamed grittiness that is increasingly rare in a society of yuppified conformists. I see someone wild ... someone who takes the majority of his contentment from living alone in the woods and on a farm, someone comfortable in the outdoors in almost any kind of circumstance, and someone who can't really decide whether he's a recluse or a warrior. His conflicts are not that different, perhaps, from some of the hesitations that punctuate my own life, but somehow they seem more unique. Where mine inevitably end up in the gray area of personal and organizational compromises, his seem to lead to the bright and solid colors of the land, forest, and sea.

In an album at home I have several old photographs that go back to our days at the Hawaii Bound School. In one of them, Kele is smiling as he emerges from a tent pitched on the rocky shores of Hōnaunau, the old City of Refuge where ancient Hawaiians found sanctuary from their enemies. In another he is grubbing around in a muddy taro patch in Waimea, waving at the camera with hands that I know to be thickly calloused from years of moving shovels and canoe paddles around. His face and arms are tanned the color of roasted chestnuts and his face has a long-jawed, raw-boned look to it. The rest of him is skinny. He is wearing an old T-shirt and frayed blue jeans with holes in the knees and seat. Underneath he has the build of a gymnast or a mountain climber or someone who has trained in the martial arts. He moves as if his center of gravity is a little bit lower than everyone else's, and the picture suggests this.

In all of these photographs, Kele looks tall and full of self-confidence. The pictures are deceiving. In truth, he is a scruffy five-foot-seven-and-one-half-inch alley cat. Typically, he holds himself at a slightly deflected angle when he is talking to you, arms defiantly folded across his chest, weight cocked on one hip. There is a great and mysterious tension to him even when he tries hard to relax. It is the eyes, however, that best define him. They are feline eyes — gray, tough, and flinty most of the time but with an unmistakably shy and haunted quality. When his guard is up, though, you see the change. They squint, flatten out, and turn to granite. Then they become jungle eyes, eyes that occasionally scare the bejesus out of his closest friends.

Kele's fierceness — and that is probably the easiest word to use in describing all of these currents and crosscurrents — is not easy to understand. Like everything else about him, his biography is complicated and secretive. What I know about him goes like this.

He was born a military brat in California in 1950, moved to Hawai'i when he was four years old and for a time lived in Waikīkī and then at Camp Smith. In 1958 his father, a marine sergeant, was transferred to Kāne'ohe and his family bought a house on 'Aikahi Hillside for $19,000 across from a papaya field. Kele settled into the local grammar school and roamed the hills and cow pastures of Windward O'ahu. Even then he seems to have been a loner. There were scraps with other kids and minor brushes with the law. Mostly it was fighting. Being a *haole* and a newcomer, he took his lumps. Never one to back down from a fight, Kele would beef with anybody and often stood down guys twice his size. But it was "dirty lickins," he once told me, lickins given and received, that led to a special respect for local kids.

High school graduation. Kele's father wanted him to join the marines. Kele wanted to get away from the Islands and from his family. He applied to Marquette University and was admitted on a Naval ROTC scholarship. Once he actually got to Milwaukee he felt like a foreigner. His closest friends were the cooks and dish-washers who worked in the school's cafeteria. Through them, he wound up spending most of his time in the city's black communi-ty. He also traveled. On long weekends that might start on a Thursday and end on a Monday a week and a half later, he'd pack a small duffel, don his Naval ROTC officer's uniform, stand by the entrance to the interstate and pick up rides to places like San Antonio, Texas, or Billings, Montana, or Athens, Tennessee. By the end of his freshman year, he knew a good deal about the geography of the United States first-hand. He was also finished with school.

Kele headed west and, after a brief detour picking apples in Washington, made his way back to the Islands. The Vietnam war was in full swing, and Hawai'i was thick with GIs. Having flirted briefly with being a college student, he now jumped ship completely and plunged into the counterculture. Just about that time, his father died of a heart attack. Although he never talks about it directly, one senses that it was a moment of great liberation as well as great sadness. Kele joined the antiwar movement, grew his hair long, smoked pot, and tried out different types of city jobs, none of which really suited him.

On weekends he lit out for the woods. But if Kele had changed, so too had the Islands. Tourism and in-migration from the mainland were now formidable forces in the economy. As a result, the pastures around his old house in 'Aikahi were gone and Kāne'ohe, once a sleepy little country town, was now bulging with frame houses plotted out in dozens of little subdivisions. Revisiting the mountains of his childhood in the mid-1970s, he found shopping centers and traffic jams and O'ahu's trails diminished or blocked completely. And now, slowly but surely, the strands of different aspirations — still nameless — started to twitch within him.

Bone-tired of Honolulu's mad pace and urban intensities, he moved to the Big Island. He had been there before, but this time it was for good. And with an idea: buy some land, plant lots of trees, make the land productive, strive for self-sufficiency, and use the entire enterprise as a living demonstration for local kids — kids in trouble and kids with fractured dreams. Kids that, in my own view, were like himself: ill at ease, lonely, adrift, and somehow dislocated.

The vision was one of political action and a kind of "land use social work" with Kele playing the combined cameo roles of Johnny Appleseed, Stokely Carmichael, and Father Flanagan of Boys Town all rolled into one. Before he could get started, however, he needed money. One day at the University of Hawai'i campus in Hilo he happened to see an advertisement for what looked like the job of a lifetime. Kele applied, was accepted, and spent the next two years as a ranger in neighboring Hawaii Volcanoes National Park.

The Park Service might have become a bona fide career had things gone differently. For a time, in fact, Kele thought he had stumbled into his life's work. The Park Service kept him in the backcountry most of the time doing hard, dangerous work. Kele loved it. He shod horses, killed feral pigs and goats, cut trails, built firebreaks, repaired water tanks, cleared out nonnative plant intruders, planted trees, and rescued city-slicker backpackers with fancy boots and Gore-Tex jackets who, despite state-of-the-art equipment, had fallen into lava holes or gotten lost. In his free time he wandered around the Park's magnificent and lonely stretches of grassy lava lands by himself. Once, exploring around a fence-line work site, he discovered and then excitedly reported a lava tube full of ancient Hawaiian petroglyphs. It was an especially valuable find to the Hawaiian and scientific communities. He visited the cave often and, much later, showed it to me and a few other friends.

Over time, however, the sense of belonging he felt with the National Park Service started to fade. Kele would periodically come out of the woods and find things not to his liking. Park higher-ups, for example, invited a team of archaeologists from the Bishop Museum to work on the petroglyph cave he had discovered. After revisiting his find a month later, Kele expressed his indignation to anyone who would listen; the scientists had trashed the cave and desecrated the petroglyphs by stubbing out cigarettes on the floor of the cave and stepping on the etchings. He also regularly confronted the Park bureaucracy about what he saw as poor hiring policies, equipment problems, insensitivity to the local community, and about its general kowtowing to the tourist industry.

His final battle began when the NPS announced that a new road would be built in the southern part of the park near Kalapana. Kele fired off an angry round of letters to the Park Superintendent, to the Superintendent's bosses in Honolulu and Washington, and to the Secretary of the Interior. Technically speaking, what happened next couldn't really be called getting fired. The NPS simply decided not to renew his contract.

To this day Kele believes it was the local County bureaucrats who did him in and not the NPS higher-ups in Honolulu or Washington. After a time, the anger and resentment ebbed away and he turned to other pursuits, among them hunting for land. He finally found a three-acre plot near the ocean. Now Kele's dreams asserted themselves once more. He cleared out the underbrush and used some of the straighter 'ōhi'a trees to frame a small house on stilts. He planted different kinds of fruit trees, tilled a small garden, and — off on a corner of his land — cultivated some pot. At first, it was just a few plants for home use. Then he planted a few more. He smoked some himself, gave some away, and sold some to a few friends who had discretionary income.

In short order, he planted some larger patches on his farm and in other parts of Puna, including out-of-the-way spots in the National Park, and started to work his little farm. He took a low-budget vagabondish trip down to New Zealand and traveled extensively around the Hawaiian Islands. Increasingly, marijuana was the centerpiece of his subsistence income. Kele might, in fact, have gone on to become one of Puna's bigger dope dealers but something else intervened in his life, just as it did mine. The Hawaii Bound School was the crucible that forged our friendship and that of a dozen other people as well. They are friendships now well into their second decade.

From the moment he heard about Hawaii Bound Kele knew he had to be part of it. The school's corporate purpose was to inspire confidence through the mastery of new skills and the completion of challenging experiences, all of which took place on the Big Island and in the wilderness. For a wide variety of students, ranging from corporate executives to juvenile delinquents, Hawaii Bound was to be a starting point, a turning point, or an affirming point. It was, in short, a classic "outward bound" program in the tropics for people willing to take on the physical and mental challenges of 24-day wilderness expeditions to rarely visited parts of the Islands.

Kele got to know Alan Hale, the school's director, met some of the other staff members, and then applied for a job. Subsistence farming and low-level marijuana production was healthy, fun, and modestly profitable, but Hawaii Bound had a special resonance. It had a mission and it had a soul! And vision. It awoke his big dream again. The idea of working in the woods and trying to teach people a Hawaiian land ethic appealed to him immensely. Alan, in turn, looked Kele over, and on the strength of his intense desire and his backcountry experience with the Park Service, hired him on as an instructor though not without a few reservations.

For Kele, and for me and many others who were involved, Hawaii Bound was indeed an extended adventure. It would also be — much later and with proper hindsight — one of those yardsticks that people use to measure the quality of other life experiences. Much of this was because of the people.

Hawaii Bound brought together an uncommonly intelligent, accomplished, and adventuresome group of individuals. People like Kele himself. But others as well. Ha'aheo Mansfield, a gifted Hawaiian woman with a lyrical voice and the ability to peer straight into your soul. Jeff Melrose, a land planner from Maui. John Frederick, the equipment wizard who was also a student of Asian history and religion. Audrey Sutherland, who paddled a rubber kayak up the Inland Passage to Alaska by herself at age 60. Leland "Bring 'Em Back Alive" Everett who once rescued ten teenagers from one of Mauna Loa's worst ice blizzards. Marine biologist Ann Fielding, author of several books on Hawaiian reef and shore life. Lorraine Robinson, Autumn Prebble, Barney Tsuruda, Tamar Chotzen, Todd Black, and Greg and Shena Sandler, who made the technical mysteries of map and compass sensible to kids who couldn't read or write. Phil and Nalani Haisley and my brother Bob, who handled Hawaii Bound's automotive and mechanical catastrophes. Walt Amond, who was a professional dolphin trainer, and Laura "Thunder Thighs" Wong, an artist and marathon runner. "Devil Dog" Oreskin, who had lived in an ashram in India for several years. And many others as well.

Nearly all were in their late twenties and early thirties. In addition to sheer physical ability and a knack for teaching, working with the Hawaii Bound School required expertise in mountaineering, seamanship, and emergency medical care. It also required a basic love for Hawaiian history, geography, geology, and botany.

As in any other Outward Bound program, the school's curriculum was taught on cross-country expeditions. At least two or three times a year, each instructor was expected to lead a dozen students of various ages and abilities through four rugged environments and bring everyone back safely. Nobody was paid very much to do this work. For some, being a part of Hawaii Bound meant taking substantial cuts in pay. Nonetheless, everyone loved it and, in the years I was there, nobody ever quit.

Our base camp was a ramshackle assortment of old wooden buildings in the town of Waimea. The rooms were filled with cots, bunk beds, sleeping pads, hand-built food pantries, reconstructed (but still ailing) refrigerators and washing machines, car and boat parts, tools, and — in the main building — a large living room with a fireplace and kitchen. Living and working in this base camp forced everyone into close proximity, especially during the summer months when courses were in full swing. This also forged powerful bonds. At one time or another almost all of us had hiked to the top of Mauna Loa together, swum across Hōnaunau Bay, led map and compass trips across the Ka'ū desert, rappeled down the 75-foot waterfall behind Anna's Ranch, and cleared miles of trail in the Kohala Mountains.

Kele was one of the most adept in backcountry matters. He had done more of these kinds of things and for longer periods of time than any of us. He also knew the topography of the Big Island intimately because he had hiked, fished, camped, hunted, surveyed, and guided others over most of it. Not that Kele was your average gung-ho Outward Bound instructor type; just the opposite. To people who didn't really know him, Kele was a loner who in fact seemed to prefer dogs, dope, and guns to most forms of human company. Even in his most social moments there was always the sense of the wild animal about him, as if he had been raised in a cave and wasn't quite sure if he really wanted to be around other members of his own species. People in general — and especially government officials and policemen — picked up on this ambivalence immediately. Intuitively they sensed danger.

By circumstance, Kele and I wound up working on various projects together. One of the first was a special trail crew composed of inner city kids, some of them street-tough law violators and status offenders sent to Hawaii Bound by the Family Court. The "Disco Droids," Kele called them, after two of them hiked into the forest with yard-long Panasonic ghetto-blasters. For most of a summer we had these kids clearing out trash and rebuilding trails in the Kohala Mountains. Kele worked them mercilessly. At first, they hated him, me, Hawaii Bound, and anything that reminded them of all the things they missed at home and in the city. Later, there was grudging respect and, eventually, true caring.

The program we set up was designed to push these kids hard. They'd hike all morning with 40-pound packs and then spend afternoons moving rocks, cutting logs, clearing brush, and shoveling dirt. Interspersed with all this was a social and physical "survival" curriculum that was taught on the run. They had to learn how to splint broken legs, how to use Pulaski tools, how to tie bowlines and taut-line hitches, how to pitch tarps so that you can stay dry in two-day downpours, and how to resolve disputes through communication and negotiation (something most adults don't do any better than the "droids"). Most learned things the hard way, but came to understand that our "hoods-in-the-woods" trail crew was a shot at redemption. Most of them were diligent and figured out how to solve interpersonal problems without flashing switchblades. Some never did.

During the trail crew project, on other expeditions, slumped into easy chairs at Hawaii Bound's base camp, or sitting around the embers of a beach fire, Kele and I would talk. Always our conversation was free-ranging. Much of it was armchair theology and bull-session politics interspersed with things cultural and horticultural. Kele was interested in community organizing, environmental protection, nuclear disarmament, agricultural self-sufficiency, and the use of small, home-sized technologies. Most of all, he seemed to be groping toward new forms of participation. How, he'd want to know, do you make government behave itself? How do you go about working with bureaucracies and red tape? And could you really do this without compromising yourself and the ideals that brought you there in the first place? Being an expert bureaucrat and compromiser, I'd share my secret horde of understandings on the subject with him freely.

My interests were more mundane. I wanted to know how to fillet and dry fish, for example. Or what phases of the moon you used to plant taro the way the old Hawaiians did. Or how to sharpen a double-headed ax in the one true way such a thing should always be done. My curiosities ran to self-sufficiency. Not, mind you, as a philosophy of living, but as a set of rediscoverable technologies that would probably be essential to the world our generation must soon relinquish to the next.

Out of this long, slow, simmering stew pot of interactions, I learned many practical things from Kele, including the basic rudiments of net laying, taro pulling, and hog butchering. I greatly admired his perseverance, his native knowledges, and his burning desire to go his own way and yet help the world at the same time. Though his restless and contentious attitudes toward society were obvious, I was confronted by veils of mystery on personal matters. In certain situations and in the company of particular people, he could be prickly, morose, or withdrawn or, alternatively, charming, innocent, and outgoing. Much of what lay behind these chameleonlike qualities was and still is in the realm of private history.

As with the National Park Service, Kele's instinctive contrariness got him in trouble at Hawaii Bound too. Basically, he is an anarchist who hates people telling him what to do — especially regarding things he is good at. He is also a crusader. At a near-genetic level of his being, Kele likes to challenge and change the status quo.

In the Hawaii Bound office, for example, he grumbled about his low salary and the lack of advancement opportunities that the school's full-time staff and directors were offering to instructors. He formed a union and generally agitated for reform. Out in the woods there were problems as well. Complaints rolled in from certain students who had paid good money for what they thought would be a quiet, communal nature experience. On Kele's courses, things never quite worked that way.

On one trip, for example — composed of a group of professional women from the Junior League of Honolulu — he took along his carbine and hunting dogs in violation of the school's rules. Then he shot a 200-pound pig, stripped off the meat and hide, and boiled down the animal's head for several days to separate its tusks from its skull. The women complained. Blood, guts, and a large stew pot filled with a boar's head weren't what they had expected. Alan Hale registered the Junior League's grievances, fended them off with great diplomacy, and added them to a small pile of other problems in Kele's file.

Alan, however, had bigger concerns. Directing everyone's collective dream of a wilderness school was exciting, but it was also a little bit like being the business manager of the Children's Crusade. The school was perennially long on expenses and chronically short of cash. Twenty-four-day courses were, in fact, very expensive propositions. There were food, salaries, liability insurance, equipment, a base camp, a business office, two trucks, four boats, and several thousand interisland air fares to be considered. There was always the additional temptation to take it big — to cut back on the length and quality of the curriculum, to commercialize the venture, and open it up to a potentially large tourist market. Nonetheless, staff, alumni, boosters, and the school's Board of Directors all recognized that touristification would defeat the school's basic purpose. Keeping it "local" was a conscious, strategic, and unanimous decision. It meant maintaining the precious emphasis on local kids, local support, and local impacts. Unfortunately, the numbers didn't work.

In 1980, after more than seven years of running extraordinarily successful backcountry expeditions, the grand experiment finally came to a close. The school would struggle on for another year and a half, but functionally and fiscally, the end had come.

Gathered around the fireplace in the living room of the Waimea base camp, Alan broke the news on a cold, rainy Saturday morning at one of our last summer staff meetings. Expenses had outstripped revenues for too many months in a row, he explained, and the school was going down. For a long time, no one said anything.

As Hawaii Bound spiraled to a close, the staff dispersed into new pursuits, many of them in Honolulu and in California. Kele's path led back into the forests of Puna to his land; to farming, fishing, and itinerant carpentry; to his private dream of creating a self-sufficient wilderness shelter program for runaways, delinquents, and law violators; and to some occasional low-level marijuana growing. We stayed in touch for awhile, but those powerful, wonderful days of working in the mountains and forests of the Big Island — of chasing our collective and individual wilderness dreams together — had come to an end. Hawaii Bound was indeed a starting, turning, and reaffirming point. It was also an ending.

*   *   *

The car scrapes along. I navigate it as best I can over the two muddy ruts, pretending it is actually a large truck. Every once in a while I hit one of the mid- to jumbo-sized boulders sticking out of the mound of soggy dirt in the middle. Carolyn, wide-eyed, asks me if I really know what I am doing. I assure her that I do and that the rent-a-car people ought to be paying me for the successful road test I am giving their new Thunderbird. Axle groaning, oil pan clanking, exhaust pipe dragging, I drive on.

Four turnoffs and a good deal of forest later, we finally come to Kele's place. There is a bony, wall-eyed horse tethered to a bread-fruit tree, and a couple of black dogs are running around. Kele's ambivalence about the world outside his own property starts at the entrance gate. There is a wooden board tacked to a tree that says in large, hand-scrawled letters: Aloha! Nearby is another sign that says: Keep Out!

We turn into the driveway and pull up in front of Kele's pole house. Two more ugly dogs with severe cases of mange sniff me up and down as I climb out of the car. Nobody is home, but there is a note tacked to the side of the porch:

Dear Peter and Carolyn and Kids,

Hope you're having a nice fun trip and sorry about not being here when you arrive. Unforeseen circumstances as I had to go to Hilo to spend the night in jail. I got busted for growing weed. I have an early morning hearing and then I'll be back by noon. Stick around. I really want to see you.

Regards,

Kele

Since it's already midmorning, we decide to stay even though a little voice in the back of my head is telling me Kele may not be back today. To pass the time, we walk around Kele's three-acre homestead.

His place is laid out in traditional Hawaiian style. Rather than one large building, there are a number of smaller structures spaced well apart. There are homes, one of which Kele lives in and two of which he rents or loans out for short periods of time in exchange for work. All three have been constructed on platforms six feet off the ground and have high, sloping, corrugated iron roofs. The roof on Kele's house drains rainwater into a catchment tank. Nearby there is a canoe shed, an uncompleted garage framed with 'ōhi'a poles, an outhouse, and several large storage boxes. The houses have all been positioned in open, grassy areas. All of them have fruit trees growing nearby. About half of Kele's land is visible from his house. The rest is obscured in a scramble of trees and vines.

Our three city kids, wide-eyed, have been prepared. I've told them that Kele doesn't believe in the fopperies of middle-class America so they shouldn't expect to find all of the bourgeois amenities we have gotten accustomed to in Honolulu. "It's simple country living...," I tell them. Based on this innocent clue, Carolyn has taken a few precautions. She has rubbed all three kids down with disinfectant and bug repellant and, with stubborn, vigilant encouragement, made sure that none of them will have to go potty anytime soon.

We start with Kele's place. It is two rooms: an outside lānai, kitchen, and sitting area, and an inside bedroom and storage area. The distinction between inside and outside is somewhat theoretical. Two rooms are divided by a barely visible, semipermeable membrane consisting of a chin-high wall against which are attached a sink and various shelves. The entire house, for that matter, is open on all sides: no window glass, screens, or doors. Black clouds of mosquitoes lurk nearby. In this egalitarian community, bugs, dogs, horse, renters, and visitors are all expected to form alliances and get along with each other.

I walk through the kitchen area holding hands with Dana and Kelly. They don't quite know what to make of all this. "Is this a museum?" Dana asks me. I laugh but the museum analogy is not that far off. Kele's larder, for example, could be an Andy Warhol exhibition. It consists of a long shelf containing a can of pork and beans, a box of baking powder, a can of coffee, several bottles of orange juice, a stick of Old Spice deodorant, a jar of peanut butter, a zip-lock bag with four sprouting potatoes, some tins of sardines, a bottle of spaghetti sauce, a bag of brown rice, and a box of 22-long bullets. Above this shelf is Kele's own art gallery: pictures cut from magazines and stapled into the wood. I notice some new ones since I was here last: magazine photos of Elvis Presley; some American GIs under fire at Khe Sanh in Vietnam; dusty Zulu warriors doing a circle dance in the middle of their village; and a pencil drawing of Diana, the Greek goddess of the hunt, holding a bow and arrow with two large dogs, neither of which has mange, looking up at her lovingly. Like all lived-in places, the house reveals the visions and eccentricities of its owner.

The girls look at everything with wonder and, for a moment, I think of Kele on his visits to us in Honolulu. He had the same general look: curiosity and caution with a tinge of culture shock. A stranger in a strange land, trying to "grok" the meaning of his surroundings. I recall Kele's discomfort at being in a fully enclosed living room, at sitting in soft chairs, at walking on rugs. I remember him in the kitchen, staring at the stove-top grill, at the food processor, at the microwave oven. I imagine him moving through our house, even as we are walking through his, and trying to fathom the strange, domesticated, crowded lives of the people who live there. What would he be thinking and how would he explain it to his kids if he had some?

We climb down the ladder and out of Kele's house and move on to a tool shed. Here we find a makeshift table on sawhorses with the hull of an old lawnmower on it. The guts of the machine are nowhere to be seen. The rest of the room is full of ropes, chains, tools, machetes, cane knives, pruning saws, spare parts for automobiles, an old, out-of-use beehive, and a saddle for Keala, the bony-looking strawberry roan standing in the driveway. Nearby we see the body of a 1951 Chevrolet that Kele has been thinking about restoring for the past three years. It's clear that the matter has not yet been fully decided because vines are growing out of the trunk, giving it a potted plant look.

Everywhere possible, Kele has fruit trees or productive ground plants growing. There are clumps of bananas — Williams, Chinese, Bluefields — and at least three distinct varieties of bread-fruit. There are papaya, cherimoya, avocado, coffee, coconut, and jackfruit trees. He eats some of what these trees produce, sells some of it, and gives a lot to neighbors and friends. There are also small experimental plots of taro and scattered patches of vegetables. On other parts of his land Kele grows various ornamentals: hedges of hibiscus, neat rows of impatiens and coleus, and clumps of monstera and dieffenbachia.

We meander around the property to get a look at the rental houses, cut through a hidden pathway to explore some of his private jungle, and then head back to Kele's place. The black dogs scratch at their mange and feebly wag their tails in the sticky heat. Because the volcano is firing off up-rift, the air is hazy and still. We settle into easy chairs on the porch-kitchen-sitting area and wait.

Pretty soon, a bearded, hatchet-faced man emerges out of the jungle, comes up, and introduces himself. He is dressed in 1960s Berkeley garb: baggy pajama pants, leather sandals, and a beaded cloth shoulder bag filled with fruit. His name is Mike. Mike the Renter. He is subletting one of Kele's pole houses for a few months. "Until I figure out what's happening," he explains. I tell him I can't quite solve that one myself.

With his big smile and gracious manner, Mike seems like a pleasant enough fellow. Kele spent most of the last week in jail on old *paka lōlō* charges. Growing with intent to sell, he thinks. Kele will be back any minute, he tells me. No question. I happen to know that "any minute" in Puna could mean today, tomorrow, next month, or never. We strike up a long rambling conversation.

He says that living in Puna is really fine because there's lots of good food on the trees and nobody bothers you very much. Mike is a drummer. When he needs some money, he plays drums in Hilo for a few weeks. As for dope, there used to be a lot more of it in Puna than there is now and other things are changing. Land values are going up and a lot of Honolulu people are moving in.

"Most of the really heavy duty dealers," he says, "they've moved away... although there's still a few hardcore lowlifes and scumballs hanging around Pāhoa."

I ask him about Kele. "Kele, he's stubborn," says Mike. "He's not what you'd call a big-time dealer but he's hard-headed. And hard-assed. He just won't play by the new rules. He hates rules. And people who like rules, they don't like him."

We talk about mosquitoes and water shortages and then we drift back to the subject of Kele. Kele's current run-in with the law is pretty serious, says Mike. They could put him in jail, fine him $50,000, and take away his land and vehicles.

"That would kill him," I say to Mike. Mike looks at me and solemnly nods in agreement.

The silence that follows is punctuated by the sound of a breadfruit crashing down through the branches and landing with a thump near the house.

"More free food," says Mike the Renter with a huge smile. We shake hands and say our good-byes, and then he slips off and silently disappears into the forest.

Carolyn and I stay in the easy chairs on the *lānai* while the kids wander around. Half an hour later, Kele himself pulls into the driveway, parks his car, jumps out, and greets us. He hugs Carolyn, pumps my hand, and pats the kids on the head. Glancing at the rented Thunderbird I'm driving, his eyes scrunch up and he says with a grin, "Stepping up in the world a bit, aren't you, Adler?" For a man who has just spent the night in the pokey and who may be headed for hard time, Kele is in remarkably good spirits. I ask him what's going on.

The charges, he explains, are old ones. Trial is still a month away and this re-arrest is actually a formality. Despite the casualness of his reply, I can tell that Kele is worried about the outcome. He talks about it more seriously, and, as contemptuous and dismissive as he is of authority, it becomes obvious that the whole affair has shaken him to the core. The threat of heavy fines, loss of property, and hard time is serious. Kele tells us that he is finally ready to make some changes. He looks me in the eye and says: "I'm going to clean things up and turn it all around. Maybe I'll finish my B.A. and go to law school. Or become a journalist. Who knows," he says with a flourish. "I might even get married."

He seems optimistic and determined, but I also wonder if all of this is wishful thinking. I've heard it before. "You mean if you can find someone to put up with you," I tell him. Kele smiles and changes the subject by asking if we've met Keala. I tell him we've seen each other around although we haven't been formally introduced. We saunter out to the driveway while Kele tells us about his horse.

"He's got a mean streak, no question about it," says Kele with a laugh. "In fact, he sort of thinks like a human. Like me, anyway. One day I was inside the house washing up when I realized I'd forgotten to give him water. I walked down with no clothes on and started filling his water tub. You know what the bugger did when I bent over? He bit me in the ass!"

Kele whistles for Keala. The dogs leap up out of the dust and race over, four tails and heads wagging in syncopated rhythm. The wall-eyed horse totally ignores us. Then he looks up from his grazing, cocks his ears, snorts, stares at us with large, piggy eyes, and, with a swish of his tail, lowers his nose back into the grass. Kele laughs and bows to reality. We pet Keala for awhile and then walk around other parts of the farm. Kele talks casually about his banana crop and the dry taro plants he is testing and about the chickens he occasionally keeps around to eat centipedes. Corey, Kelly, and Dana listen intently. "These fellahs," he says, spanning the forefingers on both hands, "are 10 inches long and have a sting worse than a scorpion. And they're all over here." With a grin, he tells them: "I like to grab them centipedes by the neck and pinch their nasty little heads off."

As we walk, the talk turns to politics. And when it does, Kele's entire demeanor transforms. A visible hardening. The granite look. Arms folded across his chest, Kele tells me about the giant hotels and condominiums that are being built in North Kohala.

"You remember when we used to camp at 'Anaeho'omalu Beach, Peter?" he asks. "The Sheraton has built the biggest, ugliest hotel you could possibly imagine up there." Kele suddenly slams his right fist into the palm of his hand. His face twists into a sneer. "I'd like to bomb those bastards into oblivion," he snarls.

I counter the anger with banter. "If I ever get to be president, Kele, I promise you that the very first thing I'll do is make the Sheraton Company tear it down. I'll make them put every last little lava rock, *kiawe* thorn, and beer can right back where they found it. And when they ask me why, I'll tell them it's because they pissed off my friend Kele!"

Kele laughs and we amble on. As we walk, the girls ask him questions. Kele is at his absolute best when he is with children. He is, in fact, a different man: patient, relaxed, gentle. For example, Corey is interested in his dogs. He tells her how all four of them are descended from Keoki, the hunting dog he lost in the Kohala Mountains when we were still with Hawaii Bound. Talking about his lost dog brings back an old sadness. He tells her what a brave hunter Keoki was and about pig hunting and how some dogs are trained to be "trackers" and others are "grabbers." As he explains all this, I watch him and listen. With adults, myself and Carolyn included, there is always a certain reticence, an unease, a holding back. I know that constellation of emotions also. It's a reluctance to engage in the chatter of cocktail conversations and the jousting of first impressions. With kids, though, Kele is different. He smiles a lot and gives freely without being patronizing. As if he knows that a child's apolitical world is a more guileless place that is less likely to hurt him.

After a time, the talk turns back to the land and its future. Walking around with his hands in his pockets, Kele says: "You know, half of my idea has been to fill this place up with lots of fruit trees and make it as totally self-sufficient as possible. The other half has always involved bringing kids who are screwed-up out here to live and work. I keep believing that being outdoors and learning about Hawaiian culture and about the land are the keys to long-term survival for these kids."

We stop. Kele bends over and plucks a strand of grass and sticks it in his mouth. I ask him if he is still working toward that goal. Does the dream still stand?

For a moment, there is no answer. With an audible sigh, he says: "Couple of years ago I thought it was going to be easy. We'd raise a little money from some rich foundations and start another school like Hawaii Bound. I still want to do all that but, god, it just gets harder and harder...."

Then Kele's voice fades off. I've touched a nerve. He knows that I know it. He pulls back. I want to follow him as he retreats along some cobbled, inner trail of yearnings and memories, but Kele is alone. It is impossible to be with him. Very suddenly, he seems old and tired. As if all of the spirit, all of the life-loving, world-hating, rule-bending, authority-questioning energy inside him is in jeopardy. As if life itself is just too hard and complicated and dangerous to deal with.

*   *   *

In the early afternoon, I fix a plate of Hawaiian Malnutrition Prevention Sandwiches and serve them up with glasses of orange juice. Each one of these delectables is made up of a single slice of heavy-duty seven-grain bread with a huge gob of homemade peanut butter slathered down on top of it. Each sandwich also has half a banana pressed down firmly into the middle of the peanut butter. The entire mucoid mass is then lightly glazed with fresh, mashed avocado. We eat cross-legged on straw mats in the dust, scratching, sweating, and swatting as we share our food with a small airborne armada of gnats, mosquitoes, fruit flies and house flies.

After lunch, Carolyn and I load the three girls into the T-Bird and follow Kele, who drives his own car, to a small beach a few miles down the road. There is a communal canoe there that belongs to Kele and a half dozen other New Punans who have built a canoe shed and purchased the boat for fishing and diving. The kids want to take a ride. We carry the 200-pound hull over some large boulders and down to the black-sand beach. Then we put life preservers on the little kids and launch off between 3 foot wave sets. Carolyn watches from shore.

Kele steers. I'm in the bow. It's been a long time since I was in an outrigger canoe. I lean into the rhythm of the ocean slowly. Gradually, long-unused paddling muscles start to remember. The canoe rises and falls with the swells as we head out into open water. As we plunge through a wave, spray sweeps over the boat. The girls squeal with delight as they grip the gunwales. Several hundred yards out, we stop paddling. Time for a swim.

I turn around and see Kele balancing on the deck of the stern. He is standing at attention, arms down, fingers curling toward his thighs. I see the concentration in his face and I notice the two tattoos on his shoulders, a fish on one side, an eagle on the other. He relaxes and then executes a perfect backflip into the warm, blue water. I dive in from the bow and Corey jumps over the side from the middle. Dana and Kelly stay in the boat. The rest of us dive and swim around the canoe and then climb back in and just float and talk in the bright sunlight.

Kele tells another story about Keoki. Corey, who loves dogs to the point where she wouldn't mind being one, props her head on her arms and listens intently. The story is about a canoe ride off the northwest corner of the Big Island. Kele and Alan Hale had checked out one of the school's 18-foot outriggers and launched off from Kawaihae for the day with a sack of sandwiches, two fishing poles, and Keoki. Three or four miles out from shore, the dog started barking madly, as a good hunting dog does when it picks up the scent of game. Kele looked around and couldn't see anything. Then, a few minutes later and a short distance away, a pod of humpback whales surfaced. Kele says he had to hold Keoki down to prevent him from leaping into the water after them.

An hour later, we paddle to shore, wait for the right moment, and then land the canoe between building wave sets. We haul it back up to the canoe shed, hang up the life preservers, paddles, and bailers, and then go back down to bodysurf along the shore wash and dry ourselves in the sun. For a time, we lie in the sand talking. Slowly all of us drowse off into sleep.

In the late afternoon, the sun starts its descent. Kele and I swap memories and preoccupations and then, slowly, hesitantly, he asks me if I would consider doing him a great favor. He wants me to write a "To Whom It May Concern" letter that will eventually be placed before the judge at his sentencing on the old marijuana charges. In it, he wants me to act as a character witness and, in effect, ask the court to be lenient.

Kele's request puts me in a quandary. I happen to know the judge involved. I have great respect for him and I think he, in turn, has good regard for me. So if I write the letter and Kele screws up, my own credibility is shot. On the other hand, Kele is a special friend. If I don't stand by him, who will? I sense the dignity and desperation tugging at each other inside him. Kele doesn't belabor the matter. He simply asks me to consider it. I ask him a few questions as we walk up the trail from the beach and when we get to the cars, it's time to say good-bye.

The fastest way back to Waimea for us lies west on Old Ocean Road and then north through Pāhoa. Kele's house lies the other way. We shake hands where the road forks and mumble about getting together again soon. Neither of us quite knows what "soon" really means, but both of us know it will happen when it happens. Kele hugs Carolyn, then the kids and then, shyly, awkwardly, he gives me a hug too. Then he gets into his car and takes off. We climb into the Thunderbird and, with a setting sun in front of us, begin the long drive back to Waimea.

Some days later I compose a letter to the judge. I tell him that I've known Kele for close to fifteen years, that he is at heart one of the more honorable but hard-headed human beings that I've ever met, and that incarcerating him would probably not do Kele or society very much good. Moreover, I suggest, it would squander a talent that is much needed in Hawai'i. His dream, I continue, is to salvage kids who are in trouble, take them into the woods, and guide them through some of the challenges of the wilderness and of their own impending adulthood. It is a good dream, I write, and perhaps with the court's help he can begin to achieve it.

A month goes by and finally Kele drops me a card. He has at last been convicted and sentenced. The verdict, however, is Kele's last shot at redemption. Eight weekends in jail, 200 hours of community service, a one-year suspended sentence. The implications are clear. One more screw-up and Kele will be facing longer-term time. The card is signed, "Aloha Pakalolo! - Kele" but, when I think about it later, I can't tell whether "Aloha" means hello, love, or good-bye.

* * *

Kele and I don't see each other as much as we used to — two or three times a year at most and then by accident. Our paths are different and my work keeps me in Honolulu. I mediate conflicts, among other things. I get involved in disputes and fights as the middleman. I enter the frays that rend our community, that embroil us in controversy, that tear at the fabric of our Island society. Once there, I search for the common ground and try to help people negotiate. I move between and among the forces in conflict seeking to build consensus. It is my work and my nature and the results are usually pragmatic. When I succeed, everyone gains, but no one gets everything he or she wants. In this role, in the constant swirl of these disputes, I strive to stay neutral and calm. I am the eye of the hurricane.

But sometimes I think of him. I'll read something — about the progressive destruction of the Earth's ozone layer, for example, or the further diminishing of native animals and plants. Or I'll hear an old Beatles song from the late 1960s, or maybe I'll pick up a copy of Mother Jones Magazine. Or I'll be listening to the ten o'clock news and hear about the manipulations and gambits of people fighting with each other over public decisions. Suddenly, I'm with him in Puna, watching the world from a slightly different angle and worrying whether the human species can survive its own successes. And then I worry also about the neutrality of my involvement and whether all those meetings and deals I help create make a difference to anyone. And I wonder, when the last word is said and the rubber hits the road, about the dreams of fifteen years ago and whether I haven't truly sold out.

And Kele's goal of starting another wilderness school on his farm in Puna? It's possible, of course, and surely he'll pursue it in his own serendipitous manner, but somehow I don't think it will happen. The other dream, though, the big one behind it, the one that's a process and not a destination, that one he's already achieved. Kele may be a doper and a daydreamer, but he is also descended from a deeper tradition that runs through the philosophical veins of certain Americans. Walt Whitman, for example. Tom Paine. And, especially, Henry David Thoreau. Inherently such people take the notion of independence personally. They "resist much and obey little" and they refuse to run with the pack.

I recognize that for the Keles of the world, the quest for freedom is a constant struggle and is rarely, if ever, completely realized. More often the search is ephemeral, filled with solitudes that verge on despair and a stubborn pride that too often turns on self and others in anger. Authority and bureaucracy don't tolerate such people lightly. Nonetheless I know that the Keles of the world are critically important to who we are as a people.

But I confess, finally, that I don't truly understand Kele very well. Nor do I think that living in Puna in his manner is inherently healthy. Quite the opposite. Sometimes I think that Kele and all the others like him in Puna are *mō ka piko* or burdened with *'olo* gourds, those ancient "garlands of waiting." Still, I know that Kele's world has been — and continues to be — a part of my own vision of a fork in the road ahead. At that juncture, one path leads to heaven and the other to an endless mediation about heaven. I am uneasy not only about his choices, but about my own. "The universe is like a safe to which there is a combination," wrote Peter DeVries, "but the combination is locked up in the safe."

In my dream, the one that I catch short glimpses of through Kele, Carolyn and I and the kids finally leave the city. We find our own small patch of forest by the ocean or in the mountains or down in the desert lands of the island of Hawai'i and we simply disappear. We leave the regimented world of eight-hour office days behind us and we say good-bye to television and current events. We search out and find a place to grow in better ways, a place greener and somehow more fundamentally honest.

And there, maybe — with luck and imagination and with a few other people like Kele — we will wait out the twentieth century to see if our souls really do catch up.

8

Wounded Island

*Wake up! Our islands are slipping away.
While you sleep, we are standing on the
edge of darkness.*

Uncle Luther Makekau

THE HAWAIIAN ARCHIPELAGO REACHES UP FROM THE OCEAN FLOOR and spreads out like a necklace of emeralds — 132 pinnacles, reefs, and shoals stretching 1,500 miles across the central Pacific basin. Of these landfalls, eight islands make up 99% of the land area. Seven are permanently inhabited: Ni'ihau, Kaua'i, O'ahu, Maui, Moloka'i, Lāna'i, and Hawai'i. The eighth is Kaho'olawe, a 45-square-mile island situated eight miles off the southern coast of Maui. By most measures, Kaho'olawe is the driest, windiest, and least habitable of the major Islands. It has also been one of the most controversial pieces of real estate in the United States.

To understand the saga of Kaho'olawe, what it means to different local people, and what it may come to mean in the near future to everyone, requires a bit of patience. It is not just one story but many stories that cascade into one another, mingle, fold, mix, and finally amalgamate into something that is greater than the sum of its parts. Some of these accounts center on events that happened centuries ago. Others are still occurring.

To begin, the island is small — 11 miles long by 6-1/2 wide — and off the main tourist path. Casual visitors are not allowed, and few would want to go there even if they could. There are no rain forests, waterfalls, or quaint plantation towns. Most often it is described as a wasteland, a barren and forgotten landscape made up of eroding hills, crumbling sea cliffs, grass, cactus, and mesquite.

On windy days, clouds of red dust rise up from the Island, shrouding it from view. Centuries ago, geologists tell us, Kaho'olawe was fully forested, but today 15 feet of its topsoil has been lost to erosion and 85% of its surrounding reefs are drowned in silt. Nonetheless, there are some folks on Maui who claim that Kaho'olawe offers the best offshore fishing in Hawai'i. Then again, there are some lifelong residents of the state who could not tell you precisely where Kaho'olawe is.

Kaho'olawe's cultural and political history is also complex. Some chants remembered by the Hawaiian people refer to the Island as a landmark on the old Polynesian voyaging route to Tahiti and as the mother Island that gave birth to all the other Islands in the chain. Its earliest, most ancient name means "the shining vagina of the sea."

At various later times, records show Kaho'olawe to have been a fishing station, a prison colony, a sheep farm, a cattle ranch, and the proposed site for a thermonuclear power plant. From the early 1950s to 1990 the Island was used as a U.S. Navy bombing and gunnery range — a large target for combined air, sea, and land assaults. Today, it is still controlled by the Federal government and the military but the bombing has been stopped, at least temporarily. Moreover, the people of the State of Hawai'i are expecting to see the Island returned to local control sometime in the very near future. The navy — a formidable economic and social presence in Hawai'i — is not pleased with this.

Baked ocher by the sun, swept low by wind and age, Kaho'olawe was bombed and shelled continuously for nearly fifty years. The navy's justification for its use of the Island was — and still is — based on national defense. "There really is no other place in the Pacific where shore bombardment can be done simultaneously with ground fire," explained ex–Third Fleet Kaho'olawe Project Officer Charles Crockett. "The roughly 8,000 acres that are used as an impact area provide a valuable variety of realistic targets including airfields, actual truck convoys, and pin-point targets."

The navy's preemptive use of Kaho'olawe has not gone unchallenged. Since 1976 a group of young Hawaiian activists calling themselves the Protect Kaho'olawe 'Ohana have sought to halt the bombing and return the Island to the Hawaiian people. In its short lifetime, the PKO — or simply the 'Ohana, which means "family" — has become the navy's nemesis by turning the target island into a rallying point and the spearhead of a much broader cultural clash.

The issue of Kaho'olawe is fraught with contradictions. Owned by the State, leased to the military, and governed by a 1953 Presidential Executive Order, the Island was, for several years, the subject of a massive lawsuit. The litigation, *Aluli v. Brown*, charged the Department of Defense with violations of (1) Federal standards for water, noise, and air pollution; (2) the First Amendment rights of Hawaiians; (3) laws that guarantee marine mammal and endangered species protection; (4) laws designed to protect historic places; and (5) the rights of religious access promised under the American Indian Religious Freedom Act.

Arguments over Kaho'olawe have also not been restricted to the courtroom. Depending on whom one listens to in the 50th state, the issue can be viewed either as a minor, regional controversy instigated by a few late-blooming student radicals or as one of the major front lines of the new Hawaiian revolution. Abandoned and forbidden to most people, Kaho'olawe has elicited a steady chorus of rumblings from the 'Ohana, the navy, local archaeologists, politicians, judges, reporters, and the larger Hawaiian community, which remains divided over the issue. Kaho'olawe is the center of one of the most rancorous controversies in the Islands and because of this, it attracts rhetoric the way a picnic draws ants.

Charles Kenn, an elderly part-Hawaiian denying Kaho'olawe's religious significance at a 1977 trial: "There is no such thing as Hawaiian religion today." An exhortation from an 'Ohana brochure: "Kaho'olawe will become the model of an alternative value structure for the Hawaiian people of today, as well as for the U.S. and the rest of the world." And a West Coast correspondent for a syndicated chain of newspapers: "In my opinion, these Hawaiians are going to shove that island, rock by rock, to the Navy."

Or take Elmer Cravalho, former mayor of Maui County, which includes the island of Kaho'olawe: "My position is that the bombing should stop immediately and the Island be turned over to the state at which time we can decide its future use." Or U.S. Senator Daniel Inouye in 1978: "Without wanting to be the Navy's apologist, I think they have been very cooperative." Or former Rear Admiral Thomas B. Hayward: "I am disturbed by the absence of appreciation for the Navy's need for Kaho'olawe." And a poetry class at the Kamehameha III Primary School in Lahaina, Maui:

> Kahoolawe, I love you
> Kahoolawe say you love me too
> I've only seen you from a distance
> I wish I could see you up close.

> Robin Bodinus, Grade 5

and:

> Kahoolawe
> poor island of Hawai'i
> it must be painful
> when all those big bombs hit.
> Unfortunately they don't miss.

> Keith Karlo, Grade 5

* * *

If geography, as is sometimes asserted, is a prime determinant of destiny, then the fate of Hawai'i is inextricably linked with its isolation. Island life is life in an echo chamber, a self-contained universe in which cultural traditions, politics, and public opinion resound back and forth in barely predictable ways. Sometimes the reverberations come roaring into the lives of people like a hurricane. More often, they take the form of hearsay, gossip, equivocation, and suspicion.

Each Wednesday at 5:00 p.m. in a conference room at the Legal Aid Society, the Protect Kaho'olawe 'Ohana comes together to plan strategy. The sessions begin with a four-way conference call to 'Ohana supporters on the neighbor islands. If the press of Kaho'olawe business is light, the meeting is likely to turn into a party with music, food, and story. If more serious affairs need attending to, a fierce, eloquent, and slightly unruly tactics session will ensue, inevitably lasting late into the night.

Because the 'Ohana is a coalition that defines itself in both spiritual and political terms, it attracts an unusual assortment of people. Nearly all are Hawaiians or Asians. Most are Christians, but there are also Buddhists, Pele worshippers, and other native traditionalists who follow 'aumākua, their family gods. There is David Ka'iwi, the leader of a Judeo-Hawaiian cult, who occasionally stops in from Kaua'i. There are Secessionists, Socialists, Democratic Monarchists, Maoists, Democrats, and — once in a great while and seemingly by sheer accident — some tortured version of a Republican.

There are the kūpuna, the elders, like Peggy Ha'o Ross, an articulate, full-blooded Hawaiian who considers herself to be the Queen Pro Tem of the Sovereign Nation of Native Hawaiians. In 1990, she ran for Governor, and Willie Nelson gave a benefit concert to raise funds for her candidacy. Many other 'Ohana members are students or blue-collar workers. There are also babes in arms. Old and young alike, no constitution binds them together. There is no formal roster of membership and no set of bylaws. The 'Ohana is "family," a kinship of people descended from the first taro stalk planted in the mythic past and bound together by blood. Grounded in cultural history and adapted to the present, 'Ohana is a living concept with its own rules and its own built-in mechanisms for resolving disputes. Older Hawaiians are addressed with great honor as "Aunty" or "Uncle." Each person, of whatever age or status, is given time to speak. Every meeting begins and ends standing in a circle holding hands, with a prayer spoken in Hawaiian.

One of the meetings I attend is a debriefing of the fifth "access." Two dozen men and women crowd into the conference room, half of them sitting on the floor. Someone has a jar of homemade pickled mango slices, thick red chunks of sour fruit that get gobbled down as fast as they are passed around. Aunty Mallaca, the oldest kupuna present and a woman much loved for her sincerity and wit, gives the opening prayer. The meeting begins. There is considerable tension. The most recent landing on Kaho'olawe has gone badly and a rift has developed between the O'ahu and Moloka'i Hawaiians.

Monthly access to Kaho'olawe is a concession wrung from the navy under the American Indian Religious Freedom Act, but each trip must be separately negotiated and coordinated with the navy's official Third Fleet spokesman and Project Officer for Kaho'olawe. During an access, the 'Ohana typically sets up a base camp and spends three to ten days clearing trails, searching for historic sites, and seeking blessings for the desecrated Island through dance, chant, and prayer. The amateur archaeological work is important for cultural reasons and also strategically. The 'Ohana hopes one day to qualify Kaho'olawe for the National Register of Historic Places, a move that potentially would curtail the navy's use of the Island.

On the fifth access, however, something went wrong. A contingent from Moloka'i overstayed its time on the Island, forcing the navy to postpone a day of training and evacuate 26 'Ohana members by Coast Guard cutter. It was a diplomatic and public relations blunder for the Hawaiians, who — according to the agreements they have forced the navy into making — must scrupulously abide by the terms for lengths of stay.

This access appears to have been a victim of poor planning and disorganized leadership. Richard Kinney, one of the designated co-leaders for the trip, reads a written report explaining why he found it necessary to abdicate his role because of a personal religious crisis. Aunty Peggy Ha'o Ross, proud, poised, and iron-willed, defends the Moloka'i contingent from accusations by the O'ahu people. After 45 minutes of angry and impassioned remarks, the dialogue ends in tears and mutual apologies. Bo Kahui, chairman for the meeting, moves on to new business.

There are several small items, each of which generates debate. An accounting for revenues from the sale of "Stop the Bombing" T-shirts is given. A resolution of support for another group of activists is passed. Then come the plans for the next access. Among those invited are several local botanists who will search for rare and endangered plants, an archaeologist from the Bishop Museum, a marine mammal specialist who will document the off-shore migrations of humpback whales, and an ordnance disposal expert who will try — unofficially — to estimate the cost of clearing the Island. Distrusting the navy's opinions on this subject, the 'Ohana is bringing in its own consultant from Arizona.

Late in the meeting, Emmett Aluli arrives, his plane delayed by bad weather. Leadership in the 'Ohana is shared by many people, but Aluli, a young physician from Moloka'i, is the group's foremost strategist, spokesman, and visionary. Aluli inherited his chief organizer role in 1977 from George Helm, the 'Ohana's founder. Under other circumstances it would be Helm's name appearing as plaintiff in the lawsuit against the navy. Instead, it is Emmett's. Calmly, quietly, he reports on a mainland meeting with Indian tribal leaders fighting issues similar to those of Kaho'olawe: the misuse of, and denial of access to, traditionally sacred lands. After more discussion, the four-and-one-half-hour meeting comes to an end. Aunty Mallaca says the final blessing and prays for the health of the 'Ohana and the renewal of Kaho'olawe.

*   *   *

Although the Protect Kaho'olawe 'Ohana is one of many groups advocating Hawaiian rights, it has often been recognized as one of the most clearly focused, the most vocal, and the most confrontational. Many apolitical Hawaiians who might disagree with the 'Ohana's tactics are also in strong sympathy with the 'Ohana's purposes. They may quarrel about the future of the people of Hawai'i, but they share a common and passionate view of past injustices. Hawaiian history, they argue, is nothing less than a series of betrayals by the English, the French, the Russians, the Americans, and the Japanese. Hawaiians will also acknowledge the greed and shortsightedness of some of their own chiefs who traded away precious land for whiskey and silk. The result of all this, they point out, is a culture and homeland that has been steamrollered by explorers, missionaries, sugar and pineapple planters, and, most recently, investors from foreign countries.

Today most Hawaiians seek some form of redress. Influenced by the movements of other native peoples and the civil rights struggles of Blacks and Hispanics, aware of their own disenfranchisement, many are demanding direct compensation like the billion dollars and 40 million acres of land that have been awarded to native Alaskans. Hawaiians claim an enormous inheritance. Reparations and sovereignty measures for Hawaiians continue to be introduced in Congress and are gaining momentum.

For many Hawaiians, however, a strategic cultural victory is just as important as compensatory dollars. And the place to begin, says the 'Ohana, is Kaho'olawe, the most abused Island in the Hawaiian archipelago and the most obvious symbol of U.S. domination. More than any other piece of land, the rescue and restoration of Kaho'olawe should serve as the beginning of a formal apology to the Hawaiian people. Those 'Ohana members who have actually spent time on the little Island during legal and illegal accesses speak of it in reverent terms. "Kaho'olawe," says a Hawaiian professor from the University, "is the vanguard of our renaissance. We're working our way back to our artistic, agricultural, and ocean-oriented roots. The next step is to reclaim what every other immigrant group has sought to acquire and keep for its own descendants — the land."

Within the 'Ohana, Kaho'olawe represents many things. For some, it is simply a means toward other ends they find more important. For others, it is a maximum assertion of ethnicity. In the dreams and visions of the most mystical Hawaiians, Kaho'olawe is not just a piece of inanimate real estate to be haggled over with the navy, but an evocation of deep racial memories, a way of life in which the heart blood of an entire culture can be renewed. Even for the pragmatists, land has crucial cultural meanings because it is understood to be "alive."

Kaho'olawe represents all of these traditional and contemporaneous thoughts brought together. It is a vision based on hunting, fishing, farming, and living on the land in the manner of one's ancestors. Precisely where politics and mysticism intersect, the 'Ohana has developed a strategy that speaks to these most fundamental beliefs of all Hawaiians: that the land and the people of the taro are intrinsically connected, and that they flourish or perish in mutual proportion. As they always have. As they always will.

* * *

"Without question," a political science professor at the University of Hawai'i once remarked, "the 'Ohana is the most persistent, articulate, and successful group of activists operating in the Hawaiian Islands today." Although such a statement might generate debate from other groups, few observers would deny the 'Ohana its triumphs. In just a few short years the 'Ohana has scored key political, legal, and media victories. It has gained legal access to Kaho'olawe, forced the navy to file and comply with an environmental impact statement, discovered numerous archaeological sites, and halted — at least for the time being — the navy's bombing. Yet success for Hawaiians in their homeland never comes easy. The 'Ohana has paid dearly, and no price was more painful than the deaths of George Helm and Kimo Mitchell.

In 1975, the bombing of Kaho'olawe was a routine event in the Islands, publicly unquestioned but for a few grumblers living on Maui's south shore who were upset by the thumps and thuds of daily bombing runs. The Protect Kaho'olawe 'Ohana did not exist. Instead, a few scattered residents on the island of Moloka'i (some 30 miles away) were engrossed in issues of their own. Led by Emmett Aluli and Walter Ritte, then students at the University, the Moloka'i people sought to open public rights-of-way to beaches traditionally used by Hawaiians for foraging and fishing but closed off in recent times by developers. The right of "access" seemed pertinent to other lands as well, and someone — nobody quite remembers who — suggested Kaho'olawe, which had been off-limits to local people since 1941. "I don't remember whose idea it was," says Charlie Warrington, an early 'Ohana leader. "We just became aware of what was happening and decided to make it a symbol of misuse of the land."

Early in 1976, George Helm, an up-and-coming musician from Moloka'i, joined the fledgling group and helped instigate a series of illegal landings on the target Island. The first — not yet called an "access" — was more a Bicentennial stunt than a serious intrusion. Of the nine people landed on the Island, seven were picked up and hauled off by the military as soon as they arrived. "You know the only reason we didn't get caught immediately?" Walter Ritte said rhetorically, describing the 48 hours he and Emmett Aluli spent on the island. "I had to go to the bathroom." Ritte and Aluli took some toilet paper and walked off.

After discovering what looked to be ancient temple sites, Ritte and Aluli, powerfully moved by their experiences, gave themselves up two days later. Realizing that Kaho'olawe was an exceptional "access" issue because of the potential confrontation with the military, the Moloka'i group began to organize more earnestly and the Protect Kaho'olawe 'Ohana formed. Small supporting chapters were founded on each of the major Islands. It was a youthful movement; most older Hawaiians refused to join, arguing that Kaho'olawe was worthless.

As the 'Ohana began to gather momentum, most of the fundraising and political effort shifted from Moloka'i to Honolulu. From the first access, however, and until his death in the waters off Kaho'olawe in 1977, Moloka'i-based George Helm served as chief strategist. Aluli, Ritte, Warrington, and others recognized his dedicated and energetic leadership. According to those who knew him well, Helm was a charismatic man with a brooding and passionate intellect. He was also known for his lilting voice and his ability as a slack-key guitarist. Brought up on a Moloka'i farm, he was sent off to school in Honolulu, where he was duly dubbed a "country boy" and teased for his homemade clothes and pidgin English.

In the 1960s, he became a college dropout ("I couldn't see much sense in anything they were teaching"). Talented and driven by forces he couldn't fully articulate, Helm drifted deeper into his music and, through it, into a search for his spiritual and cultural roots. He was also a voracious reader. At his death, his extensive library included volumes on politics, philosophy, Hawaiian language and history, art, Zen, Jungian psychology, and world religion. As the Kaho'olawe issue came into focus, so did Helm. He began to view the troubled Island's destiny as inextricably entwined with the fate of the Hawaiian people. He pursued the issue relentlessly.

Jackie Leilani, an announcer known as the "Honolulu Skylark" on KCCN, the only all-Hawaiian radio station at the time, and an outspoken leader in the 'Ohana of the 1980s, remembers George with admiration. "It was as if the Island possessed him. Once when we were talking he told me he thought he would die for it — and I said, please George, don't do that. We need you." From his reading and his talks with *kūpuna*, the elders he revered so much, Helm sought to distill his knowledge and reconcile the sometimes conflicting forces working within him. Eventually, the strands of his thinking — some mystical, some political — fused in the concept of *aloha 'āina*: the enormous love Hawaiians feel for the land and the historical and cultural imperative they have to protect it. *Aloha 'āina* became the 'Ohana's guiding philosophical principle.

A pragmatist as well as a visionary, Helm pushed the 'Ohana into big-time politics. For a time it appeared Helm had won over the State legislature and Hawai'i's congressional delegation. Senior Senator Daniel Inouye led efforts to halt the bombing from Washington, but the 'Ohana's trust in Inouye evaporated when he proposed compromises unacceptable to them. Then, in 1976, Helm and other PKO spokespeople flew to Washington to seek new allies in the Departments of Justice, Defense, and the Interior; in the Council of Historic Places; and in what was then the Federal American Indian Program. They found no tangible support but returned to Hawai'i armed with new information.

A two-pronged strategy evolved. Claiming that Kaho'olawe was of enormous religious and historic importance, the 'Ohana filed its fourteen-point lawsuit against the navy. Then, to call attention to the suit, they decided to stage a well-publicized but clearly illegal "access" onto the Island as an act of civil disobedience.

In January, Helm, Ritte, Richard Sawyer, and several others landed on Kaho'olawe covertly. Ritte and Sawyer carried enough food and water for a two-week stay. The others, lightly provisioned, returned to Honolulu after two days to announce that Sawyer and Ritte intended to stay on Kaho'olawe until the bombing was stopped once and for all. During the first two weeks of their access, Ritte and Sawyer hid out in the high brush and scrub on Kaho'olawe's northeast slope, moving down to the ocean at night to fish and bathe. Three weeks into their "occupation," the navy dispatched 100 marines and a fleet of helicopters to track them down. Playing a constant game of hide-and-go-seek, Ritte and Sawyer managed to evade the marines. The weeks turned into a month. On the thirty-fifth day, with food and water low and bombing runs resumed, they decided to declare victory and give themselves up. The point, they believed, had been made. But it was not quite that simple. Walter Ritte would later remember the irony. "For two days, with jets shrieking over us, we tried to get off the Island, lighting bonfires, sending smoke signals, flashing mirrors. Nobody saw us."

Even as Ritte and Sawyer were making every effort to get captured, George Helm was preparing to go find them; he had dreamed that they were in trouble. Others had dreams as well. Emma de Fries, known, respected and even feared by some for her powers of vision and foresight, warned Helm of danger, rough waters, and a failure to heed the signs. Concerned for the safety of his friends and worn out from months of frenzied organizing, Helm disregarded her advice and went ahead.

On March 5, Helm, Billy Mitchell, and Kimo Mitchell (one of the best watermen in the Islands) landed on Kaho'olawe in a small powerboat driven by Sluggo Hahn of Maui. They carried with them four canteens of fresh water, swim fins, an inner tube, a transistor radio, spare clothing, and two seven-foot surfboards. Hahn returned to Maui with an agreed-upon pick-up time — but because of boat problems, the pick-up never occurred. For two days, Helm and the Mitchells combed Kaho'olawe's underbrush unsuccessfully searching hiding places known to the 'Ohana. On March 7, they made their decision to return to Maui by surfboard.

About the time Sawyer and Ritte finally were being picked up by the military, George, Kimo, and Billy were putting their boards in the water at the opposite end of Kaho'olawe. The events of the following hours remain a mystery. According to Billy Mitchell, Helm — injured by a rock while entering the water — seemed to be racked by spirits but was still capable of paddling. With Billy on one board and Kimo and George on the other, they headed southwest across the 8-mile 'Alalākeiki Channel. The literal meaning of

'Alalākeiki is "child's wail." Three miles short of Maui they en-
countered high winds, rough waves, and a strong offshore current.
Somewhere in that turbulence, Billy lost sight of George and Kimo.
Realizing the futility of pushing on to Maui, he turned back to
Kaho'olawe, landed, found a squadron of marines, and reported
that George and Kimo were in trouble.

The search started immediately. The Coast Guard, the navy and
a flotilla of local fishing boats hastily organized by the 'Ohana
scoured the waters off Kaho'olawe for days. When George's surfboard turned up 13 miles southeast of Lana'i the search area was
expanded. Twenty-one days and 7,500 square miles later, the
Coast Guard called it off. George Helm and Kimo Mitchell were
listed as "missing at sea" and presumed drowned or killed by
sharks off the coast of Maui. Those tense twenty-one days were
marked by an ironic and bittersweet alliance between the 'Ohana
and the military. Uncle Harry Mitchell, a 60-year-old farmer, carpenter, and fisherman, recalled, "When I was searching for my son
and George on Kaho'olawe, I was sitting down and two marines
looked at me. I say, you guys no more cigarettes? No, they say, two
days now. Here, I say, take this full pack and look good at my face.
Some day you gonna hunt me down on this Island too. When you
catch me that day, I like my cigarettes back."

In the wake of George's death, the 'Ohana floundered and
almost dissolved. Accusations that his death was engineered by a
local "godfather" were leveled at a part-Hawaiian politician. The
charges generated a libel suit, which was later dismissed. Daniel
Inouye again offered proposals that would allow, temporarily, joint
uses of Kaho'olawe. The proposals were rejected by the 'Ohana.
Tensions boiled to the surface and two factions within the 'Ohana
fought for leadership. The losers — Walter Ritte and Richard
Sawyer — moved their families to remote Pelekunu Valley on
Moloka'i "to live like our ancestors."

Exhausted from grieving and infighting, the 'Ohana reorganized
and Emmett Aluli assumed the leadership role left vacant by the
untimely death of George Helm. The PKO then turned its attention to the lawsuit issues — but with a new strategy: prove beyond
the shadow of a doubt that Kaho'olawe is archaeologically and

historically important. With this in mind, the days of illegal trespass came to an end.

* * *

Very few things seem to happen at the right time and of their own accord. The rest, suggested Herodotus in 400 B.C., never happen at all. He went on to argue that it is the job of the historian to correct the defects inherent in understanding the past and make sensible what is otherwise nonsensical. Most historians fill such voids with thoughtful theories and speculations. Archaeologists, on the other hand, are the pathologists of history, and they proceed more directly to the evidence. To them falls the task of exhuming bodies.

One hundred miles northwest of Kaho'olawe, about thirty minutes' flying time, is the island of O'ahu and the city of Honolulu, the State's nerve center. When a final resolution of the Kaho'olawe dispute emerges — and such a resolution is now in sight — negotiations will be concluded, not from the embattled Island itself, but in Washington, on Maui, and on O'ahu. The critical decision involves, among other things, an ultimate determination of Kaho'olawe's historical worth.

It is on O'ahu that the Kaho'olawe debate erupts in its most acerbic forms. In a steady stream of press releases, the navy studiously downplays Kaho'olawe's possible historic value, pleading its case for future military training needs. The 'Ohana, for its part, routinely lambastes the navy for dropping bombs on valuable Hawaiian artifacts. The navy likes to think of itself as the defender of the 'Ohana's right to dissent. The 'Ohana, in turn, seems to revel in the image of disenfranchised natives pitted against professional (but inept) soldiers and of local browns versus newcomer whites. Beneath this morass of images, at a deeper and more complex level, lies the truly soft ground: the multiple and often conflicting interpretations of patriotism and Hawaiian history. For most of us, the clash of arguments is a bit like walking through quicksand.

Like its future, Kaho'olawe's past is mired in speculation and controversy. During the 1977 trespass trials that sent Walter Ritte and Richard Sawyer to jail for six months, the 'Ohana repeatedly claimed that Kaho'olawe was a historically valuable Island, a place of worship and pilgrimage to which Hawaiians came from other Islands to pray, make offerings, and bury their troubles. Not so, argued others. The distinguished "dean of Hawaiian anthropology," Kenneth Emory, was quoted as saying that Kaho'olawe was, at best, of marginal importance. The part-Hawaiian Charles Kenn, a lifelong amateur student of archaeology, stated unequivocally that Kaho'olawe was never more than a temporary shelter for fishermen. The standard texts on Hawaiian history — Malo, Kamakau, and Fornander — suggest little more.

Swept into the issue more recently (and gingerly trying to pick their way through the navy's intransigence and the 'Ohana's exhortations) are a group of scientists from Hawaii Marine Research, Inc. (HMR), a private consulting firm contracted by the navy and headed by Dr. Maury Morgenstein. Morgenstein's six-figure contract calls for an intensive archaeological survey of Kaho'olawe culminating in three written end products: a summary of all findings, a set of management recommendations for preserving and protecting whatever archaeological sites are deemed valuable, and individual site forms submitted by the navy to the National Register of Historic Places.

Bill Barrera is HMR's part-time Field Director. His job is to supervise the actual site work. Dropped off by marine helicopters and accompanied by ordnance disposal escorts, Barrera and his team single out a particular area on a grid and start walking. When a potential site is discovered, members of the team converge to map, photograph, and describe the specific archaeological features. Wherever possible the sites are left undisturbed. There are two exceptions. If an artifact is endangered by erosion, it is removed for safekeeping in such a way that it can be returned to within centimeters of its original position. And if samples of basaltic glass (obsidian) are available, they too are removed for hydration-rind analysis, a dating method — more accurate than the better known carbon-14 process — that has been adapted and calibrated for Pacific materials by Maury Morgenstein.

"What we are doing," says Barrera, "is the data gathering that comes prior to study and classification — a basic mapping of surface locations." Barrera — bearded, portly, and professorial — maintains his own cluttered and dusty laboratory a few blocks away from HMR's main office in Honolulu. His company is called CHINIAGO, Inc., a Navajo word that means "It's time to eat!"

Barrera likes to talk about food. "In the last two years I've eaten a total of 100 cases of navy C-rations while on Kaho'olawe. I figure 95 of those have gone right through me without being digested." Barrera plucks at his beard and talks about Kaho'olawe in short, scolding bursts of conversation. "Everyone wants to know how many sites there are on the Island but 'site' is a geographical designation that may not have any real scientific interest." More important to Barrera are the three to four "features" that make up a site: charcoal remnants from some ancient fire, bird bones, intentionally constructed mounds of stone and coral, or chips and flakes from a piece of rock destined to become an adze. "I can't tell you with absolute certainty, but I'd say we've already described 600 sites and at least 2,000 features. The work isn't done yet."

Like all of the scientists associated with Kaho'olawe, Barrera is cautious when it comes to statements that might reveal personal feelings about the navy and the 'Ohana. I want to know about the dangers of working on an Island full of unexploded ordnance. "If you want to poke into that kind of stuff, you better go see Morgenstein." So Barrera talks about the weather. He shows me a photograph of his tent being washed away by floodwaters on what is reputedly the driest major Island in the chain. "Most of the time our biggest problems are sunburn, heat stroke, and mosquitoes. Kaho'olawe only gets 30 inches of rain a year, but last February we were camped up near the center of the Island and it started to pour. I called Third Fleet headquarters in Honolulu for a forecast and some joker asked me how long I could tread water."

Down the street at HMR, Maury Morgenstein can be found immersed in the details of several complex projects; Kaho'olawe is his biggest. HMR is a consulting firm that provides technical assistance on environmental impact statements, excavations, geological surveys, and undersea mining. Morgenstein is founder and president. Like Barrera, he bristles with nervous energy. Born and raised in New York, he holds a Ph.D. in geology and geophysics from the

University of Hawai'i. Morgenstein's particular niche is sedimentology. His office is wallpapered with maps of Kaho'olawe that show the Island's soils, drainages, and bombing zones. Hawaii Marine Research employs a dozen people, including several well-known local archaeologists and the now-retired Captain Charles "Davy" Crockett, former Third Fleet Kaho'olawe Project Officer. Crockett is HMR's administrative vice-president.

Morgenstein, his hair kinky and bleached from months in the field, chain-smokes Marlboros as he talks. His carefully chosen words are delivered as if he has said it all before. His manner is precise and technical. Working under contract to the navy and within the climate of anticipation generated by the 'Ohana, he says, makes HMR's findings political and not just scientific. Morgenstein does not want to be misquoted.

"Above and beyond the reports, our major concern is not to lose — and in fact to protect — valuable information." Kaho'olawe is the first real chance archaeologists have had to study the pattern and impact of early Hawaiian life on an entire Island over time. The major problem with archaeology in Hawai'i, he goes on, is that most sites have been indiscriminately covered by concrete and glass or have simply been lost in thick, impenetrable vegetation. In effect, the navy protected Kaho'olawe from the shovels and bulldozers of developers. "That makes Kaho'olawe one of the most unique and discrete research sites in the world," he says. "The real irony is that the high quality of archaeological work is being made possible by Kaho'olawe's dramatically eroded condition."

That erosion, explains Morgenstein, is the result of a series of successive environmental insults. First, Kaho'olawe is naturally dry because it is situated in the rain shadow and wind funnel of Maui. Second is the fire. Morgenstein has found evidence of a major burn horizon over a stable set of soils. "We know that there was a massive fire, or series of fires, sometime around A.D. 1450. We can't tell whether what happened was due to war, slash-and-burn agriculture, or lightning, but we can say that, whatever happened, it covered most of the Island and was uncontrollable." A third factor, says Morgenstein, was the disappearance of vegetation and subsequent salt-water encroachment into the water table.

"The entire system was probably weakened even more by the widespread planting of mesquite in the late 1800s." The final and most drastic insult, in his view, was the introduction of thousands of goats and sheep, which effectively eliminated most of the endemic and indigenous plants.

Despite these problems, or perhaps because of them, HMR's archaeological work has been exciting and fruitful. "What we've found on Kaho'olawe," says Morgenstein, "is a pattern of prehistoric occupation similar to that of the other major Islands. The earliest dated remains come in at A.D. 900 plus or minus 50 years — about the time of the major migrations from Tahiti." There is evidence of a heavier utilization of the Island's interior sometime after A.D. 1300, probably for agriculture, bird hunting, and tool making. The findings include adze quarries, basaltic glass mines, fishing shrines, housing complexes, burial sites, petroglyphs, storage caves, dancing platforms, interred bodies, several kinds of *heiau* or temples (at least one of which was sacrificial), and untold numbers of obsidian chips, which, according to Bill Barrera, were Hawaiian "all-purpose pocketknives." At one site Morgenstein's crews uncovered evidence of probable cannibalism.

Based on these findings, it is possible to make reasonable guesses about what life on Kaho'olawe was like six centuries ago. Before the fires of A.D. 1450, the Island was probably covered with grass and thin strands of dryland forest; gentle, sloping valleys, now eroded into jagged gulches; and sheltered small settlements of pole, thatch, and stone structures. Larger settlements developed along the coast and sugarcane and sweet potatoes were cultivated intensively inland. Endemic birds, many now extinct, probably roamed the hills and forests. It is likely that fishermen and bird catchers from other Islands came to Kaho'olawe, and that the people of Kaho'olawe went to Maui or Lāna'i to gather plants, hunt, fish, and trade.

Temples and altars were erected along the sea on prominent points and near beaches that in pre-erosion times were made of white sand. Some were for the worship of major deities, others for individual fishing and family gods. Some may have been designed to house visiting chiefs and priests. There is at least one site that knowledgeable Hawaiians recognize as an important navigational landmark. The shrine, containing four perfectly matched compass points correlating with similar structures on Maui and Moloka'i, is at the western tip of the Island, at the channel called Kealaikahiki, "the road to Tahiti."

Like any new research, HMR's work poses new questions even as it answers others. Why, for example, are so many seashells found inland? Why are there so few sites dated after A.D. 1500 along the coast? And why did Kaho'olawe's population and, in fact, the population of all the major Islands, take a nosedive around A.D. 1600? Is HMR's work conclusive enough to corroborate any of the 'Ohana's claims? "The sheer number of sites," Morgenstein says, "indicates a wide range of activities and confirms its historic importance. It dispels the notion that Kaho'olawe was uninhabited." Morgenstein, however, is also quick to disavow any inference that he might somehow side with the 'Ohana. "The evidence we've uncovered does not necessarily justify what many contemporary Hawaiians would like to do with the Island."

Morgenstein's (and by extension, HMR's) relationship with the 'Ohana is at best tenuous and occasionally openly antagonistic. Maury is skeptical of the 'Ohana's emotionalism and leery of the tendency of some of the younger Hawaiians to revise their culture as they see fit. He views the 'Ohana as a kind of cultural revitalization movement; like the cargo cults that occurred on some South Pacific Islands after World War II, he sees them as trying to recreate a certain type of cultural identity that may never have existed in fact.

The 'Ohana, for its part, is equally suspicious of HMR. They are critical of Morgenstein for not using more Hawaiians as archaeologists, as cultural consultants, and as technical assistants. The cultural consultant issue is particularly thorny because Hawaiian history, genealogy, and mythology come down through an oral tradition that most Western scientists will accept only as tertiary or, at the very best, secondary evidence.

The 'Ohana also dislikes Morgenstein for hiring ex-Third Fleet Project Officer Davy Crockett, an obvious navy plant in their eyes. Crockett denies any conflict of interest. "I do HMR's administrative work," he says. "My only connection with the navy is my monthly retirement check."

Adding to the complexity are several older, educated Hawaiians who, although sympathetic to the 'Ohana's overall goals, refuse to be a part of their efforts. Loyalties divide in unpredictable ways. Rudy Mitchell, for example, is a Hawaiian who has visited Kaho'olawe twice, once with the navy as an ordnance disposal expert and once as a guest of the 'Ohana. Mitchell is an archaeologist who has worked on O'ahu's north shore. As a Hawaiian elder, he has befriended many younger Hawaiians but, like Morgenstein, he is skeptical of the ends he hears so many of them espousing. "Basically, they want to recreate a golden past without really knowing what it is they want to go back to." He is equally skeptical of Morgenstein and HMR.

Sitting under a shade tree at Waimea Falls Park on O'ahu, Mitchell produces photographs of artifacts found in areas HMR had already swept through and missed. One is of a mortar and pestle, perfectly preserved, found sitting in the dirt. Then, discoursing on the origins of the Hawaiians, he draws a diagram of what he believes to be a pre-Polynesian shrine. Mitchell himself located the shrine on Kaho'olawe through instinct and educated cultural guesswork. That kind of intuition, he suggests, is something only a Hawaiian can understand. Mitchell is convinced Kaho'olawe's prehistory can never be fully appreciated by white scientists trained exclusively in Western methods.

Though repeatedly invited, Rudy Mitchell declines to work on Kaho'olawe. "It's such a beautiful Island but, my god, everything about it — everyone who touches it — gets sucked into the politics and fighting. The truth can't help but suffer." Mitchell also says he is getting too old. "I just don't have the same stamina I used to. My job now is to pass on what I know to the young so they can carry on the work themselves." Kimo, Mitchell's young apprentice, is an anthropology student at the University of Hawai'i. Hair matted down by the rain and eyes riveted on Mitchell, he nods in agreement.

* * *

For more than a century, the United States has used the Hawaiian archipelago as a staging ground for its Pacific forces. Hawai'i is part of North America's strategic western perimeter, a first line of defense, and a toehold and jumping-off point for treaty involvements in the much larger theater of Asia. As a result, the U.S. military has constituted a major presence in Island life for more than a hundred years. It pours more than a billion dollars annually into the local economy, is the second largest employer, and is one of the largest landholders in the State. Thirty percent of O'ahu alone is under military control.

The social and political impacts of having major air and sea commands located in one of North America's smallest and most land-scarce states are enormous. "You better believe that the military is a serious power broker out here," says a well-decorated and well-known naval Captain who prefers not to be named. "And I can also tell you that the 'Ohana has shaken things up. Some of the people who could make decisions on this are starting to consider that Island an albatross around our necks." If this is true, the military would not be the first group of outsiders to be jinxed by Kaho'olawe.

In the half century that followed the Western discovery of Hawai'i by Captain Cook in 1778, Kaho'olawe remained a bleak, little-known, and isolated snippet of land, uninhabited by any permanent population and apparently of no appreciable interest to anyone. In 1830, however, the Hawaiian monarchy began to see possibilities for it. Queen Ka'ahumanu, a Protestant convert filled with anti-Papist indignation, thought about banishing Catholics to Kaho'olawe, but the mass exile never came to pass. Instead, the Island became a penal colony for thieves and adulterers.

As prisons go, Kaho'olawe seems to have been an easygoing affair. Led by a banished chief from Maui named Kinimaka, several dozen exiles maintained eight huts and an adobe church, raised melons, pumpkins, and livestock, and periodically conducted foraging raids on neighboring islands for potatoes, taro, and women.

In 1843 the law banishing criminals to Kaho'olawe was rescinded. Four years later, the last prisoner, a *haole* shoemaker convicted of stealing, was removed from the Island in poor health.

From 1858 on, the Hawaiian monarchy — and, later the Territory of Hawai'i — issued a succession of leases to groups interested in establishing farms and ranches. The various enterprises, run mostly by politicians rather than farmers, tried and failed. By 1909 Kaho'olawe's population consisted of 40 head of cattle, 40 horses, 3,200 sheep, 5,000 goats, and no humans. A year later, Governor Frear proclaimed Kaho'olawe a Territorial Forest Reserve. A research expedition in 1913 catalogued sixteen native and fifteen introduced plant species and noted the proliferation of *Nicotiana glauca*, a tobacco tree that even the goats found inedible. In an effort to retain some of the Island's ever-eroding topsoil, the Forestry Department planted hundreds of trees. Like most early State conservation efforts on Kaho'olawe, the project failed.

In 1918, Kaho'olawe's destiny took a new turn. The Territorial reclamation project came to an end and Angus McPhee, an ex-Wyoming cowboy, secured a lease on the Island for $200 a year. McPhee, the most determined and energetic of Kaho'olawe's would-be ranchers, invested $300,000 and the better part of twenty years in his attempt to make the Island productive. Working with a dozen Hawaiian cowboys, he exterminated every goat he could find; built cisterns, watertanks, fences, corrals, boat landings, and a house; planted 5,000 trees, hundreds of pounds of Australian saltbush and grass seed; and developed a modestly successful herd of 600 cattle. In a remembrance filled with old photographs, Inez Ashdown, McPhee's daughter, recalls her years on the Island.

> We worked like mad on Kaho'olawe... I shaded a vegetable garden with coconut palms and papaya seedlings. I started the first watermelons from seeds strewn under the 10,000 gallon redwood tank by the house. My carrots, beets, cabbage, eggplant, string beans, sweet potatoes and Irish potatoes were bountiful.

The beginning of the end for the McPhees came with the bombing of Pearl Harbor in 1941. Eight days after the Japanese attack, their fishing sampan, the *Mazie C*, was commandeered by the army and the McPhees were removed from the Island. Ironically, McPhee had turned his first profits from Kaho'olawe just a few years before. Considering it his patriotic duty, he subleased the Island to the military and waited for the end of the war to reclaim his property and receive compensation for lost holdings. He got neither. In 1953, Eisenhower signed a Presidential Executive Order giving complete and permanent control of Kaho'olawe to the navy — with provisions, however, that assured soil conservation, limitation of "cloven-hoofed animals," the transfer of Kaho'olawe back to the State once the Island was no longer needed by the military, and the removal of all undetonated explosives upon its return. Kaho'olawe quickly became one of the most shot-at places in the world.

In the heady, prosperous days that followed the war, Hawai'i experienced its first surges of tourism. A strong military presence in the Islands lent weight to those who favored statehood. With an expanding economy and an influx of immigrants, local people took little cognizance of the bombing.

In 1968, however, the navy encountered its first organized resistance. Maui's feisty mayor, Elmer Cravalho, motivated in part by a 500-pound bomb found in one of his cow pastures, spearheaded an attack aimed at opening the waters off Kaho'olawe to Maui fishermen. Cravalho's other concern was to protect the developing tourist trade on Maui's south shore, a scant 8 miles from the daily bombing runs. Cravalho got nowhere. Rear Admiral Thomas Hayward and Secretary of the Navy John Chafee made separate trips to the Islands to lobby on the navy's behalf. In a speech to the Maui Chamber of Commerce, Hayward strongly hinted that withdrawal from Kaho'olawe might force drastic cutbacks in military spending in the Islands.

In 1970, Kaho'olawe again made front-page news. Kaare Gundersen, a professor at the University of Hawai'i, proposed a comprehensive plan for the construction of a thermonuclear power plant on the target Island. The plant, he wrote, could meet all energy needs plus desalinate seawater for agricultural irrigation. Had Gundersen made the same proposal ten years later, during the gas shortages, it might have been given more consideration. As it was, he ran into the same arguments the 'Ohana would inevitably encounter: too much unexploded ordnance and the navy's continuing need for a training area. His ideas received a brief flurry of attention and then faded away. Round one (Mayor Cravalho) and round two (Professor Gundersen) were decisive knockouts for the military. Round three — the Protect Kaho'olawe 'Ohana — proved to be an entirely different story.

* * *

Beginning in 1941 and continuing on into the litigation brought by the 'Ohana decades later, the Department of Defense and the navy pinned their use of Kaho'olawe to four basic arguments. First, military planners consider the Island indispensable because it is the only mid-Pacific site they deem suitable and available for joint training by ships, planes, and land forces. Because of its strategic location, argues the navy, it is the only place where such exercises can be done safely, economically, and in combination with each other. Second, the navy considers Kaho'olawe a death trap, so riddled with unexploded ordnance that it is virtually impossible to restore to a safe, usable condition. Third, the loss of such a major training area would result in a consequent withdrawal of troop strength and an economic loss to the State. And finally, says the navy, the military has served as a steward and custodian for Kaho'olawe by providing demolition-trained escorts for visitors, by monitoring and abating noise levels, by opening the Island's waters to fishing and boating, by maintaining anti-erosion and goat eradication programs, by exploring the feasibility of clearing unexploded ordnance, and by initiating archaeological preservation work. The navy maintains that it has tried to minimize unnecessary negative impacts, accommodate local interests, and — in general — to be a good neighbor.

One of the men responsible for defending these positions to the public is Captain Leo Profilet, Third Fleet Spokesman and Kaho'olawe Project Officer, a former professor of naval science at the University of New Mexico and a veteran of 100 missions in Korea and five years in a Vietnamese POW camp. Profilet assumed Davy Crockett's old job in 1978, at which time a Maui newspaper headlined the story with "Navy Appoints New Flak-Catcher." "When the navy was filling this post," chuckles Profilet, "they specifically wanted an ex-POW on the theory that such a person would have learned how to be patient."

Profilet's office at Third Fleet headquarters sits on historic Ford Island in the middle of Pearl Harbor. Surrounded by destroyers, frigates, light cruisers, and their attendant docks and shipyards, Profilet can look out his window and see the nerve center of one of the largest unified military commands in the world. CINCPAC — Commander in Chief Pacific — takes in the Third and Seventh Fleets, parts of which have stood duty in the waters of the Persian Gulf and other places equally far from Honolulu. In the foyer outside Profilet's office stands a polished wood and glass trophy case enclosing a bronze ship model emblazoned with the Third Fleet's motto: "Readiness."

Leo Profilet and his assistant, Lieutenant Jamie Davidson, are more than eager to talk. They are convinced that Kaho'olawe is basically a public relations problem. "Our given," says Profilet, "is that we need strong conventional forces and we need them in Hawai'i. Hawai'i is pivotal to the Pacific basin and continuous training is absolutely essential." As he launches into the conversation, Profilet begins to reveal the depth of his own emotions. "What most people don't realize is that sentiments about Kaho'olawe run high in the military as well, especially among troop commanders who've been in combat. They are the ones who really understand the need for training. In Korea, we just didn't have it, and because we didn't, we suffered terribly."

Although Profilet and his staff coordinate what happens on Kaho'olawe during training exercises, the actual use of the Island is spread out across five service branches. The heaviest users (85% of the time) are the marines, who conduct artillery practice, small arms training, amphibious landings, and aerial attacks by planes and helicopters. The navy's use is generally confined to ocean gunfire and air cover. The army sends ships over for shore bombardment. Once a year, joint training exercises are held with American allies in the Pacific. Other countries are occasionally invited to shoot at the Island as well.

Profilet and Davidson readily acknowledge that the navy comes off poorly in the public debate over Kaho'olawe. Profilet explains it this way: "In Hawai'i, we are always made out to be the villains. Part of this stems from a long history of social antagonisms with local people and the military's inclination to stick to its own community. There is also the shadow of Vietnam and a core of outright militants in the 'Ohana." The locals, says Profilet, want things both ways. "They want us here because we pump a lot of money into their pockets but at the same time they tell us we are destroying their land." Ironically, for Profilet as for many Hawaiians, Kaho'olawe is a symbolic issue, a microcosm of other tensions and strains that have been building for a long time. "There are no fast and easy answers," he says with a sigh.

Although the loudest and shrillest critics of the navy have been the PKO, the most compelling arguments against the military have not come from the 'Ohana, but from the local chapter of the American Friends Service Committee, a Quaker pacifist group. Ian Lind, one-time head of the Committee and author of a paper on Kaho'olawe, believes the navy vastly exaggerates the Island's importance as a training site and has failed to conduct a meaningful search for alternatives. To begin with, says Lind, the navy claims to have "considered" and then rejected sites in California and on Kaua'i as alternatives but is unable to produce any data for either place. Those "considerations" are complicated by the fact that the Department of Defense has no specific criteria for evaluating the type and amount of land needed for training.

Then there is the fact that use of Kaho'olawe as a military training facility was declining steadily between 1969 and 1977 but increased more than 300% after the 'Ohana began its protests. The increase, Lind believes, was a clear response to local political pressures rather than an accurate representation of training needs. Sitting in his former office at the Honolulu Quaker House, trade winds blowing through the patio, Lind explains why he thinks the navy is so vehement about keeping the Island. "Vested interest and rampant careerism," he says. "The Pacific Command has traditionally been the launching pad for big promotions. No commander wants to be the first to give up land in Hawai'i."

Profilet, of course, disagrees. The expansion of training, he maintains, was a result of pulling back American forces from

Okinawa at the end of the Vietnam war. As for alternatives to Kaho'olawe, he says, there simply aren't any. Profilet likes to refer to a seventy-page report on the target Island that includes evaluations of other sites. With Kaho'olawe as the standard for comparison, the alternatives are dismissed as too costly, inadequate, or simply not feasible. Because the navy's argument for retaining the Island is based largely on the claim that Kaho'olawe is the only place where combined land, sea, and air operations can be conducted simultaneously, I ask Profilet what percentage of the training time is actually used for combined arms operations. Offhand, he says, he really doesn't know.

The conflict between the 'Ohana and the navy is, on the bottom line, a clash of American subcultures. Between the two lies a gulf of misunderstanding, a reflection of fifty years of local military pride, and a newly discovered ethnic vitality among young Hawaiians. Leo Profilet is an intelligent, decorated, and dedicated military administrator nearing the end of a distinguished career. But like some of the hotbloods in the 'Ohana, he can be curiously naive. "Why is the military's training on Kaho'olawe a desecration?" he asks, genuinely puzzled. As much as that question rankles many Hawaiians, it may be central to the entire dispute.

Cynthia Thielen, at one time the 'Ohana's lawyer, believes the bombing will ultimately be stopped on a permanent basis. "The issue won't die and it won't be swept under the rug... when the navy was forced to grant religious access to Kaho'olawe, it was the beginning of the end. For the first time they had to surrender some of their control." Profilet disagrees. "Stopping the bombing is an oversimplification. Any solution will have to take account of the military's on-going need for training in the Pacific."

Whatever the resolution, Captain Leo Profilet won't be a part of it. He retired from the navy and returned to civilian life a few months after our conversation. When I asked him whether there was any outside possibility he might end up working with Hawaii Marine Research like his predecessor, Davy Crockett, Profilet shook his head and waved his pipe at me. "Of course not," he said with a laugh.

* * *

Kaho'olawe rears up on the horizon like a gray-green whale, not radically different in shape and color from the real humpbacks that are breaching and sounding off our starboard side. Next to us, one whale slides directly beneath the boat, raises its flukes, and dives. The sixth (official and legal) access of the Protect Kaho'olawe 'Ohana begins aboard *The Charger,* a fishing sampan out of Lahaina skippered by Uncle Harry Mitchell, father of Kimo Mitchell, who died in the waters off Kaho'olawe along with George Helm. On board *The Charger* are some forty 'Ohana members headed for the tiny Island.

Under a rain-splattered canoe shed the night before departure, there is a briefing. "Prepare yourself for your first visit," says Uncle Harry. "Kaho'olawe will capture you. She has plenty *mana,* she does. The ancientness is there, buried in the rocks, the temples, the walls of the old houses."

Under that same canoe shed, Dr. Emmett Aluli shows slides and talks about the history of the 'Ohana. Over dinner, I talk with him and begin to get a sense of the man. Aluli is three-quarters Hawaiian, short, tanned, and muscled like a surfer. For a medical man, his credentials are unusual; for a leader in the 'Ohana they are probably normal. Noa Emmett Aluli is originally from Moloka'i but was raised much of the time on O'ahu. He spent sixteen years in Catholic schools in Honolulu, then four years at Marquette University studying biology and philosophy. Another nine years (off and on) went into completing an M.D. at the University of Hawai'i. Along the way to being a doctor, he spent time teaching school, doing kidney research, working with Navajo and Hopi Indians, and serving regular stints in the Coast Guard Reserve. Why, a reporter once asked him, haven't you settled your medical practice in Honolulu, where you logically could be making $250,000 a year? "Because," answered Aluli, "I choose not to."

At the moment, nothing is more important to Aluli than ensuring that this sixth access, made up of young and old Hawaiians from every Island, comes off without a hitch. Already on Kaho'olawe are Rick Jackson and Mark "Monty" Montgomery, the navy's explosive ordnance disposal team. Every step taken on the Island, every rock turned over, or tree planted must be with their permission. It is part of the deal. In exchange for the several bomb-free days that are allowed each month for religious purposes, the 'Ohana agrees to be accompanied and supervised by the "EODs."

Because of strong currents and a full load, the trip across the cobalt waters separating Moloka'i and Kaho'olawe takes eight hours. It is a gentle journey, with light swells and foam, trade winds, whales, and an eagerness to "touch the land," a phrase much used by the 'Ohana. "On these trips," says Jackie Leilani as we near the Island, "we give and receive in equal proportions. You can't help but be touched by the experience."

Kaho'olawe is a surprise, a victim of years of bad press. It is neither waterless nor barren — descriptions that have been used by many people, but especially by the navy's spokespersons, who would like the bombing to seem inconsequential. Access base camp — a small village of tents and tarps — is pitched at Hakioawa Bay, a sheltered valley on the northeast side. From the windswept cliffs above it, one sees three other Islands and the outline of 10,000-foot Haleakalā looming over Maui. Above the bay the valley steepens into grass-covered hills that become, on the top of Kaho'olawe, a plateau. This flat highland is crisscrossed by rain-worn trenches and gulleys eroded down to the clay hardpan. Punctuating this red and ravaged desert are islands of grass 4 feet high, bristling like little tufts of hair on an old man's head.

Hakioawa Valley itself is a thick green forest of mesquite, with ancient wells and waterholes slowly being restored by the 'Ohana. A little more work is done on each access. Everyone pitches in. It is part of the reason for being there.

Trails connecting different archaeological sites in the valley are cleared. Small mounds of stones, possibly fishing shrines, are restored rock by rock. Trees and shrubs are slashed out of ancient house sites. Hale o Papa, "the forbidden temple" on the northern slope of the valley, is cleaned of debris. Someone finds a half-worked adze blank under a large boulder. It is photographed and noted in a journal and left alone. Mealtimes, everyone gathers to discuss the day, to hear stories from the *kūpuna*, to sing songs, dance *hula*, share feelings, and argue about Kaho'olawe's future.

The weather over the five days of access is exceptional: misty dawns, occasional showers, bright hot afternoons, and star-spangled nights. Although the navy views this as a "religious" visit, it seems to be simultaneously a cultural, educational, and archaeological pilgrimage. It provides for both the data gathering of amateur archaeologists and a classroom for the older Hawaiians to offer their knowledge and remembrances. One such elder is Charlie Ke'au, a Maui fisherman and self-taught archaeologist with nine years of field experience on Maui and Kaho'olawe. Charlie guides twenty of us around Hakioawa Valley, pointing out the remains of shrines and temples, picking up bits of shell and bone, detailing their ancient uses and explaining, with infinite patience, the critical ecological balance between humans and the rest of nature in old Hawai'i.

Later, in the pink afterglow of sunset, Charlie walks on the beach with me and talks politics. Like so many other older Hawaiians, Charlie's views on Kaho'olawe differ from the 'Ohana's:

> Couple years ago, after I been to the Island a few times, the military asks me, Charlie, what's your idea? You have any notions on what should be done? Remember now, I spent plenty years in the Army. So I say to the Colonel, here's my management plan. I don't want to have to choose between my Hawaiian heritage and our national defense. I say, leave 'em like it is. We need the navy and I like it that they are protecting me. Just let us Hawaiians come to this Island so we can learn more and pass it on to the next generation.

Like the waves of Hawaiians who have come before, most people on this trip have brought seeds and shoots to plant on various parts of the Island. Near the large well that is slowly being restored in the valley, the 'Ohana has fenced off a quarter-acre of land to sprout coconuts, ti plants, and young *kukui* trees. On a hike to the top of the Island, Keoki Ka'a'lau carries a bag of *wili-wili* seeds that will, in thirty years, be magnificent, red-berried trees providing shade and helping to restore Kaho'olawe's parched water table. If, that is, they survive the heat and the goats. Keoki — lean, tanned, and bearded — hikes all day in the sun without drinking water. He is a taro farmer on O'ahu by trade and used to the heat. To quench his thirst he chews the mildly narcotic root of the 'awa plant. He offers the 'awa around and, mouths tingling, we dig small holes in the tough, red hardpan soil, drop in a few seeds, and sing the planting chant Keoki has taught us:

> E lalo la wiliwili
> E luna la
> Na ulu
> Mālama
> Mālama Kaho'olawe

The words mean: "Go down into the ground *wiliwili*, come up and grow and preserve and support Kaho'olawe."

The planting expedition with Keoki takes us to the top of the Island and on to Kaho'olawe's dust-bowl plateau. Everywhere we go there are the remains of bombs, shells, and bullets. Kaho'olawe is a military junkyard, with 50-calibre machine-gun shells strewn across the Island like pebbles. Hiking all day, we are escorted by Monty Montgomery, one of the navy EODs. Montgomery has been on several of these accesses. He is twenty-eight years old, a former Idaho logger and ex–Colorado Outward Bound instructor who is half Nez Percé Indian. Montgomery has strong and conflicting feelings about the 'Ohana. "I'm caught in the middle on these trips. I can sense the way the Hawaiians look at me as a symbol of what they are against, and a part of me — maybe the Indian part — can understand how they feel. But this is my job. I'm good at it and I like it. I'm here to make this place safe for them and to keep them from being blown all to shit." Montgomery knows the Island intimately. "Two marines died not far from where we are now," he says perfunctorily as we walk through the brush. "Stepped on a live grenade."

The planting trek takes us up and across some of Kaho'olawe's most bombed and eroded slopes. Rounding a small rise, we see what looks to be a lone tree sticking up on the horizon. It is, on closer inspection, an 8 foot bomb stuck point down in the hardpan. Montgomery says it is an undetonated 2,000 pounder.

Emmett Aluli says it is a nuclear simulator. The ordnance is every-where: half-exploded parachute flares, pieces of fragmentation bombs, chunks of large mortars and rockets, and twisted slivers of corroded metal that are impossible to identify. Whole bombs, mostly 500 and 1,000 pounders, lie rusting in the harsh sunlight. I ask Montgomery how all this could possibly be cleaned. It can't, he says. "We could clear the surface, but no one knows how much live stuff lies underground. Some of it may be 15 feet down. It would take millions of dollars and many years. The 'Ohana doesn't really believe this. They think the navy uses this as an excuse to keep the Island to themselves."

Trudging across Kaho'olawe's upland plateau planting trees and staring at bombs, we head south toward Luamakika, the Island's highest point. It's a three-hour walk in the heat. Luamakika is an adze quarry, an ancient toolmakers' workshop where Hawaiians pried out top-grade basalt blanks for adzes, bowling rocks, ham-mer stones, and small chips to be used for knives. A large shrine sits on the highest knob of land. Two triangular rocks have been set so that they form an arrow pointing directly at Maui. Keoki Ka'a'lau says the shrine was probably used only by the men who came to make tools, but no one is quite sure what the stones really signify.

Shrines like the one at Luamakika abound on Kaho'olawe. Some are nothing more than a few rocks stacked on top of each other. Others are more elaborate constructions of bleached coral stones set amongst dark, volcanic boulders. The ones at Kealaikahiki on Kaho'olawe's west end are the best known. From here, in the tenth and eleventh centuries, so it is said, Hawaiian navigators made their long journeys back and forth to Tahiti in double-hulled sailing canoes, crossing the Pacific at a time when most Europeans were afraid of being gobbled up by sea monsters or of falling off the edge of the world where their maps ended.

Theoreticians of old-time navigation believe the Hawaiians sailed along a visible demarcation of the sea extending 2,500 miles from Tahiti to Hawai'i. Trained from childhood, these navigators — perhaps the best the world has ever known — would tack their way north or south along this "Kāne-Kanaloa Line" fixing their positions by the taste of the water, by star paths, and by dead reckoning. Kealaikahiki — "the road to Tahiti" — was the known jump-off point for the southbound journey.

Other evidence of Kaho'olawe's history can be found on the hardpan as well. There are rotting fence posts from Angus McPhee's cattle-ranching efforts in the 1930s. The tobacco plants *Nicotiana glauca*, reported by the 1913 Territorial research expedition, are still thriving. Here and there, sitting on the hardpan or half buried in the dust, are bleached cowrie, cone, and oyster shells, the mysterious shore materials that logically don't belong there. All the archaeologists, amateur and professional alike, have puzzled over these shells, but no one has offered a conclusive explanation.

Part of the time we hike along a two-tracked convoy road that follows the general contours of Kaho'olawe's high, central section. Off to the side are occasional plots of tamarisk and ironwood trees hanging limply in the heat. The trees, stunted but surviving, are part of a joint Navy-State conservation effort aimed at halting the incessant erosion. "The top of the Island is simply weathering off," says Monty Montgomery, "and the only thing that will stop it is to rebuild some kind of watershed." The trees chosen for this effort are not native to Hawai'i, but they have a strong tolerance for heat and salt. On their twice-a-year planting trips, Montgomery and other EODs fly over from O'ahu by helicopter, plant shaped charges in the ground, and then blow out about five hundred holes at a time. Seedling trees are removed from plastic vials, watered, and left. Less than half survive. Keoki, most of his red and yellow *wiliwili* seeds now planted, is disgusted by this. Exploding holes for planting, he believes, is an insult to both the trees and the Island.

In the evening, back at Hakioawa Valley, we find our numbers increased. A chartered helicopter has landed on the beach, bringing over lawyer Thielen, Bishop Museum archaeologist Patrick Kirch, and a brawny Arizonan named Dennis Marketic, who has been hired by the 'Ohana to give a private and independent estimate on how much it would cost to clear the bombs off Kaho'olawe.

Dinner is ready. The EODs, camped down the beach, are invited over. Tired of C-rations, they gladly accept. Grace is said in Hawaiian and dinner is served: pots of stew, rice, and roast pork;

three kinds of steamed fish; sweet potatoes, bananas, and fresh coconut; spinach (taro leaves); *poi* (taro root); chopped octopus in seaweed; water, coffee, and juice. Seven large bags of potato chips disappear as fast as everything else. We retire early, worn out by the day's activity.

In the days that follow, different people are engaged in different activities, all of which are central to 'Ohana aims and purposes. Jim Hudnull, a whale specialist from Maui, spends his days perched on top of a ridge with a high-powered telescope tracking and recording the migrations of the humpback whales. Dorothy Tau, a librarian from Kaua'i with an encyclopedic knowledge of Pacific botany, searches for rare or endangered plants — which she finds, in the form of a fragile white *'ilima* blossom. Charlie Ke'au, Pat Kirch, and several archaeology students from the University of Hawai'i scour Hakioawa Valley itself trying to piece together a sense of what was obviously a major village. Warren Onishi and Mike Teruya, fastidious recorders of nearly everything, drag around 70 pounds of cameras and tape recorders. They are making a documentary to be shown to high school students across the state.

Everyone, regardless of specific interests and background, is caught up in "stone fever." This is the result of Charlie Ke'au's demonstrations and talks on archaeology and Hawaiian history. "You can look at them all," he says. "Pick them up, feel them, taste them if you want, but just put them back exactly like they were!" Under Charlie's practiced eye, random rocks take on new meanings. They are the remains of old campfires, house foundations, fishing shrines, and cairns. Most everyone walking around Hakioawa Valley, even on the way to the one-hole outhouse set back in the bushes, walks head down, looking at the stones. People are constantly asking Charlie to "check this one." Most of the time, it is nothing. Once in a while, a broad smile cracks across his brown face. If someone is nearby, Charlie will say, "Come look over here at what this brother has found for us!"

A dozen of us beat our way back up the hardpan and then turn south to Kanapou Bay. Kanapou is a steep, boulder-strewn cut on Kaho'olawe's east end, a precipitous descent that only five of us make. Emmett Aluli wants to go back to a spot he remembers from one of the first, illegal accesses. Pat Kirch is searching the valley's stratified walls for fossil land snails. "If we can find the shells buried there, it will tell us what the original forest was like on Kaho'olawe. We know the kinds of trees the different land snails lived on." Kanaina Smyth, a forest ranger from Kaua'i, wants to go for a swim. I'm going because I want to see everything and I can't sit still. Monty Montgomery has to accompany us because no one other than a trained EOD is supposed to hike alone.

On the way down, I ask Aluli what the 'Ohana would do with Kaho'olawe if the navy gave it to them tomorrow. "We want to be the permanent stewards of this Island," he says. "The Hawaiian word for this is *kahu* — the guardians and custodians of the land." Aluli's vision for Kaho'olawe is a cross between a religious sanctuary for Hawaiians and a National Park. "Kaho'olawe is a living treasure, full of history, full of meaning. I want Hawaiian kids — in fact, all kids — to be able to come here and see how the old people lived. No one will ever be denied access, as we have been, but it is especially important for Hawaiians."

Aluli is a soft-spoken yet intensely passionate speaker who can make the simplest and lightest conversation crucially important. There is humor and gentleness but no frivolity. He is direct and clear in everything he does. On this access, he is either in constant motion — talking with people, coordinating with the EODs, organizing logistics — or he is flat on his back in a hammock, exhausted, asleep. "When we finally do stop this ridiculous bombing, when that finally happens, you are going to see an incredible celebration in the Hawaiian Islands. It will mark a transition for us: full access to our past and new certainty about our future."

At the bottom of Kanapou, we swim, rest, talk further, and then climb back up to the waiting group. Pat has found no land snails. Emmett points out one of the places Walter Ritte and Richard Sawyer hid during their month on the Island in 1977. "If you look around, you can see that this was a temple." It was a refuge for the 'Ohana as well. Keoki Ka'a'lau asks if he might say a special prayer. We gather in a circle holding hands. Monty and Rick Jackson, the other EOD, join us. "Bless this place, bless the spirit of this place. And bless all of us for the work we are doing. It will last as long as there is wind and sea and land."

Back at base camp on our last evening together we eat dinner in small, huddled groups. Once again, there is a mammoth spread of food. I join a group that includes whale watcher Jim Hudnull and the red-nosed Arizona demolition man who has brought along a fifth of bourbon. He has spent the day surveying Kaho'olawe by helicopter and on foot. "This Island could be made guaranteed safe if you bulldozed the heavy impact areas down about eight feet. You can see what the problem is. We can get rid of the hardware but we are also going to get rid of a lot of archaeology. It would be a hell of a trade-off." The conversation wanders off onto bomb clearance, whales, and land snails. The bourbon is excellent.

After dinner, everyone gathers around a blazing bonfire. The tinder-dry mesquite sizzles and snaps, sending a shower of sparks up into the night. It is cloudy and cool. Forty people sit around the fire shoulder to shoulder. Emmett Aluli asks if we could all, on this last night together, share a few words or ideas on what this trip has meant. There is a long silence and then the thoughts begin to pour out. It is a propitious moment, a time for summing up. Tamara Wong, an 'Ohana organizer from Kaua'i:

> This Island has been hurt for so long and I've never felt it more than this trip. When we first landed, I almost drowned in the surf and then I cut my foot on the coral. I thought maybe Kaho'olawe didn't want me here but now I know what it means. We have to put back into the Island. Everyone else has taken from it. We have to give back to it, our work, our *aloha*, and even our blood.

Others speak. There are tears and half-choked sobs. The depth of feeling is profound. Eric Cato, an electrician from Kaua'i:

> What I've learned is that Kaho'olawe is a living being and when it gets killed, we are killed. Our purpose as an 'Ohana, as a giant family of people, is reaffirmed. It is to live!

And Jackie Leilani:

> How fortunate we are! How wonderful and important!
> Think of it — all of us from the other Islands gathered
> here on this one. It is good to find things and good that
> we can help give life back to the land. My friends, we
> are Hawai'i!

And Emmett Aluli:

> It's a sweet moment to be here listening to you. I thank
> you for making it special for me as well. When we first
> came here in 1976 we didn't know what all this
> meant. All we had was this deep feeling that it was
> important. Now we know about the stones. Thank you
> for that, Charlie Ke'au! For myself, I've been thinking
> about George Helm and Kimo Mitchell and thinking
> how Uncle Harry over there and I and so many others
> have carried on because of them. I think they would
> appreciate the change that has taken place in the
> 'Ohana since 1977. It is no longer just *aloha 'āina*,
> loving the land. Now it's *mālama 'āina*, helping it
> revive, nourishing it, bringing the people back so they
> too can be nourished and revived by it.

Late into the night there is music and dance, loud at first, but later, soft songs and gentle *hula* that praise the Island for its magic. There are chants and stories and then, finally, most everyone drifts off to their tents. In a few hours we will pack our gear, haul it out through the surf, load it back into *The Charger*, and return to Maui. Before sleep, I walk down to the beach and look out across the flat, cool sand. The weather has cleared. Stars are out. Trade winds are blowing out of the north, cleansing the sky, settling the bittersweet passions of the evening. A lone figure comes over and stands with me, digging bare feet into the sand. "You know," says Emmett, "we don't really have to retake this Island at all. It has always been ours and it always will be anyway." Tired and relaxed, it is Emmett Aluli.

The next morning, all of us — 'Ohana, guests, navy — depart from Kaho'olawe in calm seas.

*   *   *

In March 1981, after a month of last-minute maneuvering by the 'Ohana and the navy, the entire island of Kaho'olawe, containing more than 500 designated archaeological sites, was deemed eligible for the National Register of Historic Places. At a press conference in Honolulu, Emmett Aluli announced that eligibility for the Register would ultimately lead to a cessation of all bombing on the target Island. Lieutenant Jamie Davidson, in his own press release, suggested otherwise. Military operations, he said, would not be affected if a part of the Island or even the Island in its entirety was named to the Register.

A few months later, after one of their survey trips to Kaho'olawe, Hawaii Marine Research reported the discovery of what may be the largest known petroglyph field in the state of Hawai'i. Soon after, Congress approved legislation providing for a demonstration program to clear some of the unexploded ordnance. Then, in October 1990 — under mounting pressure from Hawai'i's congressional delegation, the Congress, the Governor, the State Legislature, and the County of Maui — the President declared a two-year bombing moratorium. Congress then established a high-level entity called the Kaho'olawe Conveyance Commission and mandated it to recommend the terms and conditions of the Island's return to the State of Hawai'i. Emmett Aluli is a member of that Commission.

Barring serendipitous circumstances and the vagaries of politics, permanent cessation of the bombing, the return of Kaho'olawe to Hawai'i, and the creation of a special protected status now seems inevitable. That status may also be linked to the assertions for sovereignty that are starting to unify the Hawaiian community and the rising tide of sentiment among non-Hawaiians who also want to see some of those demands granted. "For a nation," said a high-ranking State official recently, "there needs to be a 'corpus' of land — beginning, in my opinion, with Kaho'olawe — managed and controlled by a Hawaiian government."

On Kaho'olawe itself, under the court-ordered Consent Decree with the navy, the 'Ohana continues to mount monthly visits for "scientific, archaeological, educational, and religious" purposes.

When the Island is finally reclaimed by the State, the 'Ohana seems destined to play a major role in running it. Meanwhile, on a recent trip to the wounded Island — and in anticipation of that day — the 'Ohana scoured the Island for archaeological sites, discovered several new ones, and planted coconut trees on Kaho'olawe's northeast side.

9

Millennium

Ask the questions that have no answers.
Invest in the millennium. Plant
sequoias.... Swear allegiance to what is
highest in your thoughts. As soon as the
generals and politicos can predict the
motions of your mind, lose it. Leave it
as a sign to mark the false trail, the way
you didn't go. Be like the fox who makes
more tracks than necessary, some in the
wrong direction. Practice resurrection.

from "Manifesto" by Wendell Berry

RISING UP A SMALL SADDLE OF VOLCANIC HILLS AND ESCARPMENTS, Kōnāhuanui is the highest peak in the Ko'olau range on the island of O'ahu. An odd word, Kōnāhuanui. Literally translated, it means "large fat innards." According to people knowledgeable in these matters, the name derives from a legendary Hawaiian man who had very large testicles and threw them in a fit of anger at an escaping woman. Drive over the Pali Highway and you'll notice Kōnāhuanui's hatchetlike shape sticking out from its surroundings. Look carefully and you'll also see that the mountain's sides are precipitously narrow. Thin enough, in fact, to cut off a giant's privates if he happened to slip over the side.

The real mountain is unapproachable from the Pali lookout. Occasionally people try. Some of them end up dead or crippled. The rest turn back or get stuck and have to be rescued by the Honolulu Fire Department. This doesn't mean that the mountain can't be climbed; it just means you have to take a different route, which is what I am in the process of doing; climbing the tallest peak in the Ko'olaus — a hatchet-shaped, ball-whacking, knee-wrenching slab of rock — by the back way (supposedly the safe and easy way) on a Wednesday morning on the last day of the year. Alone.

I am playing hooky from the office, something I very rarely do, although my absence probably doesn't matter much — especially today. Christmas is gone, New Year's Eve coming, and most everyone in Honolulu is avoiding work for one reason or another. If I were a more conscientious and persevering type, I suppose I'd be back in the office with the last of the obsessives tidying up year-end reports and studiously preparing for what lies ahead. There are, however, three reasons why this is futile.

First, my desk resists tidying. It has an invisible vortex, kind of like the Bermuda Triangle. Things disappear, rise up months later when I'm not expecting them, and then disappear again just before I really need them. Second — and perhaps as an antidote to my perpetual personal disorganization — I need to clear the cobwebs and rust spots from my brain. Seeing the mountains will help do this, as it has many times before. And finally, there are bigger things afoot. We are, after all, not just nearing the end of the year, but the end of the twentieth century. This seems to require commemoration, or at least a pause to wonder what's in store for us around the bend.

Millennia are no small events. The last time this happened, Vikings were ravaging English coastlines, cholera was decimating German cities, and Saracen pirates controlled most of southern France. In Japan and China, kingdoms had just gone up in flames and new empires were rising from the ashes. In South Asia, India was being invaded by Muslim Turks. Throughout Europe, visions of destruction haunted people. According to the Book of Revelation, the world was to be consumed in a blazing holocaust "when the thousand years are expired." As A.D. 1000 approached, famines, earthquakes, plagues, and eclipses of the sun were confidently predicted. The Four Horsemen of the Apocalypse were on the verge of riding, so it was assumed, and Pope Gregory confidently announced, "these signs of the end of the world are sent... that we may be solicitous for our souls, suspicious of the hour of death, and may be found prepared with good works to meet our judge."

Despite the barbarians and cholera and notwithstanding the pessimism of the Pope and his Book of Revelation, the world muddled on. Here in the Pacific, Hawaiians and other Polynesians, not to mention the Micronesians and Melanesians, were operating on entirely different calendars. Horses weren't yet present in Hawai'i; of apocalyptic visions, less is known.

Now the year 2000 approaches. It is the last day of the year, the last decade of the century, the last century of the millennium, and a major birthday for humanity. All of this makes a little ramble up Kōnāhuanui seem appropriate. It also postpones the chaos on my desk for a few more hours.

The hike is in the neighborhood of six miles. It starts a mile from Honolulu proper, just left of a telephone company access road on the mountain the Hawaiians used to know as Pu'u'ōhi'a. Today we all call it Tantalus. The path wends around the mountain's back, skirts the hillsides of Mānoa Valley, and then opens at a lookout above the State's Water Reservoir no. 4 in Nu'uanu Valley. At this point you jump a fence and then more or less whack and wonk your way up the hogback that leads to Kōnāhuanui's summit. Near the top, the trail rises in a manner that would make our ancient Hawaiian Big Man's fabulously oversized genitals contract in fear, which is probably what happened a long time ago anyway.

On the way to the scene of this almost-forgotten and maybe-never-happened biological event, however, there are interesting things to see, such as gulches and hillsides filled with guavas and mountain apples, a few creeks and small waterfalls, some adventuresome geological formations, and a number of views that will sooth away the tensions of the week. Along the trail, I shuffle down into a scramble of bananas, coffee plants, guava, and *koa* and then rise up a hillock tufted with ferns. Yonder from that, the trees form a jungle canopy, filtering the light and casting portions of the forest in deep shadows. Underfoot, thimbleberries, *naupaka*, *moa*, fungi, mosses, small grasses, and lichens grow in luxurious profusion.

In the steady rhythm of morning walking, I find myself transfixed by the landforms and lifeforms associated with these hills. "Once in a lifetime," wrote Loren Eiseley in *The Immense Journey*, "if one is lucky, one so merges with sunlight and air and running water that whole eons, the eons that mountains and deserts know, might pass in a single afternoon without discomfort." Less than half a mile down the trail I am plunged into a stately, silent world more or less untouched by the daily comings and goings of humans. True, many of the animals and plants here are "exotics," the result of accidental or intentional introductions that have had devastating impacts on local flora and fauna, but all of which seem to fit in now. The only two-legged beast in view, I feel blissfully alone.

The trail rises up, then drops. I walk on, absorbed in my own feelings and thoughts and entranced by the deep green woods about me. Here and there boulders peep out of the vegetation like sentinels. Elsewhere, water trickles out of a crack; a fallen log and some jammed rocks turn it into a little waterfall with a small pool at the bottom; frogs, crayfish, and 'ōpae shrimp abound; and taro plants root alongside. Occasionally, birds whistle low overhead and then, when they see me, streak into the brush. A Shama Thrush trills a song in the distance. Along the trail, spiders who have seemingly studied Gary Larson's cartoons have strung huge webs across rocks as if they are hoping to snag a rhinoceros for dinner. Slowly, just a few brief miles away from the hurly-burly of Honolulu proper, I make my way into the forest.

*   *   *

After an hour of easy walking I find myself in a huge clump of green and yellow bamboos — acres of the stuff. Most of the vegetation of the Koʻolaus is non-native, as is true of much of the rest of this Island. If I'm to see any real stands of endemic flora, they will be at the top of Kōnāhuanui. Here, the thick-rooted, slender-stalked bamboo has crowded out all the other plants completely. The effect is oddly disturbing. A forest shouldn't be just one thing, even if it's something strong, flexible, and beautiful like bamboo. I meander away from the main path, into the grove, and then stop and listen to the stalks creaking in the wind. I cut a few small pieces for future use. Maybe they'll become Hawaiian nose flutes or a New Year's kadomatsu for Carolyn, or small flower holders for the girls.

Farther into this uncanny forest, I come to a large outcropping of rock encircled by bamboo spikes. Slowly, inevitably, the stone is giving way to the plants. Left to themselves, bamboo shoots are known to push their way through reinforced concrete. Here, however, the rock, seems to be fighting back. With both it is a matter of time. Wind, water, and alternating spells of wet, cool, dry, and hot weather will eventually pulverize the rock into loam. The bamboo will thrive for a time and then be succeeded by other plants. Whole generations of forests will come and go. After enough successions, the rock's home will become a marsh or a knoll or a hummock of grass — or, if some developer gets hold of this land, a bunch of condos or maybe a hotel.

Meanwhile, the eerie little forest of bamboo, the twisted gulches, the imperturbable boulders, the whistling wind, and my own weird proclivities trigger a chain of thoughts. I imagine a perilous and primitive place, a smoldering brown landscape vaguely reminiscent of the Australian Outback, but more extreme. There are craggy mountains, raging rivers, cyclonic dust storms, gunmetal gray volcanoes, strange mists, bizarre vapors, and — off in the smoking distance — the wreckage of old cities.

My soul — locked into continuous paper sorting and bureaucracy mongering these past weeks, but now liberated by my brief foray into the woods — conjures up a complicated plot. A nearly normal hero (me, for example) is fighting off radioactive rednecks as he crosses the last mountain range to bring humanity-saving serum to his family and friends. There are deep, dangerous canyons and dense jungles filled with poisonous lizards. There are hideous snakes, packs of feral dogs, rivers full of alligators, and wandering bands of half-humans who take unusual pleasure in torturing others. Our hero is captured by mutants who intend to boil him in oil. He steals a cutlass and barely escapes. Then, finally, he...

I make my way back through the bamboo, find the main path, and continue through the forest for another thirty minutes or so. Finally, I emerge from a tunnel of trees. Vistas stretch three directions into the distance. I see the Pali Highway and Pearl Harbor to the west, most of Nu'uanu Valley to the north, and Diamond Head to the east. The temperature is in the low eighties, the air smells sweet, and a few fat clouds provide contrast to an otherwise strikingly blue sky.

All and all, it is a tranquil and comfortable setting. Peace, however, is a relative condition. Show me a moment of serenity and I'll guarantee there is some vexatious little problem just waiting to pop its ugly head up the very moment you are most relaxed. Consider this one. After several hours of rummaging around on the mountain, I have just eaten a juicy Kona orange, knocked back a swig of cold water, and followed both of these with half of a very delectable medium-sized bag of peanut M&Ms. A fine chaser or bracer, M&Ms, and one that I've been taking with me on hikes for years. Unfortunately, I didn't bring enough.

To understand the full ramifications of this as a scarcity economics problem, you need to appreciate some fundamental facts about M&Ms. M&Ms are an esteemed (and in some circles, required) part of hiking in the woods. Eaten straight from the bag (the way REAL men do it), Vitamin Ms are a supplement for the malnourished, an antidote for the weak-willed, and a well-known modifier of deportment for the misbehaved. Mix some of them into a gorp with a few Brazil nuts, raisins, and sunflower seeds, and a bag of M&Ms rises to transcendental proportions. It becomes a sanctuary for the contemplative, a reward for the virtuous, and a promise of things to come in the next life for those who aren't doing so well in this one.

If all of this sounds a bit highblown, you should know that, in addition to being a lifelong M&M consumer, I am also a true student of the history, science, and art of M&M making. I could, if time allowed, explain the process by which all these candies are rolled, "panned," and coated into existence and how they are then off-set printed with the little "m." I could tell you how M&Ms were invented by two gents named Forrest Mars and Bruce Murrie, who built an M&Ms factory in Hackettstown, New Jersey, in the 1940s; how this factory now generates over 100 million of the little buggers every single day; and how the entire enterprise came to be Mars, Inc., maker of Milky Ways, Munch Bars, Skittles, Kudos, Starbursts, Snickers, Holidays, Three Musketeers, and, of course, Mars Bars. I could tell you, with absolute confidence, that the average package of peanut M&Ms like the one I have just consumed contains 30% brown, 20% each of yellow, red, and green, and 10% orange M&Ms, and why — every once in a very great while — an accidental white one shows up. I could expound on the recent introduction of peanut butter M&Ms (excellent!) and almond M&Ms (so-so), and on the flowering of other M&Ms for Easter and Valentine's Day (strange). Finally, I could share the results of my own personal taste-testing experiments and illuminate the very special psychogenic effects that eating green M&Ms is reputed to produce in rats, kids, and humans.

All of this, however, would be an even longer digression from the question at hand, which is: do I give in to gluttony and gobble down the rest of my M&Ms this very instant or do I save the remaining little nuggets for the end of the day or, heaven forbid, when I might actually need them?

It's a quandary and not as minor as it might seem. Self-restraint does not come easy to twentieth-century Americans like myself. I know I and others consume disproportionate amounts of the world's resources, but it's hard to stop. I like driving cars at high speed, eating hamburgers, and popping M&Ms, even though all of these may very well have negative consequences for me and the rest of the world. Hence I tend toward guilt and anxiety, the forerunners of *angst* — which is precisely what I don't want on a trip to the woods on the last day of the year on the eve of the millennium. I take off to places like Kōnāhuanui to escape dilemmas. But here I am again, hoisted on my own mental and ethical petard. (I don't really know what a petard is, but mine always seems to get hoisted pretty high or, worse yet, to spiral back down into what some smartone once called "the paralysis of analysis.") I put the remaining half-bag of M&Ms in my pack and march on.

Now the trail rises sharply. Here and there the volcanic contours of the mountain become more apparent. Climbing steadily, I start thinking about this stone on which I am walking. The lavas of the Hawaiian Islands make up an odd world. They seem to confide in each other in their own low-frequency voices. Most humans don't understand rocks very well, and even in our most sensitive moments, we participate in geologic conversations only proximately. We know the histories, chemistries, and geologies of these stones, but our greatest obstacles to understanding seem to be the illusions created by our own mechanical knowledges. Sometimes when the moment is right, however, we sense the mysterious and porous spirit within and celebrate it in our own anthropomorphic ways. So it is for me.

In their cooling, some of these particular lavas have assumed compelling shapes — a matter of permeabilities and viscosities perhaps; nonetheless, I see faces in the stones. I see the contours of animals and plants. I see the inspirational wellsprings of ancient artistic images from the time of the bone-scratchers and bark-shapers on through to the impressionists and surrealists and postmodernists. I see textures and forms that echo unspeakable and wondrous happenings to and in the land, and to and in all of the peoples who have inhabited the land since time immemorial. I see the profiles of noses, the curvatures of chins, the outlines of skulls. I see petroglyphs and Zen brush strokes and Chinese hexagrams striated into the rock. I see fortunes, past and present. I see whole ancestral lines of myths and legends going back to the beginning, to the first light and the greening of the planet, and then back farther into the primal darkness, and then finally into the void. At least I think I see them.

Can stones be all of these things? The possibility exists and in Hawai'i even the most hurried visitor can discover it, perhaps where it is least expected.

In the middle of noisy, bustling Waikīkī, for example, there are four fabled rocks called the Wizard Stones. Most people — residents and visitors alike — aren't aware of them, but they are there. Most people, for that matter, aren't aware that the original Waikīkī was full of springs, streams, and creeks. The name itself reveals this: "Wai Kīkī" — Spouting Water. For centuries, the 'Āpuakēhau Stream flowed down from the mountains above Honolulu and emptied into the ocean next to the original Waikīkī village that stood, surrounded by sacred sites, approximately where the Moana Hotel stands today. It must have been a magical place. Near the current Royal Hawaiian Hotel was the sacrificial *heiau* of Helumoa and, next to that, a great athletic field where chiefs and chiefesses engaged in the equivalent of Olympic games. At the other end of Waikīkī, near the foot of Diamond Head at Kapi'olani Park, stood a different *heiau*, this one built to celebrate battles and conquests by chiefs who lived long after Helumoa was erected but nearly a cen-

tury before Kamehameha the Great ruled. Large and highly productive fish ponds dominated the area. Aquaculture may in fact
have been the most prominent feature of Waikīkī. At the time of
Captain Douglas's meeting with Oʻahu's high chiefs in 1790 there
were at least fourteen separate ponds where the Reef Hotel now
stands on Kālia Road. Salt marshes filled with water birds were
plentiful, along with taro patches, gardens, and plantations that
extended more than a mile inland.

Today, all of this is gone, obliterated by the digging of the Ala
Wai Canal in 1919 and the steady building of modern Waikīkī.
The *heiau* have been reduced to rubble and the fish ponds filled to
make way for hotels, shops, and restaurants. Even the ʻĀpuakēhau
Stream and other freshets that once flowed into Waikīkī have been
severed and channelized. In fact, the original watercourses no
longer reach Waikīkī at all. The mountains' water slides through
culverts and drainage ditches and into the canal, along with many
of the memories of what existed before.

The only material reminders of the ancient past of Waikīkī are
the Wizard Stones. "If you should be walking through that part of
Waikīkī," says Lucia Tarallo-Jensen, a gifted local writer, "and perhaps have a mad desire to experience something original... something ancient... something not of our world today... something
that bespeaks a culture from whose origin the essence of these
Islands emerged, you might want to stroll over to the Waikīkī
Beach Center, on the land once called Nanapua, just beyond
Ulukou." That is where the stones can be found.

The Wizard Stones, she tells us, commemorate the arrival and
departure of four soothsayers from Tahiti who were famed for their
powers of healing. The wizards, whose names were Kapaemahu,
Kahaloa, Kapuni, and Kinohi, made their way to Hawaiʻi in the
sixteenth century, stayed for a time, and, when they left, transferred their *mana*, their power, to the Islands in general and to
these rocks in particular. It was their gift and legacy and helped
shape the destiny of Hawaiʻi.

Go and look at these stones. Stare at them. Put your hands on
them and feel their cool, rough texture. Despite the crowds of
people that will be streaming around you, despite the beachgoers

and sunbathers, despite the multitudes of cars and buses pushing down Kalākaua Avenue — despite all these things — you will feel the core of silence emanating from them. The timeless dignity of these boulders will hush you. They are surreal and quieting and through them, if you have a mind that is receptive, you will briefly connect with the roots of this archipelago and its people.

Stumping up the trail — stride after stride, yard after yard — I think about the fashioning of human temperaments by the land. The rocks, trees, shrubs, watercourses, and animals that surround us are a living birthright to which we owe allegiance. It is a heritage we must protect so that the future may know it also. To do this we need to link ourselves back to the ground and water and sky. Not an easy task; in an age of upward aspirations, in a time of mobility and transience, most of us no longer have the kind of physical or mental foundations that are forged by geography. We are city-things. We tend to live in the imaginary centers of our own social constructs, which are generally devoid of wild nature. We have families and friends, colleagues, networks, significant others, and voluntary social companions. We have our houses and offices, amped-up sound systems, and "data bases" that allow us access to fast-breaking information and quick transactions. All of this, individually and cumulatively, has some positive and far-reaching effects. We don't, however, have wild roots, the kind that sink down into the earth, that keep us in touch with natural and nonhuman intelligences.

It is an odd state of affairs. What culture, after all, would be so presumptuous, so soulless and self-limiting as to cease caring about the shimmering, spectral spirit-lights of a long arctic night or the deep and ceaseless green of a jungle rain forest? Or the muddy fertility of a river delta? Or the dusty veldt of an African savanna? Or the ranges and divides of the American West? Or the moods of a stormy Pacific Ocean on a sun-soaked, rain-drenched, wind-whipped island? Staying warm and dry is one thing, but cutting oneself off from nature is another. Given our planet's magnificent and compelling landscapes, why would anyone choose to hole up on the forty-fifth floor of a paper-filled, hermetically sealed office building by day and in a lint-free, Raid-sprayed suburban ranch house by night?

Nonetheless, that is what much of the world is coming to and what the rest of it is being taught to want. Gregory Bateson once said that it is impossible to imagine the world as it is, because the world comes into being by what we imagine. Today, on New Year's Eve, on the edge of the millennium, as I'm ascending the summit of the rocky face of Kōnāhuanui, these imaginings look dark indeed. The predictions are clear. In the spare words of Pulitzer poet Gary Snyder, our noses are pressed against the "slopes of statistics" that exist in front of us, "the steep climb of everything, going up, up, as we all go down." In Hawai'i, these inclines and declines translate into the loss of the Islands as we know them today. The pressures of economic growth, the reduction of travel time, development and full build-out, the in-migration of more and more people, and the unabated exploitation of cultural and natural resources will, without a doubt, seriously alter the character of this place.

Some of the danger also comes in the form of ozone depletion and global warming, phenomena that may sound distant but in fact are not, especially if you happen to live close to the equator or in the middle of the ocean. The greenhouse effect — a set of "feedback loops" resulting from steadily increasing levels of carbon dioxide, methane, and other gases — is affecting global temperatures at a rate that is now measurable and alarming. Much of the hard data on this — the so-called "Mauna Loa Curve" — comes from thirty years of continuous carbon dioxide monitoring at the 11,200-foot level of Mauna Loa on the Big Island. Here, Dave Keeling of the Scripps Institution of Oceanography and other scientists have found a significant rise in the concentration of carbon dioxide in the middle layers of the troposphere. Extrapolating from this, modelers in other disciplines have been able to project future climate conditions.

The world appears to be getting warmer. Like my little backyard compost pile in which heat generates decay that in turn generates more heat, one of the greenhouse loops involves the creation of more and more water vapor in the atmosphere. Heat stays trapped and this leads to an additional rise in temperature. In other words, we may be headed for a conservatively estimated — but according to some, irreversible — global warming of between five and ten degrees in mean temperature by the year 2030. Worse and worst-case scenarios are much more dire but these may be prone to the same kind of alarm mongering and doomsaying that Pope Gregory was indulging in a thousand years ago.

Then again, maybe not.

We now appear destined for slow but inevitable climatic changes: less sunshine, more dust, more desertification, more carbon dioxide, more shifts in rainfall, more alterations in snow and wind patterns, and — as a consequence — more disruption of the Earth's present growing seasons. In the world's larger forests (which are nature's oxygen producers; in effect, the planet's lungs), we will see an increased number of reproductive failures, slow diebacks, and even occasional wholesale biomass crashes. The impacts of all of these factors in conjunction with each other are not entirely clear. Most likely, there will be a rise in sea level and major changes in the way coastal populations live. Eventually and if left unabated, say some scientists, all of our natural atmospheric, hydrospheric, and ecospheric systems with their intricate compensations will have been turned topsy-turvy and the planet itself will no longer function in ways consistent with past experience or predictive of sensible futures. Maybe change will be such that we can adjust to it before it's too late… maybe not.

None of this is happening overnight nor are we likely to see in the next decade something that looks distinctly "cataclysmic" — a huge meltdown of the polar caps, for instance. Perhaps it would be better if there were a catastrophe. That at least would serve as a serious warning and rallying point. For the immediate future, though — from now through 2050 — there will be a steady, insidious deterioration of the complex and beautiful surroundings that sustain us and that we refer to simplistically as "the environment." Some arid places will get wetter and some wet spots will dry up. Rivers and streams will shift courses and many may cease to flow. Temperate forests will retreat north and equatorial forests will wither in the heat. Without a doubt, the pace of animal and plant extinctions will increase and we will see small and then progressively larger human impacts through starvation and disease.

In the face of these threats, humans will struggle to make adaptations and some will succeed. But if the current thinking is correct, none can truly stave off the collapse of what we have come to know and expect as our natural inheritance. We can envision ingenious domed cities, factories full of gene-spliced production animals that look vaguely like a chicken or cow used to, and helmeted spaceworkers poised to inhabit other stars that are healthier-looking. We can further guess — and there are any number of sociologists and political scientists making the same point — that the lives my Corey, Dana, and Kelly will lead as adults, here in Hawai'i or elsewhere, will be more severely administered and regulated than the childhoods they have today. Inescapably, says Bruce McKibben in a book of the same title, all of this means "the end of nature."

In using this phrase, McKibben isn't suggesting the end of the world. The rain will continue to fall and the sun will still rise, and many of the rhythms of life as we know them will continue without skipping a beat. But more and more the measured realities of science will clash with our notion of "nature" as something eternal and foundational. We are on the edge of a fundamental break with the historical order. A walk in the woods, a stroll by the seashore, or a hike in the Ko'olau Mountains will surely be something different than it is now. There is, says McKibben unequivocally, no future in loving nature, because the very idea of nature itself will soon be obsolete.

* * *

Over the years I have found a special pleasure in hiking alone. It's not that I don't like the company of other people, because I do. In fact, the small amount of time I spend in the backcountry is usually with a few like-minded, escape-crazy friends. In slightly smaller proportions, the women in my house also have adventure-lust in their hearts. Whenever possible, all of us head toward some of the remote and stunning wild areas of the Islands. In my bones and in my soul, I enjoy those family times immensely.

Solitary hiking, however, along with its dangers, has its own peculiar rewards, among them an absence of external authorities and the freedom to come and go where and when one wants. When things go right, all of this yields pleasurable observations and ruminations. Occasionally — and especially because trails in Hawai'i can be treacherous — there are unanticipated costs. Today is one of those occasions.

Lathered from my trudge up the mountain, I stop to catch my breath, draw down some of the fresh water in my canteen, recycle some previously-consumed water onto a nearby shrub (shrubs seem to invite this), and then settle down to do some general repairs necessitated by a fall. My shirt is ripped, my arms are covered with mud, and my right leg is slightly bent and bleeding in several places. A minor set of inconveniences caused by taking "freedom" one step too far. Cutting across a switchback (which even Cub Scouts know is a no-no), I once again have relearned one of life's fundamental lessons: there are no shortcuts.

In addition to repairs, it is time to take stock of where I am — which, to be precise, is on the narrow ridge line that leads to Kōnāhuanui, roughly 500 feet below the summit. From here, the route is basically a scramble over rocks, roots, limbs, and a few muddy indentations that can, with a certain stretch of imagination, be called handholds. It is now late morning. A half-hour more and I'll be at the top. My plan is to rest here out of the wind, take an hour at the summit to look around, and then head back down by a slightly different route.

Sitting on the ridge, licking my wounds (figuratively), and looking down the mountain, I notice how much the city has encroached on the Ko'olau Mountains since my previous trip here; how more of O'ahu's hills and watersheds have been given over to development; how, in fact, not a valley is left on this side of the Island that isn't spidered with streets and clogged with tracts of houses and stores and choked with automobiles. All of which — in one form or another and depending on your disposition to examine such matters — can be translated into "the end of nature."

Global warming is not a galvanizing issue, particularly in Hawai'i. It is too far removed from daily experience. People in America don't normally start to worry about things like ultraviolet radiation and water pollution until it interferes with TV reception or the national beer supply. As for increases in carbon dioxide, what difference can a few more degrees of mean temperature mean for a bunch of little islands stuck away in the middle of the tropical Pacific? Can these kinds of small atmospheric changes really presage a change in something as physically grand as the Hawaiian archipelago? Are these forests on Kōnāhuanui really doomed because of it? Hard to believe, but if so, so what? Will a few less birds and bugs make a real difference to Corey, Dana, and Kelly in the decades beyond 2000?

Consider this. The year is 2025. At home in the Islands, Corey, Dana, and Kelly are in their forties. Having navigated the normal bumps of adolescence and young adulthood they have arrived, more or less intact, at the same point in life at which Carolyn and I are today. They work hard, take pleasure from the things that surround and ground them, and strive to make some kind of contribution to the Island society they inhabit.

Hawai'i, however, is a very different place. The coastal and dry upland forests are completely gone as are almost all of the once endemic plants and animals. Global sea level has risen, as many had predicted, causing shifting currents and the chilling of the mean water temperature surrounding Hawai'i by ten degrees. Low-lying areas like Waikīkī, Hawai'i Kai, and Kāne'ohe have been diked, resulting in a loss of beaches and waterfronts. Hawai'i's fresh water supply is diminished because of salt-water intrusion into the basal lens. Most offshore reefs are dead, victims of sewage spills, construction runoffs, and the new currents.

On the Big Island, heavy industry — particularly the processing of ocean-extracted oils, gasses, and minerals — now dominates the formerly agricultural areas surrounding Hilo. East Hawai'i has been de-watered to support a few large hydroponic and agricultural monocrops. Urbanized O'ahu and Maui look like dilapidated Hong Kongs. They are studded with aging skyscrapers and otherwise paved over with concrete. In fact, the only large tracts of wilderness left in the Islands are Volcano and Haleakalā National Parks and a few arid places held dear by nobody except a handful of Hawaiians, scientists, backpackers, and crazies.

As a result of overdevelopment and shifts in the earth's wind patterns, smog is now a serious problem over Honolulu (which extends to Ka'ena Point) and across the fully developed urban corridors of Hilo-Pāhoa, Kona-Waimea, Līhu'e-Hanalei, Wailuku-Kīhei, and Lāna'i City-Mānele. "Quality of life" — an ephemeral set of opinions in the best of times — is at an all-time low. In measurable terms, streets, bridges, sewers, and water mains are in disrepair, traffic has been close to gridlock for more than a decade, and public housing — including the once premier "Diamond Head Project" adjoining Waikīkī in the former Kapi'olani Park — has deteriorated beyond repair. Global depression coupled with population pressures and the failure of certain regional industries (including the seesawing fortunes of tourism) have created a Los Angeles in the middle of the Pacific. Hawai'i has true slums and a highly marginalized polyglot of immigrants living in welfare camps and public housing projects. The "super-rich" own all the private land and spend much of their time in high rises and offshore casinos for which the Islands are now famous. The market for personal bodyguards — usually referred to as "security valets" — is booming.

Farfetched? Probably, but also not outside the realm of possibility. Tossing the bones, reading palms, and studying tea leaves is a time-honored tradition. Today's version uses large data bases, statistical modeling, and trend analysis. Pollsters, pundits, and "hard" and "soft" science prophets — Bruce McKibben, Gerard O'Neill, Ravi Batra, Peter Drucker, and Johann Galtung to name a few — have conjured up plausible scenarios very similar to these. Not all of the prognostications are this bleak. Nonetheless, every credible long-range projection posits more people, more violence, more state-imposed regulation, more environmental destruction, and a life that is more complicated and less comfortable for everyone.

Huddled on the ridge, immersed in small wounds and mud, it's easy to get gloomy. There isn't very much that people like Carolyn and me can do to alter the future. Even the smart people who make full-time livings as prophesiers don't seem to have any pragmatic solutions to these impending problems. But then, neither did Pope Gregory. This doesn't mean we are powerless, however. Bleak scenarios about the future don't confer some kind of larger philosophical license to wallow around in a pit full of despair. In fact, the only true antidote to what John Hersey calls "the creed of greed" is contrariness, something that at least affords us the exercise of free will, some passion and dignity, and a few small measures of occasional entertainment.

Resistance — opposing the flow of "progress" as we've known it this past century — happens in many ways. Hiking up Kōnāhuanui and staring the ugliness of the coming maelstrom directly in the eye doesn't qualify, but planting serious gardens does. So does turning off air conditioners and using bicycles. Uprooting survey stakes and chaining yourself to old-growth trees as the loggers rev up their chainsaws is another way if you are of the monkey-wrencher persuasion. But so also are teaching your children not to be afraid of worms and frogs and forcing the big shots downtown to pass bottle bills and land-use controls. Or writing good nature poems that stir dormant emotions in others. There are, in fact, hundreds of little purposeful and self-directed things that can be done that individually might not amount to a hill of beans, but cumulatively might at least stockpile some bean seeds for the future.

One of the most valuable is changing our attitudes about travel and rejecting the worst traits of mass tourism — the quick, pre-packaged, predigested getaway in which you visit some other place but learn nothing about the land or its people. This is something we can easily act on, both as travelers ourselves and in the ways we collectively plan for and greet tourists. If "tourists" are our "industry," let us texture their experiences more richly and with greater thought to impact on traveler and host and on the local ground and sea traveled upon.

In another day and age, not so very long ago, the norm for many types of travel was the "purpose-filled pilgrim," someone who set off to explore the world beyond familiar boundaries. Such travelers were searching for deeper encounters. Entertainment and diversion were by-products, not goals. In this context, travel was a moratorium from the mundane and a spiritually transforming adventure. The pilgrim sought to probe the world in new ways and, in turn, was usually touched by it in ways never anticipated.

It was, under the right conditions, what Joseph Campbell called a mythic journey. With this approach, even the most ordinary of people — you and me, for instance — depart from our everyday circumstances, get initiated into deeper realms of experience, and return home with the boon of knowledge.

Modern tourism is different, but the purpose-filled pilgrimage is still possible. I know because it's happened to me in Hawai'i, in my own neighborhood.

I rearrange my socks and tie my boots. The weather, ideal until now, is changing. Appropriate to my mood, dark clouds are building and the wind is rising. I look back and see the city far below, where it belongs, and where this cheerless deluge of thoughts about the coming century belongs as well. Albert Camus once said that if a person has a sad philosophy and a happy face, you can conclude that their philosophy is not really sad. The reverse is true, too. So what is it that I really feel? Things indefinable and contradictory: the delight of fresh raspberries, the taste of chalk; the rich, thick smell of baking bread, and the acrid odor of a bloated rat carcass; the sound of a thrush singing in the morning and the clamor of burglar alarms and breaking glass. Pleasure and pain. The world is changing but it's the only one we have. What we see is what we get and what we have is worth the agonies of the times.

Gazing at the ridge and sky, at the scrubby trees and bony rocks, at the beautiful light that is illuminating the archipelago and bathing it in wonder, I know it is all fleeting. Time and the incoming tide of human affairs will drown much of this with it, or send it out on the ebb. Hence these bittersweet emotions that are too confusing to sort out. There ought to be more; there should be some kind of clarity or insight or even the vague outline of a plan of action. But there isn't. Just the summit.

I shoulder the pack and turn toward Kōnāhuanui.

* * *

The crest of "large fat innards" comes unexpectedly. One moment I am clambering up the skid mark that serves as a trail, and the next minute I am standing on the spine of the Island in a thick haze staring down. There is wind, height, expectation, and the usual ten-degree drop in temperature. The summit is ghosted over with wind-blown fog. I pull out a raincoat and bundle up. Low, fast-moving clouds stream over the ridge leaving brief glimpses of the blue-green peaks of the windward side of O'ahu in their wake.

On the ridge that forms the summit, squishing through puddles, I carefully navigate my way across a fragile flora. Disregarding the bright blue and orange sprigs of lantana, most of the trees and shrubs I see here are unique to the bogs and the narrow ridges of wet upland forests in Hawai'i. 'Ōhi'a lehua trees with their gnarled roots, twisted branches, bright red flowers, and dark green foliage dominate the landscape. Many other native plants are thriving here as well: mountain naupaka, tree ferns, white hibiscus, red lobelia, Hawaiian holly. Although I can't knowledgeably explain what is technically occurring in this ecosystem, I have to believe that most of these plants are in retreat, that this place is the botanical equivalent of Little Big Horn.

But up here among the lichens and ferns there are also surprises. Rising up out of the spongy remains of an old 'ōhi'a stump is a 10-foot 'ōlapa tree. Special trees, these: used long ago by bird catchers who needed straight poles to hold their sticky glues; by kapa makers, the clothiers who made blue dyes from the fruit and leaves; and by hula masters who saw the quivering of the 'ōlapa's pale-green leaves and inspired their students to similarly graceful movements. Also special are the colorfully banded endemic snails I find on the underside of some 'ōlapa leaves. Called Achatinella, or "little agates," these small, harmless, and highly endangered land mollusks survive on certain rain forest trees and quietly graze their lives away on microscopic detritus. In the early 1900s they were gathered by the bucketful and collected or sold as novelties. Today, the greatest problem is predation by rats and alien snails. Another threat is habitat loss. They are almost gone.

The fog thickens. I am soaking wet. I study a large brown bracket fungus growing out of a branch and then clamber across the ridge line another 200 feet to the highest point on Kōnāhuanui. Enveloped in fog, there is really nothing to see except the ghostly, paleozoic shapes of the 'ōhi'a and the spectral spray of cloud-blown haze splattering drops of dew against the dark background of my raincoat. I stand for a moment, listen to the precious silence, and then start back down the trail. Just before I descend, however, I remember something.

M&Ms. Yep, those luscious little nuggets calling to me... reaching out... waiting and wanting to be eaten. I slip off my pack, reach in, and caress the stiff yellow package with the large brown letters. I contemplate the sublime taste and smooth texture of all those bright-colored lumps. Half a bag left. I visualize myself giving in, impulsively tearing open the sack, pouring a few M&Ms into my muddy scratched-up palm, savoring one or two ever so slowly, and then, in a moment of total swinishness — in a convulsion of gluttony — seizing the bag in both hands and pigging the whole thing down as fast as I can.

Such is not to be.

With pride and regret — considerable regret, in fact — I put the bag back, sling my pack over my shoulder, and head down the slope. I've decided to view the M&Ms as a supreme test of willpower and personal integrity. The challenge is to see just how long I can resist them. In fact, if I can resist them all the way to the end of the hike, I'll share them with the very first person I meet who looks in need of a sugar fix. Then I'll declare the whole episode a twentieth-century triumph over temptation. Man over M&Ms; in the greater scheme of things, an innocuous accomplishment. On the other hand, it could be the start of something big. In the face of manufactured needs and marketed desires, even small acts of voluntary simplicity might be considered proud acts of recalcitrance. Gandhi would understand. So would Thoreau and Thomas Merton and Loren Eiseley.

Ever so carefully, I pick my way down the slope of Kōnāhuanui avoiding the fascinations and allures of shortcuts, keeping to the main trail, and thinking about resistance. Despite the predictions of what lies in wait for us at the millennium, there are still things to be done and quite a few people who are dedicating their energetic talents to doing them. These "defiant optimists," as McKibben calls them, espouse very different philosophies ranging from stepped-up large-scale technological development (Julian Simon), to stepped down "permacultures" (the late E. F. Schumacher and Bill Mollison), to complete planet management (James Lovelock and the late Buckminster Fuller), to the "deep-ecologists" (Raymond Dasmann and Gary Snyder) who argue for a return to fundamentals and a "future primitive."

All of these contain ideas worth studying and, in most cases, practices worth implementing. Small-scale changes in food production, housing, and personal transportation are possible. You don't need a Ph.D. in physics or economics to evaluate the short-term costs and long-term benefits of certain behaviors and then, as a consequence, to make sensible choices. We can avoid buying aerosol products that contain chlorofluorocarbons and we can recycle newspapers, aluminum cans, and glass bottles. We can raise carrots in window boxes, compost our coffee grounds, plant young trees on eroding hillsides, and collect all the beer cans junking up the park. We can screw in energy-efficient light bulbs, carpool with other people, and cut back on a few of our air conditioners without giving up tremendous amounts of comfort. All of these things are easily within our grasp.

I march on down the mountain, mindful of where I am putting my feet, but thinking about territories, geographies, and ecosystems as replacement concepts for political nation-states. It is a fantasy, of course, but if you can't go out to the woods on the last day of the year in the last decade of the century and in the last century of the millennium to indulge in a few daydreams, then what the hell have we come to?

What, then, if we actually had an archipelagic citizenry that was awakened to the rich complexity of this place, to its climatic uniqueness, to its native possibilities, to the innate sanctity of its biota? What if we could somehow come together and work toward a cleaner landscape for our children, one with smaller technologies, more diversified cities, plenty of farms and ag lands cultivated with things eaten locally, and lots of fresh, clean, and unpolluted waters percolating free through miles of wilderness? What if we could make the Hawaiian archipelago a model for other places, something replicable, something demonstrable and true in a world that is getting tackier and phonier by the day? And what if Hawaiian tourism were based on helping other people to think about these things so they could return home refreshed in body and spirit and ready to transform their own surroundings?

Pipe dreams?

Historian Daniel Boorstein, writing about the cartographers of the seventeenth and eighteenth centuries, says the greatest obstacle in discovering the true shape of the earth was not ignorance but the illusion of knowledge. The world was flat, monsters ruled the perimeters, and scholars, kings, and clerics scoffed at any ideas to the contrary.

Pipe dreams? Maybe and maybe not.

Beyond the protests of defensive environmentalism lie some odd, fragmented, and only partially articulated intuitions. At the moment they are more of a set of frustrations and dreams than anything else. With time, however, they could be the basis of a possible vision, something around which we might begin to forge a true consensus.

When such agreement emerges, which it no doubt will, the hard work will have been done by a few tinkerers, activists, and political pioneers with a distinctly "local" temperament (whether they were born here or not). These people — like the Keles and Thoreaus of this world — will be married to their place and willing to fight for it with all of the stamina they can muster. They will be people of different origins, ages, and genders. They will have different backgrounds and upbringings. And they will be people with diverse talents — farmers, civil servants, hotel workers, lawyers, stockbrokers, truck drivers, doctors, and poets. What they will share, though, is simple and unifying: a burning desire to keep calling this northern tip of the Polynesian triangle "home" and the courage to stand against the forces that want to turn it into someplace else.

Pipe dreams? I don't think so. Increasingly I catch glimpses that tell me these folks are among us right now. The millennium is not an ending; it is the start.

I thread my way down Kōnāhuanui, down the shank of the mountain, past the overlook, through the bamboo, and back into the thick forests of Tantalus. Scratched up and tired, I descend slowly, taking little pleasures from things inside and out. I see water moving in freshets and thick trees holding firm. I see birds, bananas, and centipedes. I think of a Japanese scroll poem talking to us through time and telling us how only rock and wind remain through generations (even though the poem has too). I remember a Hawaiian chant beholding these lovely Islands and urging us to sing out in all directions. I walk through the woods meditating on things firm and infirm and then, after a time, give in to exhaustion and simply move down the trail.

Finally, I emerge from the forest. My car is where I left it at the trailhead, safely nestled under a large flowering mango tree by the side of the road. I fish the keys out of my pocket, open the trunk, flip my pack in, and lean on the fender. And then I notice it. The bottom section of my pack is open, the one that contained my water bottle, pocketknife, and spare T-shirt. The section that also held my bag of M&Ms. All of which, with the exception of one lonely M&M rolling around in the bottom of the compartment, are now gone.

I think back to try to find the point where I screwed up and then I remember: at the summit. My M&M lust. I visualize my belongings sitting on the ground at the top of the mountain with the fogs rolling in and the clouds blowing over and for a moment I'm tempted to go back up. Too far, of course. So I'll let them be offerings. A perfectly good Shrade-Walden pocketknife, a 1 quart water bottle, and an old Hawaii Bound School T-shirt for some other hiker playing hooky from business-as-usual. And almost half a bag of M&Ms. For the critters and the elements. For the mountain.

I strip off my muddy boots, climb in the car, and pop the last M&M in my mouth. It's a green one. I start the engine and head for home.

10

Passage

Gather up the fragments that remain,
that nothing be lost.

John 6:12

WE ARE WALKING ALONG KUALOA BEACH on the windward side of O'ahu, the five of us, courting the edge of land and sea. The morning sky is muted and gray and the sun has yet to appear. Nonetheless, the day holds promise.

Last night's storm, full of furious rain and spray, has given way to gentle combers that are rolling up the beach. The tide is out. The high-water line is a long jumbled berm of driftwood, plastic jugs, old fishnets, pieces of tire tread, and coral rubble. The symmetrical, cone-shaped island of Mokoli'i, better known as Chinaman's Hat, is off to our left. Between the sets of waves and just ahead of our footfalls, ghost crabs skitter back to their holes in the sand.

Carolyn and I walk slowly, stiff from spending the night in a tent in the rain. Corey and Dana saunter along next to us rubbing their eyes. Kelly, however, is jumping around like a flea. She runs ahead, chases a crab, catches it, releases it, stops to inspect something else, brings back a piece of beach glass, and then shoots off again in search of more treasures and adventures. The rest of us are in slow motion.

Dana: "Dad, where are we going?"

"To look at the baby fish."

"What's so special about the fish over here?"

"Everybody says the fish are disappearing. I just want to make sure they're still here. Besides, its a nice walk."

There is more to it than this, but what else can I say? How do I begin to articulate to my children the tangled truths that are beating on the margins of their childhood? How do I explain about animals and plants, this place, their roots, our home? How do I explain what I barely understand myself?

There is a meandering continuity here that desperately needs explanation, an intricate spiral that connects the waves, the sand, the shells, the crabs, the fish, this Island, Carolyn, myself, and each of them. It is unfiltered education, the lessons about causes and effects that no school can teach. Words too easily diminish the power of the instruction. We cannot cause insight or understanding, says Anne Dillard. All we can do is put ourself in its path. Which is always straight ahead.

Corey: "Dad, how far is it?"

"About a mile."

She groans and then we walk in silence.

"What's there?" she asks eventually.

"Well, this stretch of sand leads around an old fish pond. Then, where the beach makes a bend, there used to be a little estuary. An estuary is like a cove. Actually, it was a fish pond at one time but now its just a little lagoon with a creek flowing in. Unless the currents and stream flow have changed, that's where the fish will be."

Dana: "We should have brought fishing poles."

Corey: "They're baby fish. They're too small to bite a hook."

Dana: "We could still try to catch them."

"No fishing this morning," I tell them both. "We're just looking to see if they are there. There used to be a lot of little hammerhead sharks around here too. It would be neat to see one."

Kelly comes tearing back to us with more beach glass, lovely red and blue pieces that have been scratch-polished by the sand. The colors are pastels, the edges smooth and rounded.

"Mom, why do they call that place Chinaman's Hat?" she asks.

Carolyn: "Look at the shape, sweetie; what does it look like?"

"Is that the kind of hat Chinese people wear? Stephanie is Chinese and she doesn't wear one like that."

"The real name of that place is Mokoli'i," I tell her. "It's supposed to be what's left of a vicious dragon, what the old Hawaiians used to call a *mo'o*."

Dragons interest Kelly.

"This particular lizard terrified all the people that lived around here until it was finally killed."

Kelly, round-eyed: "Who killed it?"

"Hi'iaka," I tell her. "Pele's sister. You know, Pele, the fire goddess?"

She nods.

I point up to the cliffs. "Hi'iaka fought the *mo'o* all over the mountains. The tip of his chopped-off tail is that little island."

Dana: "Is that true? Did that really happen?"

"It's an old story, full of magic. Some people say it's just a tall tale, but I think most Hawaiian legends are based on things that actually did happen, that people still sort of remember. Something important happened here even though we can't be sure what it was exactly."

We walk on. After a time, Corey turns to Dana and Kelly and says: "Uncle Roger told me this was a place of refuge."

Kelly: "What's a place of refuse?"

Corey: "No, it's *refuge*. Refuse is like trash that you throw away. Refuge is a place you go to when you run away."

Kelly: "You shouldn't run away."

Dana: "There's a City of Refuge on the Big Island. My teacher said so. Maybe this is like that."

Corey: "Yeah, people used to come here when they got in trouble. Nobody could bust them if they came here because..."

...because it was sacred, I think to myself. It was *pu'uhonua*, a protected place. Defeated warriors running from their pursuers and noncombatants wanting to get out of harm's way in the perennial wars between O'ahu's chiefs were safe here; so too were people escaping punishment for violating the *kapu*: women who had eaten bananas that were reserved only for men; *ali'i* who had slept with commoners; commoners who had let their shadows fall upon an *ali'i*.

The old stories, now memorialized in written texts on Hawaiian culture but formerly passed down from generation to generation by word of mouth, tell of other things as well. Kualoa was known for both its rich fish ponds and for the ivory that was collected from dead whales that washed up on its shores. It was here that the breadfruit tree was introduced to the Islands, so it is said. And here too there was a training ground for young chiefs who were raised by wise teachers and tutored in the arts of governance and war. So sacred was this place that passing fishermen were required to lower the masts on their canoes when they sailed by...

"Dad, do people still do that?"

"Do what, Kelly?"

"Come here when they get in trouble and then nobody can bother them because they're here?"

"It's not like the old days, when there were wars going on all around this place. But people still need a place to come and rest and be with their families. That's why it's a park. That's why we can come here. So can the bugs and the birds and the lizards. This place is neutral ground for them too."

We pass the bouldered walls of an enormous, partially restored fish pond that will eventually be returned to active use by the local Hawaiian community. Nearby, a spreading mangrove thicket has taken hold, creating a mud flat. And then, we round the bend and we are at the cove.

The estuary covers several acres. It is separated from the ocean by a long spit of sand and a sand bar that keeps the cove contained but still allows a sustaining flow of sea water to enter. Inside the lagoon and along the shore, one portion of the inlet has turned into a swamp, dominated by grass, reeds, and mangroves. Other parts are strewn with pebbles and rocks that have been washed down from the mountains above. Most of the estuary is shallow and sandy.

As we approach we see movements on the beach and in the water. There are tidal currents in the cove and, on the surface, little concentric ripples that expand outward. On the beach, two small birds — probably sandpipers — take flight as we come into sight. The kids notice both of these things and quietly start to investigate the shoreline. Kelly points. Then Dana. Then Corey. Following them down to the water's edge, I see too: baby fish.

In ancient times, the bays and ponds of this area would have been filled with mullet, milkfish, goatfish, silver perch, bonefish, eels, shrimps, and other beautiful sea creatures. Caring for the ponds, sustaining them, flourishing with them, was a handsome and gifted civilization of people who knew, with great particularity, the names and origins of each living being and the intricate relationships among them. It is all different now.

Today, the old aquaculture ponds have been filled and the inshore and offshore fish populations decimated. Native flora and fauna are in retreat. Fish, limpets, and edible seaweeds are scarce. But they aren't completely gone. There are still out-of-the-way places left with small numbers of animals and plants bearing their young and poised for a comeback in the wiser days that I must believe lie ahead.

Carolyn and I sit on the sand and watch Corey, Dana, and Kelly exploring. We see them wading in, bending to look, slowly moving their hands into the shallow waters, then carefully pushing their fingers into the sand on the bottom to see how deep it is. We see them searching through the primordial elements of this obscure Hawaiian strand, groping for a different world. "I touched one," yells one of the girls. "Me too," echoes another one. On that pathway where insights sometimes hurtle past, and sometimes stop and whisper in our ear, an ancient passage is under way. Little children and little fish come together.

The sun pokes through the gray and flashes across the sand. "When you are in that blessed retreat," wrote Mark Twain after his 1866 trip to Hawai'i, "as far as you can see, on any hand, the crested billows wall the horizon, and beyond this barrier the wide universe is but a foreign land..." A bee buzzes around and then lands on a red *pōhuehue* blossom growing out of the sand. The waters of the lagoon glisten and the kids laugh and play. Even as the future rushes headlong toward us, these things will surely abide if we love them enough.